The Reference Shelf®

Representative American Speeches 2004–2005

Editors

Calvin M. Logue, Ph.D.,

Lynn M. Messina, Ph.D.,

and

Jean DeHart, Ph.D.

The Reference Shelf
Volume 77 • Number 6

The H.W. Wilson Company
2005

The Reference Shelf

The books in this series contain reprints of articles, excerpts from books, addresses on current issues, and studies of social trends in the United States and other countries. There are six separately bound numbers in each volume, all of which are usually published in the same calendar year. Numbers one through five are each devoted to a single subject, providing background information and discussion from various points of view and concluding with a subject index and comprehensive bibliography that lists books, pamphlets, and abstracts of additional articles on the subject. The final number of each volume is a collection of recent speeches, and it contains a cumulative speaker index. Books in the series may be purchased individually or on subscription.

Library of Congress has cataloged this serial title as follows:

Representative American speeches. 1937 / 38–
    New York, H. W. Wilson Co.™
        v. 21 cm.—The Reference Shelf
Annual
Indexes:
    Author index: 1937/38–1959/60, with 1959/60;
    1960/61–1969/70, with 1969/70; 1970/71–1979/80,
    with 1979/80; 1980/81–1989/90, 1990.
Editors: 1937/38–1958/59, A. C. Baird.—1959/60–1969/70, L. Thonssen.—1970/71–1979/80, W. W. Braden.—1980/81–1994/95, O. Peterson.—1995/96–1998/99, C. M. Logue and J. DeHart.—1999/2000–2002/2003, C. M. Logue and L. M. Messina.—2003/2004– , C. M. Logue, L. M. Messina, and J. DeHart.
    ISSN 0197-6923 Representative American speeches.
        1. Speeches, addresses, etc., American. 2. Speeches, addresses, etc.
        I. Baird, Albert Craig, 1883–1979 ed. II. Thonssen, Lester, 1904–
        III. Braden, Waldo Warder, 1911–1991 ed.
        IV. Peterson, Owen, 1924– ed. V. Logue, Calvin McLeod, 1935– ,
        Messina, Lynn M., and DeHart, Jean, eds. VI. Series.
PS668.B3   815.5082   38-27962
                                                     MARC-S
Library of Congress [8503r85] rev4

Cover: U.S. Secretary of State Condoleeza Rice speaks in June 2005 at the Inaugural Session of the XXV General Assembly of the Organization of America States in Ft. Lauderdale, FL. (Photo by Roberto Schmidt/AFP/Getty Images)

Visit H. W. Wilson's Web site: www.hwwilson.com

Printed in the United States of America

Contents

Preface

In the United States, election years bring a variety of long-simmering issues to boil, as candidates try to win support from voters by appealing to what they perceive to be Americans' deepest concerns, fears, and insecurities. With the incumbent president George W. Bush the Republican nominee in 2004, the job of raising those issues fell primarily to the Democrats, who wanted to win back the White House for their party. With the popularity of the war in Iraq waning, the Democrats believed their candidate, Senator John Kerry of Massachusetts, had an excellent chance to defeat President Bush, but there were other issues besides the conflict in Iraq that occupied the minds of voters. Many of these concerns are reflected in the speeches chosen for this volume.

Shortly before the New Hampshire Primary in January 2004, Senator John Edwards of North Carolina, in his pursuit of the Democratic nomination for president, began speaking of "two Americas"—one prosperous and one disadvantaged. The speeches in the book's first chapter, "A Divided America," touch on this and similar issues, beginning with Senator Barack Obama's keynote address at the Democratic National Convention in the summer of 2004. Obama discusses the significance of the American slogan *E pluribus unum*—"out of many, one"—in order to present Senator Kerry as the candidate who could unite the country as Bush never did. Reverend Kenneth S. Beldon, a Unitarian minister, next reflects upon the divisive nature of the election and encourages his congregation to abandon their anger towards the party opposing their favorite candidate. Former secretary of labor Robert B. Reich also laments the rise of America's "culture wars" and urges the nation's people to overcome their differences. The final two entries address the gay marriage issue, with a speech by Peter Sprigg against same-sex marriage and another by Evan Wolfson defending it.

The next chapter, "Church and State," covers a topic that was the subject of much debate in the United States throughout 2004 and 2005, as arguments for and against such issues as prayer in public schools and the display of religious symbols in or around public buildings continue to challenge its meaning. The first two speeches collected here, by Ronald B. Flowers and Nadine Strossen, consider the founders' purpose in prohibiting the establishment of a national religion and look at events that have tested the separation clause in recent years. Bishop Donald W. Wuerl of the Roman Catholic Archdiocese of Pittsburgh next examines the influence that religion should have in the political life of elected officials who consider themselves Christian. In the final speech, R. Drew Smith looks at the manner in which African American churches can influence government policy.

Another issue that came to the fore during the past election season was the growing importance of electronic media—specifically the Internet—in the dissemination of information and the shaping of public opinion, with weblogs, or blogs, emerging as a form of citizen journalism and an effective monitor of the mainstream press. In the book's third chapter, "Established and New Media," Jan Schaffer, Alan Nelson, and Vin Crosbie explore the various ways in which daily newspapers and broadcast and cable news programs might utilize new forms of cyber technology to reach a more tech-savvy audience. Senator Hillary Rodham Clinton also considers the myriad new electronic media, but from the perspective of a concerned adult worried about the influence of this technology on the younger generation.

Concern for the future of America's youth was also stated as a reason for President Bush's campaign to reform the Social Security system in 2005. While he insisted upon the benefits of personal retirement accounts for the younger generations of workers, others argued against privatization and claimed the system would not be as bereft of funds as the president argued it would be in the next 20 or 30 years. The fourth chapter, entitled "Seniors and Social Security," examines this debate and the people it most concerns. It begins with a speech by Mariah Burton Nelson, who encourages her audience to view the aging process more positively. Then, Peter R. Orszag discusses the long-term effect of the current U.S. budget deficit on younger generations as they age and begin to receive Social Security benefits. The radio address by President Bush that follows outlines his plans for reforming Social Security, while Mark Warshawsky, from the Treasury Department, presents a more developed explanation of the president's agenda. Finally, the economist William E. Spriggs looks at the issue from a moral standpoint.

The book's final chapter, "America and the New Europe," examines a subject that concerned many U.S. voters during the 2004 presidential campaign—repairing and strengthening America's relationship with Europe after it was so badly damaged by the U.S.–led war in Iraq. Stephen J. Dannhauser looks at that relationship from a business perspective, arguing for a better understanding of European markets. T. R. Reid then considers the social and political gaps between Europeans and Americans. Secretary of State Condoleezza Rice next discusses the importance of U.S.–EU cooperation in spreading democracy and freedom abroad, while Senator Richard G. Lugar suggests how the Transatlantic Alliance can win the battle against terrorism. The final speech, another radio address by President Bush, offers America's sympathies to and solidarity with the people of Great Britain following the terrorist bombings that occurred in London on July 7, 2005.

We would like to thank all of the speakers who graciously gave their permission to reprint their speeches here. We would also like to thank Eugene F. Miller and Paul McCaffrey for their assistance in researching and producing this book.

December 2005

I. A Divided America

Democratic National Convention

Barack Obama

U.S. Senator (D), Illinois, 2005– ; born Honolulu, HI, August 4, 1961; early education in Jakarta, Indonesia, and Honolulu, HI; B.A., Columbia University, 1983; J.D., Harvard Law School, 1992; first African American president of the Harvard Law Review; *community organizer and civil rights lawyer in Chicago; senior lecturer, University of Chicago Law School, specializing in constitutional law; represented South Side of Chicago as senator in Illinois State Senate, 1997–2004; elected to U.S. Senate, 2004; U.S. Senate committees: Environment & Public Works, Foreign Relations, and Veterans' Affairs; organizations: Center for Neighborhood and Technology, Chicago Annebery Challenge, Cook County Bar, Community Law Project, Joyce Foundation, Lawyers' Committee for Civil Rights Under the Law, Leadership for Quality Education, Trinity United Church of Christ; award, 40 under 40, Crains Chicago Business, 1993; author,* Dreams from My Father: A Story of Race and Inheritance *(1995, reprinted 2004).*

Editors' introduction: In his keynote address to the Democratic National Convention, then State Senator Obama of Illinois told delegates that "the true genius of America" is "a faith in simple dreams, an insistence on small miracles." In what some journalists called "the most memorable convention speech in 25 years," Senator Obama concluded that "it is that fundamental belief, I am my brother's keeper, I am my sister's keeper that makes this country work. . . . *E pluribus unum.* Out of many, one." Most of the delegates had convened to nominate John Kerry for the presidency of the United States. Senator Obama was introduced by U.S. Senator Dick Durbin. Senator Obama's speech followed addresses by Senator Edward Kennedy and presidential candidate Howard Dean.

Barack Obama's speech: Thank you so much. Thank you so much. Thank you. Thank you. Thank you so much. Thank you so much. Thank you. Thank you. Thank you, Dick Durbin. You make us all proud.

On behalf of the great state of Illinois, crossroads of a nation, Land of Lincoln, let me express my deepest gratitude for the privilege of addressing this convention.

Tonight is a particular honor for me because—let's face it—my presence on this stage is pretty unlikely. My father was a foreign student, born and raised in a small village in Kenya. He grew up herding goats, went to school in a tin-roof shack. His father—my grandfather—was a cook, a domestic servant to the British.

Delivered on July 28, 2004, at Boston, MA.

But my grandfather had larger dreams for his son. Through hard work and perseverance my father got a scholarship to study in a magical place, America, that shone as a beacon of freedom and opportunity to so many who had come before.

While studying here, my father met my mother. She was born in a town on the other side of the world, in Kansas. Her father worked on oil rigs and farms through most of the Depression. The day after Pearl Harbor my grandfather signed up for duty, joined Patton's army, marched across Europe. Back home, my grandmother raised their baby and went to work on a bomber assembly line. After the war, they studied on the G.I. Bill, bought a house through F.H.A., and later moved west all the way to Hawaii in search of opportunity.

And they, too, had big dreams for their daughter. A common dream, born of two continents.

My parents shared not only an improbable love, they shared an abiding faith in the possibilities of this nation. They would give me an African name, Barack, or "blessed," believing that in a tolerant America your name is no barrier to success. They imagined me going to the best schools in the land, even though they weren't rich, because in a generous America you don't have to be rich to achieve your potential.

They are both passed away now. And yet, I know that, on this night, they look down on me with great pride.

I stand here today, grateful for the diversity of my heritage, aware that my parents' dreams live on in my two precious daughters. I stand here knowing that my story is part of the larger American story, that I owe a debt to all of those who came before me, and that, in no other country on earth, is my story even possible.

Tonight, we gather to affirm the greatness of our nation—not because of the height of our skyscrapers, or the power of our military, or the size of our economy. Our pride is based on a very simple premise, summed up in a declaration made over 200 years ago: "We hold these truths to be self-evident, that all men are created equal. That they are endowed by their Creator with certain inalienable rights. That among these are life, liberty and the pursuit of happiness."

That is the true genius of America—a faith in simple dreams, an insistence on small miracles. That we can tuck in our children at night and know that they are fed and clothed and safe from harm. That we can say what we think, write what we think, without hearing a sudden knock on the door. That we can have an idea and start our own business without paying a bribe. That we can participate in the political process without fear of retribution, and that our votes will be counted—at least, most of the time.

This year, in this election, we are called to reaffirm our values and our commitments, to hold them against a hard reality and see how we are measuring up, to the legacy of our forbearers, and the promise of future generations.

And fellow Americans, Democrats, Republicans, Independents—I say to you tonight: we have more work to do. More work to do for the workers I met in Galesburg, Ill., who are losing their union jobs at the Maytag plant that's moving to Mexico, and now are having to compete with their own children for jobs that pay seven bucks an hour. More to do for the father that I met who was losing his job and choking back the tears, wondering how he would pay $4,500 a month for the drugs his son needs without the health benefits that he counted on. More to do for the young woman in East St. Louis, and thousands more like her, who has the grades, has the drive, has the will, but doesn't have the money to go to college.

Now don't get me wrong. The people I meet—in small towns and big cities, in diners and office parks—they don't expect government to solve all their problems. They know they have to work hard to get ahead—and they want to.

Go into the collar counties around Chicago, and people will tell you they don't want their tax money wasted, by a welfare agency or by the Pentagon.

Go into any inner city neighborhood, and folks will tell you that government alone can't teach our kids to learn—they know that parents have to teach, that children can't achieve unless we raise their expectations and turn off the television sets and eradicate the slander that says a black youth with a book is acting white. They know those things.

People don't expect government to solve all their problems. But they sense, deep in their bones, that with just a slight change in priorities, we can make sure that every child in America has a decent shot at life, and that the doors of opportunity remain open to all.

They know we can do better. And they want that choice.

In this election, we offer that choice. Our Party has chosen a man to lead us who embodies the best this country has to offer. And that man is John Kerry. John Kerry understands the ideals of community, faith, and service because they've defined his life. From his heroic service to Vietnam, to his years as a prosecutor and lieutenant governor, through two decades in the United States Senate, he has devoted himself to this country. Again and again, we've seen him make tough choices when easier ones were available.

His values—and his record—affirm what is best in us. John Kerry believes in an America where hard work is rewarded; so instead of offering tax breaks to companies shipping jobs overseas, he offers them to companies creating jobs here at home.

John Kerry believes in an America where all Americans can afford the same health coverage our politicians in Washington have for themselves.

John Kerry believes in energy independence, so we aren't held hostage to the profits of oil companies, or the sabotage of foreign oil fields.

John Kerry believes in the Constitutional freedoms that have made our country the envy of the world, and he will never sacrifice our basic liberties, nor use faith as a wedge to divide us.

> *There is not a liberal America and a conservative America— there is the United States of America.*

And John Kerry believes that in a dangerous world war must be an option sometimes, but it should never be the first option.

You know, a while back, I met a young man named Seamus in a V.F.W. Hall in East Moline, Ill. He was a good-looking kid, six-two, six-three, clear eyed, with an easy smile. He told me he'd joined the Marines, and was heading to Iraq the following week. And as I listened to him explain why he'd enlisted, the absolute faith he had in our country and its leaders, his devotion to duty and service, I thought this young man was all that any of us might hope for in a child. But then I asked myself: Are we serving Seamus as well as he is serving us?

I thought of the 900 men and women—sons and daughters, husbands and wives, friends and neighbors, who won't be returning to their own hometowns. I thought of the families I've met who were struggling to get by without a loved one's full income, or whose loved ones had returned with a limb missing or nerves shattered, but who still lacked long-term health benefits because they were Reservists.

When we send our young men and women into harm's way, we have a solemn obligation not to fudge the numbers or shade the truth about why they're going, to care for their families while they're gone, to tend to the soldiers upon their return, and to never ever go to war without enough troops to win the war, secure the peace, and earn the respect of the world.

Now let me be clear. Let me be clear. We have real enemies in the world. These enemies must be found. They must be pursued—and they must be defeated. John Kerry knows this.

And just as Lieutenant Kerry did not hesitate to risk his life to protect the men who served with him in Vietnam, President Kerry will not hesitate one moment to use our military might to keep America safe and secure.

John Kerry believes in America. And he knows that it's not enough for just some of us to prosper. For alongside our famous individualism, there's another ingredient in the American saga. A belief that we're all connected as one people.

If there is a child on the south side of Chicago who can't read, that matters to me, even if it's not my child. If there's a senior citizen somewhere who can't pay for their prescription drugs, and has to choose between medicine and the rent, that makes my life poorer, even if it's not my grandparent. If there's an Arab American family being rounded up without benefit of an attorney or due process, that threatens my civil liberties.

It is that fundamental belief, it is that fundamental belief, I am my brother's keeper, I am my sister's keeper that makes this country work. It's what allows us to pursue our individual dreams and yet still come together as one American family.

E pluribus unum. Out of many, one.

Now even as we speak, there are those who are preparing to divide us, the spin masters, the negative ad peddlers who embrace the politics of anything goes. Well, I say to them tonight, there is not a liberal America and a conservative America—there is the United States of America. There is not a Black America and a White America and Latino America and Asian America—there's the United States of America.

The pundits, the pundits like to slice-and-dice our country into Red States and Blue States; Red States for Republicans, Blue States for Democrats. But I've got news for them, too. We worship an awesome God in the Blue States, and we don't like federal agents poking around in our libraries in the Red States. We coach Little League in the Blue States and yes, we've got some gay friends in the Red States. There are patriots who opposed the war in Iraq and there are patriots who supported the war in Iraq.

We are one people, all of us pledging allegiance to the stars and stripes, all of us defending the United States of America. In the end, that's what this election is about. Do we participate in a politics of cynicism or do we participate in a politics of hope?

John Kerry calls on us to hope. John Edwards calls on us to hope.

I'm not talking about blind optimism here—the almost willful ignorance that thinks unemployment will go away if we just don't think about it, or the health care crisis will solve itself if we just ignore it. That's not what I'm talking about. I'm talking about something more substantial. It's the hope of slaves sitting around a fire singing freedom songs. The hope of immigrants setting out for distant shores. The hope of a young naval lieutenant bravely patrolling the Mekong Delta. The hope of a millworker's son who dares to defy the odds. The hope of a skinny kid with a funny name who believes that America has a place for him, too.

Hope in the face of difficulty. Hope in the face of uncertainty. The audacity of hope! In the end, that is God's greatest gift to us, the bedrock of this nation. A belief in things not seen. A belief that there are better days ahead.

I believe that we can give our middle class relief and provide working families with a road to opportunity. I believe we can provide jobs to the jobless, homes to the homeless, and reclaim young people in cities across America from violence and despair. I believe that we have a righteous wind at our backs and that as we stand on the crossroads of history, we can make the right choices, and meet the challenges that face us.

America! Tonight, if you feel the same energy that I do, if you feel the same urgency that I do, if you feel the same passion I do, if you feel the same hopefulness that I do—if we do what we must do, then I have no doubts that all across the country, from Florida to Oregon, from Washington to Maine, the people will rise up in November, and John Kerry will be sworn in as president, and John Edwards will be sworn in as vice president, and this country will reclaim its promise, and out of this long political darkness a brighter day will come.

Thank you very much everybody. God bless you. Thank you.

Thank you, and God bless America.

Peel Back the Label

Kenneth S. Beldon

Lead minister of a new Unitarian Universalist Congregation to be launched in Chester County, PA, 2005– ; born Brooklyn, NY, March 23, 1970; B.A., Oberlin College, 1992; M.A. in religion, Yale University Divinity School, 1994; M.Div., Union Theological Seminary, 1998; raised a Reform Jew, but has sought to combine the Jewish and Christian traditions as a Unitarian Universalist; minister, River of Grass Unitarian Universalist Congregation, 1998–2005; Hansen Award, 1998, Union Seminary, for the graduating student entering the ministry who best relates issues in theology, philosophy, and ethics to topics in contemporary society; author, "O Brother, Where Art Thou?," The UU (Unitarian Universalist) Voice, 2000.

Editors' introduction: During the weekly worship service on the Sunday after the presidential election in 2004, Reverend Beldon addressed his congregation. Aware of the "divisiveness" caused by the campaign, Reverend Beldon reminded those present that "political life in America has always been hard fought." "As a religious community," he counseled, "we have a calling as well that transcends party or politics, a mission to make our values manifest regardless of whether these ideas win or lose at the ballot box." The River of Grass congregation is a liberal religious community in Western Broward County, Florida, and is part of the Unitarian Universalist Association. The mission of the church is to provide a caring spiritual community that helps its members in the quest for meaning and purpose in life.

Kenneth S. Beldon's speech: The *New York Post* had this to say about one of the candidates: "A vote for [him] is a vote against God. If he is elected president, the people of the nation will receive the just vengeance of an insulted heaven, will witness our dwellings in flames, hoary hairs bathed in blood, female chastity violated and children writhing on the pike . . ."

Perhaps those last few archaic phrases give it away; The *Post* wasn't writing about this election, and the man referred to, whose Presidency would most surely bring about doom wasn't John Kerry or George W. Bush. The year was 1800 and the politician was Thomas Jefferson who was locked in a bitterly divided, geographically polarizing, personally antagonistic race against John Adams.

Jefferson, the author of what is universally recognized as our most holy national writ, the most esteemed and debated and revered of the Founders. From our perspective we know that Jef-

---

Delivered on November 7, 2004, at Southwest Ranches, Broward Cournty, Florida. Reprinted with permission of Kenneth S. Beldon.

ferson helped give birth to our nation, so what a silly prediction it seems to us to make that Jefferson's Presidency would bring about the end of the Republic even as it was just getting started. With over two centuries of American history in our rearview mirror, we look back at this judgment in laughter.

This history lesson is really a moral tale this morning. However we feel about the outcome of Tuesday's presidential contest—depressed, satisfied, encouraged, disappointed—we've all heard about or experienced the bitterness, the divisiveness, the supposedly unprecedented cleavage that this election revealed through the heart of America and think that somehow we're unique in the utter discord of our era; that this time America is irredeemably fractured.

But it's just not true. Political life in America has always been hard fought and electoral maps have always revealed that from among the *unum*, there is the *pluribus*, the many, varying perspectives within America that has always comprised America. Don't believe the myth that we are now so divided that we don't know how we can possibly go forward from here. Elections are contests and contests are based upon opposites. But there are truths greater than opposition in our national life.

Don't believe the myth that we are now so divided that we don't know how we can possibly go forward from here.

The great blessing of American life is that we don't lurch from revolution to revolution, we continue to exist from administration to administration, now for over 200 years, and peacefully so internally for 150 years. When you study the blood soaked history of kings and regimes and dictators, you realize what a noble experiment our nation is.

We can affirm this morning, as the President of our denomination did this past week that our faith in democracy is deserved not because of a particular outcome but because of the process of democracy itself. Unlike four years ago, in this close election, there was a clear-cut winner. There was something oddly enlivening about being a Floridian four years ago in the weeks after the 2000 election. Sort of like when a child misbehaves because s/he knows that then they'll be the center of attention, we knew that all eyes were upon us back then, on our chads and our recounts, and regardless of the reason, it was sort of thrilling to be involved in the drama.

I've a feeling, though, that if we saw a repeat this time around, whether in our own state or elsewhere, we would have been like the survivors of a horror movie who make it to the sequel, only to discover that still the monster lives, and we would have just wanted to huddle in the corner, whimpering, "Please, please just make it go away." This morning we don't have to live in the light of uncertainty. Our election went forward, and our election revealed the will of the American people who cared enough to vote and be involved. That is as it should be and is deserving of our national faith.

As for the outcome of the election itself, I've seen enough of your bumper stickers and been around enough of you this week to know that many, not all by any means, but many of you are disappointed. Personally, my candidate did not win, either. But, I'm not here this morning to preach to you as a registered Democrat; you have not called me to be your minister to perform in such a capacity, and as there are many finer places to receive election analysis you won't hear 20 minutes more this morning of those thoughts from this pulpit.

This is as good a moment as any be mindful of what Rev. Sinkford also said this week to all of us in his open letter to our Unitarian Universalist communities—that we are liberal religion, we are not liberal politics. Some of you stand to my right politically, and some of you to my left, but we all stand together this morning as Unitarian Universalists.

We don't gather every four years as political conventions do to nominate a candidate to take us through an election; we gather every week in all sorts of seasons to give testimony to our values of compassion and care and encouragement to one another, and to stand as a testament to the kind of rare and precious religious community that does not hold each other to the narrowest test of creed or practice, but instead exists to enlarge our circle of hope to all who wish to belong to this people.

In whatever emotional place you find yourself this morning in regard to the election, I encourage you to stay involved in our democratic process. Democracy happens more often than just every four years. In one of the many, many morals and meanings that still spin out of from September 11th, remember that even as people rushed to give blood after the horrific events of that day, that it was those who gave blood on that ordinary day of September the 10th whose gifts meant the most, because their blood was already there when the need was the greatest. If this election burned itself deep down into your psyche, then I encourage you to mourn, or to celebrate, as you must, and then get back to the business of being a citizen in our nation, a calling that echoes beyond just the moment of any particular election.

As a religious community we have a calling as well that transcends party or politics, a mission to make our values manifest regardless of whether these ideas win or lose at the ballot box. Jim Wallis, the editor of *Sojourners Magazine*, phrased it well this past week in his reflection on the election:

> Clearly, God is not a Republican or a Democrat, as we sought to point out, and the best contribution of religion is precisely not to be ideologically predictable or loyally partisan but to

maintain the moral independence to critique both the left and the right.

In a deeply polarized country, commentators reported that either political outcome would "crush" the hopes of almost half the population. So perhaps the most important role for the religious community will come now, when the need for some kind of political healing and reconciliation has become painfully clear. In the spirit of America's greatest religious leader, the Reverend Martin Luther King Jr., the religious community could help a divided nation find common ground by moving to higher ground. And we should hold ourselves and both political parties accountable to the challenge of the biblical prophet Micah to "do justice, love kindness, and walk humbly with your God."

Wallis knows that religion is at its best when it is not co-opted by partisan affiliation. To me the most dismaying dynamic of the campaign season was the way in which both sides played the religion card against the other.

In just the two weeks leading up to the election right here in Broward, on successive Sunday mornings Senator Kerry appeared in the pulpit of a Baptist Church and a former Republican legislator from Texas occupied central space in the worship service of Calvary Chapel. From my perspective, both messages are spiritually unacceptable, because the meaning behind each is that religious identity is easily translated into a particular political party's platform. People within a faith community can share a core set of values even if they disagree about how best to implement those values and even about whether a political solution should have any hand in the broadcasting of those values. A God who is a Democrat or a Republican is simply a God fashioned into too small a human package, an idol set up to convince us of the rightness of our cause. To me, God must always be an Independent.

This year I chose not to put a candidate's sticker upon my car. Win or lose, the sticker would have to be torn off anyway come November 2nd. Instead, as some of you may have seen, my back bumper reads, "Civil Marriage is a Civil Right," sponsored by our Unitarian Universalist Association. In states both red and blue, 11 states in all, voters denied the right for gays and lesbians to be wed. If you read the polling, you know that marriage equality is opposed by some of the core voting constituents of the Democratic Party. But I wanted a statement that spoke for the values of my religion, and this community, which is a Welcoming Congregation, and practices Universalism in both word and deed. That sticker isn't coming off, because it speaks for something bigger than a political party, and for a value that goes to the heart of my faith.

And there are other values as well that go to the heart of our faith and transcend any easy label and bind us, each to the other, qualities that allow us to speak together and be together regardless of difference. I was a first year student at an overwhelmingly left-wing college when the small band of campus Young Republicans sponsored a lecture by a group of Contras from Nicaragua. The visit barely came off because of protestors, and as the spokesperson for the Contras approached the microphone to deliver his speech, the leader of the Socialist Youth on campus began haranguing him and shouted him down, along with dozens of others.

At that point the leader of the Young Republicans stepped to the microphone and began exchanging insults with the Socialist Youth leader. Back and forth, the insults rang, "You're a fascist stooge with blood on your hands!" "You're a proletariat who serves a communist totalitarian master." "Get a life, son of the ruling class." "Get a haircut, you Stalinist moron." Back and forth it went. The Contra leader eventually spoke briefly and then left. So much for political dialogue or even effective protest.

Anyway, about two days later, I was walking through the campus center and, there, at a table before me, was the leader of the Socialist Youth and the leader of the Young Republicans, sitting together, talking, laughing, drinking coffee. First of all, it made me think that part of their show the other night was just that, a demonstration to prove their ideological bona fides to their respective followers that was, like a lot of politics, manufactured drama. As I sat and pretended to read across from them and peered at them over my book, I saw that the yelling the other night might have been the act, because what they were sharing was real and authentic; they truly enjoyed each other's company. I walked away feeling almost a sense of relief, and believing then as I do to this day, that there is a truth of human relationship deeper than partisanship that will reveal itself if we allow it to.

There is a truth of human relationship deeper than partisanship that will reveal itself if we allow it to.

It is also a psychological truth that the closer you are to someone the more pronounced your differences can become. As an example, look at two siblings who are similar in age in the back seat of a car fighting for control of who has 51% elbow room of the armrest between them and you'll understand what I mean. In any contest where the outcome is in doubt things will become heated, with the differences magnified and similarities dismissed. That's certainly true in politics. Right now red and blue seem like opposing pieces in a board game.

Clearly there is a general tide of red and blue states in this country, broken down regionally. But even in a very blue state like Connecticut, 44% of the people voted for the President. In a red state like Tennessee, Senator Kerry received 43% of the vote. In red states there are millions of Kerry voters and in blue states, there are millions of Bush voters. No state is just one thing.

More importantly, no person is just one thing. We have become so accustomed these last few weeks of seeing the American people as segments on a pie chart, sliced into segments of race, age, gender, income level, province all in the attempt to correlate voter preference to demographic profile. All political operatives have to look at the world this way, but a religious community should not. If we do, we risk losing the individual trees for our attempts to take in the whole forest. If our Universalist heritage makes a meaningful difference in our lives, if we assert that all are welcome and all matter, then to look at the world and its people as types and labels is a violation of our faith.

Our Universalism leads us in the path away from superficial understanding. In this election, both former NYC Mayor Ed Koch and Rev. Pat Robertson supported the President. Do they both see the world exactly the same? Both President Eisenhower's son and Michael Moore supported Senator Kerry; how much do we assume they have in common? On the other side, one of my best friends in the world almost always votes Republican. We talk religion, music, baseball, love, family, but don't agree on politics. But I would trust my life in his hands.

There is no such thing as a Kerry supporter and there is no such thing as a Bush voter. There is no such thing as a Republican and no such thing as a Democrat. Not absolutely. Call this my Snowflake Theology. When each of us is treated as a gift, each of us unique, then we can begin seeing what we might have truly in common. Seeing the world with labels attached is shorthand that enables us to get a quick glimpse of the world and make a judgment. It's a necessary tool for knowing which car to buy or which detergent we like, but shorthand will only reveal the most obvious aspects of our existence. Labels are never the path to wisdom.

A colleague of mine, the Reverend Barbara Merritt, tells of a day she spent in the company of a male fundamentalist minister clearing an abandoned, drug-strewn lot in Worcester, MA, where they both serve religious communities. As they carefully picked up the used hypodermics and empty crack vials, Barbara reflected on the fact that in the theology of this fundamentalist, Barbara was doubly suspect, both as a Unitarian Universalist and as a woman ordained to ministry. At the same time, though, here were the two of them sharing a common religious dedication, outside on a blustery New England day, trying together to beautify a forgotten portion of the world that had been abandoned to ugliness. What mattered more—his theology or their mutual help? As the garbage around them diminished, she had her answer, one that confirmed in her heart the Universalism to which she had dedicated her life.

Among the most beautiful portions of Scripture are the Psalms, timeless like Shakespeare is timeless because a psalm gets inside of what faith and doubt and devotion and hope feel like. Psalm 139 asks this question, "Search me, O God, and know my heart: try me, and know my thoughts." Search me, open me up, get to the core of me and see who I am.

That is not a political inquiry, for politics, as Bismarck famously said, is the art of what is possible. But religion is the realm of the imaginable, and it takes time to reveal the depths of the imagination. Much longer than a political season, much longer than it takes a person to tell you how they voted. That's just one thing about us. And far from the most important thing. "Search me and know my heart: try me, and know my thoughts"; such is an invitation into the essence of who we are, a more wide ranging call to be a religious people. Let us go forward in that spirit together.

Amen. I love you. May you live in blessing.

The Culture Wars

Robert B. Reich

University professor and Maurice B. Hexter Professor of Social and Economic Policy, Brandeis University and its Heller School of Policy and Management, 1997– ; born Scranton, PA, June 24, 1946, raised in South Salem, New York; B.A. and Rhodes scholar, Dartmouth College, 1968; M.A., University College of Oxford University, 1970; J.D., Yale Law School, 1973; M.A., Dartmouth College, 1988; assistant solicitor general, 1974–76; director of policy planning, Federal Trade Commission, 1976–81; taught at Harvard University's Kennedy School of Government, 1981–92; secretary of Labor, 1993–97; host of four-part public TV series, Made in America, *1992; writer and host PBS special,* At the Grass Roots, *1998; weekly radio commentary program,* Marketplace, *public radio; co-founder, national editor, and chair of editorial board,* The American Prospect, *1990; author some dozen books, including* Next American Frontier *(1983),* Work of Nations *(1991),* Locked in the Cabinet *(1997), and* Reason: Why Liberals Will Win the Battle for America *(2004); other books, articles, and commentaries at www.robertreich.org; Vaclav Havel Vision Foundation Prize, 2003.*

Editors' introduction: Professor Reich gave the Ralph Milliband Lecture, named in memory of the influential British politician and social thinker, at the London School of Economics, in London. The audience was composed of graduate students, faculty, and invited guests. "The political fault-line in modern America," maintained Professor Reich, "has become cultural. It is about religion, sex, and firearms (or, in the vernacular, God, gays, and guns)." "One thing is clear," he cautioned, "America's culture wars are diverting the nation's attention from dealing with the economic fundamentals."

Robert B. Reich's speech: About the same portion of Americans describe themselves as being liberal (19 per cent) as believe that the world will come to an end in their lifetimes (17 per cent). Right-wingers have so effectively besmirched the term ("wishy-washy liberals," "tax-and-spend liberals," "limousine liberals"), that only a few political martyrs and masochists publicly proclaim their allegiance to the cause once championed by Franklin D. Roosevelt.

The word preferred by left-of-centre types in the U.S. is "progressive," which hearkens back to the earlier Roosevelt, Teddy, a turbocharged Republican who whipped monopolists and gleefully asserted the power of the federal government.

Delivered on March 22, 2005, London, England. Reprinted with permission of Robert B. Reich.

FDR's robust liberalism focused on social justice at a time when one in four workers had lost their jobs to the Great Depression, and then on social solidarity when the U.S. entered the Second World War. By now, much of that twin legacy has disappeared.

> *The political fault-line in modern America has become cultural.*

But look beneath current political labels and you find a nation still clinging to several liberal ideals. Polls show, for example, that an overwhelming majority of Americans support social security, unemployment insurance, and a minimum wage, as well as Medicare for the elderly (courtesy of Lyndon B. Johnson), strong environmental protections (Richard Nixon's contribution, surprisingly enough), and a graduated income tax. Most believe that government has no business snooping into people's private lives without cause to believe that they have been involved in crime. The vast majority favour equal civil rights for blacks, women, and ethnic minorities. And George W. Bush's swagger notwithstanding, most Americans oppose unilateral assertions of U.S. power abroad. An overwhelming majority believe we should work in close concert with our long-standing allies, including France. The shrill, right-wing rantings of radio and television talk-show hosts do not reflect the views of most Americans—or the manner in which they disagree with one another.

The political fault-line in modern America has become cultural. It is about religion, sex, and firearms (or, in the vernacular, God, gays, and guns). Since 9/11, the culture war has been extended to global terrorism.

On the conservative side are Americans who attend church regularly, believe that homosexuality is morally wrong, want the government to ban abortions, take offence at out-of-wedlock births, and think they have a God-given right to own any gun they wish. They also want the U.S. to exterminate all terrorists, including anyone with terrorist leanings.

Most of the people who think this way reside in rural and southern parts of the nation, towns and small cities, and outlying suburbs. They are the majority in what are now called "red states"—states that lit up bright red on the electronic TV maps late on election day 2000, when returns showed that most of their voters had cast ballots for Bush. They dine nightly on meat, potatoes, and a vegetable, watch Fox News, shop at Wal-Mart, and enjoy NASCAR races and wrestling on TV. They earn between $20,000 and $60,000 a year—straddling the middle and working classes, doing jobs ranging from mechanic to clerical worker, beautician to physical therapist, and low-level managerial and technical work.

On the liberal side of the cultural divide are those whose church attendance is irregular at best, who harbour far more permissive attitudes toward sex, and think government should control gun ownership and ban handguns and assault rifles. They believe terrorism is a complex problem, requiring better intelligence and more effective ways to win the hearts and minds of Muslims who now opt for suicide missions.

These people tend to inhabit America's sprawling metropolitan regions in the north-east and on the west coast, the larger cities and the inner suburbs. They are the majority in the "blue states" that went for Al Gore. Their tastes in food tend toward varied national and ethnic cuisines. They watch the major TV networks or public television, and play golf or baseball. They typically earn between $60,000 and $200,000 a year or they earn under $20,000. Cultural liberals tend to be both richer and poorer than cultural conservatives—moderately paid professionals such as teachers, lawyers, and social workers, or else low-paid employees such as hospital orderlies, retail and restaurant workers, and hotel personnel. In other words, they are more cosmopolitan than cultural conservatives and more diverse.

Why God, gays, guns, and true-grit? These are proxies for two distinct temperaments that divide the U.S. like a meat axe.

On the conservative side is a moral absolutism that views the nation's greatest challenge as holding firm to enduring values in the face of titanic economic and social changes. The common thread uniting strong religious conviction, rigid sexual norms, and an insistence on owning a gun is the assertion of authority, typically by men. The task is to apply strict discipline to those who might stray from established norms, and to win what are repeatedly seen as "tests of will."

Since 9/11, this has also taken the form of patriotic bravado and stubborn pugnacity. America, say cultural conservatives, must remain the strongest nation on earth. The best way to deal with terrorists is to demonstrate toughness and never waver. Better to be feared than loved; better to be consistent than appear indecisive. The tough-talking, born-again cowboy president, George W. Bush, perfectly exemplifies this world-view. Bring 'em on, he says. You're with us or against us.

On the liberal (progressive) side of the cultural divide is a belief in tolerance, reason, and law as central tenets of democracy. Americans who hold to this view consider all public issues to be soluble with the correct and relevant information, subjected to objective analysis and full deliberation. Religion and sex fall outside the public sphere because they are inherently private matters. A vibrant democracy must tolerate different beliefs and personal choices. Gun ownership directly affects the public sphere and, as such, is subject to regulation if there are good reasons to limit it. (As there are.)

By extension, the battle against global terrorism requires that we be smart rather than merely tough. We have to get our facts straight (Saddam Hussein had no weapons of mass destruction), tell the public the truth (Iraq played no part in 9/11), apply rational analysis (our first priority must be to keep nuclear weapons out of the hands of potential terrorists), and respect international law (work through the UN and NATO, and don't torture prisoners). We also need to get at the causes of terrorism—the hate and hopelessness that fuels it. If you want to understand John Kerry, look no further.

Cultural conservatives condemn liberals as having no strict moral compass, as being "moral relativists" and "flip-floppers." Conservatives fear liberals will sell out because they don't know what they stand for. In fact, liberals do have strong beliefs (again: tolerance, reason, democratic debate, the rule of law), but these beliefs seem more about process than substance and do not lend themselves to 30-second soundbites. To liberals, most issues are complicated and nuanced. This attitude drives moral absolutists nuts. American liberals, for their part, worry that the right-wing conservatives are stubborn, intolerant zealots who shoot before they think. Recent history seems to bear out these fears.

Presidential elections in modern America have been about these contrasting world-views since at least 1964. Starting with Barry Goldwater's failed bid in that year and continuing through Nixon,

---

America's culture wars are diverting the nation's attention from dealing with the economic fundamentals.

Reagan, and the two Bushes, the new right has emphasised moral absolutes and the need for authority and discipline to enforce them. By contrast, Jimmy Carter, Bill Clinton, Gore, and now Kerry have focused their campaigns on tolerance, reason, and democracy. Republican candidates repeatedly talk about toughness and resolve, while liberals talk about being correct and thinking problems through. On balance, toughness and resolve have proved the easier sell, especially when American voters are worried about something big.

What about social justice? This part of FDR's liberal legacy has been eclipsed by the culture wars. This is especially odd when the biggest thing voters worry about is their jobs and pay checks, and the pay check (including wages and job benefits) of most Americans has been declining for two decades, adjusted for inflation. The gulf between rich and poor in America is now wider than at any time since the robber barons of the late 19th century monopolised industry and bribed the government to do nothing about it.

Yet, in recent years, Democratic candidates have not dwelt on the subject. They have bought the conventional view that economic populism does not sell because most Americans still want and expect to become rich one day. That is rubbish: upward mobility has just about ground to a halt. And it's circular reasoning. Economic populism would sell if Democratic politicians explained to the public what has been happening and why.

America is splitting into "have mores" and "have lesses" because the twin forces of globalisation and technological change are rewarding the educated and well-connected, while punishing the less educated and the disconnected.

What to do about this? There are solutions that do not require protectionism and neo-Luddism, solutions much in keeping with the liberal legacy of FDR, but too few of today's liberals have been discussing them and the American public doesn't have a clue. They center on education—from access to high-quality early childhood through affordable higher education. They also involve such innovations as wage insurance (so if you lose a higher-paying job and must settle for a lower-paying one, half the difference will be remitted to you for, say, six months). You hear them discussed mostly in the rarefied precincts of university towns such as Cambridge, Massachusetts, and Berkeley, California, whose inhabitants talk to one another and convince themselves that the rest of the nation must be saying the same things.

One thing is clear: America's culture wars are diverting the nation's attention from dealing with the economic fundamentals. History has shown repeatedly that when people are economically distressed and anxious, when everything they have known of their jobs and their communities is subject to upheaval and they have no firm ground on which to stand, they are most vulnerable to demagogues who offer them the comfort of certainty—of firm belief, regardless of fact. Authoritarianism is always most alluring to those who cannot comprehend what is happening to them, who crave simple answers. It is a dangerous attraction.

Homosexuality: The Threat to the Family and the Attack on Marriage

Peter Sprigg

Vice president for Policy, Family Research Council (FRC), 2005-; born New York, NY, 1957; B.A. summa cum laude, Drew University, NJ, 1979, majoring in political science and economics; master of divinity cum laude, Gordon-Conwell Theological Seminary, Mass, 1997; economic development assistant with U.S. Representative Robert F. Drinan, 1980–81; community energy specialist, Municipal Power Project, 1982; unit leader, Covenant Players (Christian drama ministry), 1983–93, traveling in U.S., Australia, Papua New Guinea, Germany, Austria, and Switzerland; pastor, Clifton Park Center Baptist Church, Clifton Park, NY, 1997–2001; senior director of Culture Studies, FRC, 2001–03; director, Center for Marriage and Family Studies, FRC, 2003–04; senior director of Policy Studies, FRC, 2004–05; appeared on NBC, ABC, CBS, CNN, MSNBC, and Fox News; co-editor (with Timothy Dailey), Getting It Straight: What the Research Shows About Homosexuality, *2004; author,* Outrage: How Gay Activists and Liberal Judges Are Trashing Democracy to Redefine Marriage, *2004.*

Editors' introduction: Some 2,800 delegates from 40 nations attended the World Congress of Families III (WCF III) in Mexico, March 29–31, 2004. They endorsed the "Mexico City Declaration" intended to "defend the family" against forces that "challenge the family's very legitimacy as an institution." Ms. Martha Fox, First Lady of Mexico, welcomed the delegates, declaring that "the future of mankind is forged in the family." A letter from President George W. Bush was read to the Congress. In addressing WCF III, representing the Family Research Council (FRC), Mr. Sprigg told the delegates that "homosexuality and homosexual civil marriage would rip the fabric of society in ways that may be difficult, if not impossible, to mend." FRC states its mission to be "champion[ing] marriage and family as the foundation of civilization, the seedbed of virtue, and the wellspring of society. FRC shapes public debate and formulates public policy that values human life and upholds the institutions of marriage and the family."

Peter Sprigg's speech: After individual human life itself, nothing is more precious or more essential to the survival and the success of human society than the family. The family is more important than the United Nations, more important than our individual countries, and more important than our cities, towns, or villages. The family is

---

Delivered on March 29, 2004, at Mexico City, Mexico. Reprinted with permission of Peter Sprigg.

more important than our schools, corporations, or our civic organizations.

The family is more important than all of these things, because human civilization is built from the bottom up, not the top down. The first brick of the foundation is individual human life, and the second brick is the family. This raises crucial questions: What is a family? What makes a family?

Some people answer that question by saying, "Love makes a family." That sounds nice, but while love is, as the saying goes, "a many-splendored thing," love alone is not enough to make a family. In truth, what makes a family is one man and one woman united in marriage for a lifetime, and the children born from that union.

Not every family lives up to that ideal. Some people become single parents through no fault of their own, because of death or abandonment. Some loving couples adopt children in order to create a new family structure that reproduces as closely as possible the circumstances of a natural family. But it is important for society to continue to uphold the traditional family structure as the ideal family. It is important to uphold that ideal because it is the family

---

> *It is important for society to continue to uphold the traditional family structure as the ideal family.*

---

structure most consistent with what the American Declaration of Independence refers to as "the laws of nature and of nature's God."

However, even if someone doesn't believe in natural law, or even in God, there is still a good reason to uphold the ideal of the traditional family.

The reason the married, one-man, one-woman natural family is the ideal family is that we know that both the spouses and the children in such families have a better chance in life. Such children, for instance, do better academically, financially, emotionally, and behaviorally. They have better health, and they delay sexual activity longer. The evidence for this in the social science literature is overwhelming.

It is because the family is so crucial to society that we call ourselves "pro-family." We want to do everything we can to support, encourage, assist, maintain, and promote traditional families and do everything we can to maintain that ideal of the married, one-man, one-woman natural family.

However, in order to defend what we are for—the family—we often must define what we are against. We are against anything that threatens the traditional family or undermines that ideal. That means that we are against parents snuffing out the lives of their own unborn children through abortion. It means that we are against drug and alcohol abuse, domestic violence, and child abuse.

It means that we are against illegitimacy, abandonment, and divorce. And it means that we are against any sexual behavior that would undermine the uniqueness of the faithful, lifelong marriage bond between a husband and wife. We are against premarital sex, pornography, adultery, and prostitution. And yes, we are also against the practice of homosexuality.

Now, you may ask, if we are for something so simple and profound as family, and against so many things that threaten it, why is it that one of these threats—homosexuality—gets so much attention? It's not because homosexuality is a greater sin than any other. It's not because we want to deprive homosexuals of their fundamental human rights. It's not because we are afraid to be near homosexuals, and it's not because we hate homosexuals. On the contrary, I desire the very best for them. And desiring the best for someone, and acting to bring that about, is the essence of love. However, I do not believe that engaging in behavior that is unnatural, immoral, and dangerous both to public health and to their own health is the best thing for people with same-sex attractions.

> *As one part of our broad-based efforts to support the traditional family, we oppose what is sometimes called "the gay agenda."*

And so, as one part of our broad-based efforts to support the traditional family, we oppose what is sometimes called "the gay agenda." It is an agenda that demands the full acceptance of the practice of homosexuality—morally, socially, legally, religiously, politically, and financially. Indeed, it calls for not only acceptance, but affirmation and celebration of this behavior as normal. It even demands that homosexuality be seen as desirable for those who desire it. This is "the gay agenda"—and we are against it.

This agenda has already made remarkable progress. Homosexual activists knew that their behavior would never be accepted as "normal" if doctors considered it a form of mental illness. Therefore, in 1973 they forced a resolution through the American Psychiatric Association to remove homosexuality from the *Diagnostic and Statistical Manual of Mental Disorders*. It is important for everyone to realize that the 1973 decision was *not* the result of new clinical research or scientific evidence. It was, rather, a *political* decision made in response to a vicious campaign of harassment and intimidation by homosexual activists.

Indeed, studies actually continue to show that homosexuals experience high rates of mental illness. For example, the Netherlands Mental Health Survey and Incidence Study, reported in the *Archives of General Psychiatry* in 2001, found that "people with same-sex sexual behavior are at greater risk for psychiatric disorders."[1] The fact that this is true even in one of the most "gay-friendly" nations on earth—indeed, the first nation to grant same-sex civil marriage—undermines any argument that such mental illnesses are merely a reaction to society's alleged "discrimination."

A second element in the agenda is to persuade people that those who engage in homosexual behavior are "born that way." If people are "born gay," it makes it more difficult to argue that a homosexual orientation is abnormal, or that homosexual behavior is immoral. It is astonishing how pervasive this concept has become—especially in light of the fact that there is *no* convincing scientific evidence that homosexuality is determined by either genetics or biology. Only a tiny handful of studies have ever been put forward to make such a claim. Unfortunately, the scientific critiques that discredited those studies have never quite caught up to the original media hype.

A third element of the homosexual agenda is to get "sexual orientation" added to the categories of protection under anti-discrimination codes in private organizations and under civil rights laws in the public sector. In fact, homosexuals should and already do have all of the same rights under the law as any other citizen, such as the right to vote, the right of free speech, and the right to trial by jury. Those rights are truly "civil" or political in nature, and the exercise of them does nothing to infringe on anyone else's freedom.

However, adding "sexual orientation" to civil rights laws governing private employment and housing does infringe on the rights of others—namely, the normal right of employers and landlords to make economic decisions based on their own best judgment. Governments normally interfere with such economic freedom only when the alleged "discrimination" is based on characteristics that are inborn, involuntary, immutable, and innocuous, such as race. None of those criteria apply to homosexual behavior. Nevertheless, a family-owned bed-and-breakfast in the Canadian province of Prince Edward Island went out of business because its owners refused to compromise their principles by allowing a homosexual couple to share a bed in the family's own home. In Hungary, a Christian seminary was forced to reinstate a seminary student who had been expelled as a homosexual. When "homosexual rights" are imposed, other rights of longer standing, such as religious liberty, are trampled upon.

A fourth element of the agenda is to win the enactment of "hate crime" laws that provide severe punishment of crimes motivated by "bias" against homosexuals. All of us in the pro-family movement are opposed to violent crimes, against homosexuals or anyone else. Hate crime laws, though, set a dangerous precedent of punishing people specifically for their opinions. In addition, under some such laws a person can be punished simply for intimidation—which could include just verbally expressing disapproval of homosexuality. One example comes from England, where 69-year-old Harry Hammond held a sign that said, "Stop immorality. Stop homosexuality. Stop lesbianism." Hecklers threw mud and water at him and knocked him to the ground—yet police arrested this old man, rather than his assailants, for a "breach of public order."

A fifth element of the homosexual agenda is the effort to get homosexual propaganda included in the curriculum of public schools. The intent of these efforts is obvious—to ensure that the next generation will grow up with an unquestioning acceptance of all the myths that the homosexual activists want young people to believe.

And a final element in this agenda is to redefine marriage and family altogether. They hope to achieve this by opening the door for homosexuals to adopt children and by legalizing same-sex marriage. If denied marriage in name, they hope to win virtually all the benefits and privileges of marriage through so-called civil unions or domestic partnerships.

The trend of giving all the legal rights and benefits of marriage to homosexual couples began in Denmark in 1989. Some form of these laws has since spread to Finland, Germany, Iceland, Norway, Sweden, France, and Portugal (and possibly others). In 2000, the state of Vermont became the first place in the U.S. to offer such "civil unions," as a result of a decision of that state's highest court. California's legislature voted last year to expand that state's existing "domestic partnerships" scheme into what will be essentially a civil unions registry, beginning in 2005.

The first country to open the institution of full civil marriage to same-sex couples was the Netherlands, beginning in 2001. In 2003, Belgium followed, as did two provinces of Canada in response to court decisions there. And on November 18, 2003, the Supreme Judicial Court of the American state of Massachusetts ruled that same-sex couples must be allowed to enter civil marriages, and that a parallel institution of "civil unions" would not be sufficient.

The highly publicized issuance of marriage licenses by a few local officials in California and other states since that time has been clearly illegal. However, the Massachusetts court's ruling will result in that state recognizing the first legal homosexual civil marriages in America on May 17, 2004, unless further legal action is taken to prevent it. On February 24, 2004, President Bush endorsed an amendment to the U.S. Constitution that would limit marriage to unions of one man and one woman. These developments have set off a furious debate about the meaning of marriage in the United States, which I am sure is mirrored elsewhere in the world.

The debate over whether homosexual couples should be allowed to legally "marry" is *not* about rights, equality, or discrimination, despite the often heated rhetoric to that effect. Still less is it about the allocation of an entitlement package of legal rights and financial benefits. Instead, this is a question of definition: How do we define the social institution we call marriage? To answer that we must ask, What is the public purpose of marriage?

Please note that I said the *public* purpose of marriage. The *private* purposes for which people enter into marriage may be as diverse as the people themselves. Homosexual activists sometimes argue that they want to marry for the same reasons heterosexuals do: out of a desire for love and companionship.

But are interpersonal love and companionship really the business of government? Would we even tolerate the government issuing licenses and regulating entry and exit into relationships whose only or even principal purpose is emotional attachment? I submit to you that the answer is no.

So what is the public interest in marriage? Why is marriage a public, civil institution, rather than a purely private one? The answer, I would argue, is that marriage is a public institution because it brings together men and women for the purpose of reproducing the human race and keeping a mother and father together to cooperate in raising to maturity the children they produce. The public interest in such behavior is great, because thousands of years of human experience and a vast body of contemporary social science research both demonstrate that married husbands and wives, and the children they conceive and raise, are happier, healthier, and more prosperous than people in any other living situation.

Now, I know exactly what some people say. They argue that reproduction cannot be the purpose of marriage, because opposite-sex couples that are elderly, infertile, or simply don't plan to have children are still permitted to marry. In fact, I would suggest that the actual, tangible public interest in childless marriages is not as great as the public interest in marriages that produce children.

However, to exclude non-reproducing heterosexual couples from marriage would require an invasion of privacy or the drawing of arbitrary and inexact lines. Instead, we simply define the structure of marriage as being open to the entire class of couples that are even theoretically capable of natural reproduction—namely, opposite-sex ones—and we exclude an entire class of couples that are intrinsically infertile—namely, same-sex ones.

Of course some homosexuals do reproduce (with help, of course), and some homosexual couples do raise children. But let me suggest, as an analogy, another area in which the law places limits on the exercise of a fundamental right—voting. We have a minimum voting age because we presume that adults are wiser and better informed than children. The mere fact that some adults are actually foolish and ill-informed, while some children may be wiser and better informed, does not make the existence of a minimum voting age arbitrary or discriminatory. Distinguishing between opposite-sex couples and same-sex couples with regard to marriage on the basis of general differences is equally logical.

In fact, I would suggest that the argument in favor of same-sex marriage can only be logically sustained if one argues that there is no difference between men and women—that is, if one argues not merely that men and women are equal in value and dignity (a proposition I'm sure we all agree with) but that males and females are identical, and thus can serve as entirely interchangeable parts in the structure of marriage. This contention is biologically absurd, and "same-sex marriage" is thus an oxymoron.

Nevertheless, some observers ask, What harm could same-sex civil marriage possibly do to anyone else's heterosexual marriage? One answer is, it could destroy it. Forty percent of the couples entering civil unions in Vermont include at least one partner who was previously in a heterosexual marriage—just like Gene Robinson, the new bishop of the Episcopal church in the American state of New Hampshire, who left his wife and children for a homosexual lover. I once made this point in a public forum, and a listener argued that it would be "dishonest" for someone experiencing same-sex attractions

---

I would suggest that the argument in favor of same-sex marriage can only be logically sustained if one argues that there is no difference between men and women.

---

to remain in an opposite-sex marriage. My response was simple: I would never call it "dishonest" for any person to fulfill their marriage vows.

An indirect effect is more likely, however. As the transient, promiscuous, and unfaithful relationships that are characteristic of homosexuals become part of society's image of marriage, fewer marriages will be permanent, exclusive, and faithful—even among heterosexuals. So-called "conservative" advocates of same-sex civil marriage are optimistic that legal unions would change homosexuals for the better; it seems far more probable that homosexuals would change marriage for the worse.

Some advocates of homosexual unions even suggest that if another class of couples who want to marry are allowed to do so, it would actually *strengthen* marriage. This argument has been effectively refuted by American anthropologist Stanley Kurtz, who cites the trailblazing experience of Scandinavia. In an article in *The Weekly Standard* in February, Kurtz pointed out,

> Marriage in Scandinavia is in deep decline, with children shouldering the burden of rising rates of family dissolution. And the mainspring of the decline—an increasingly sharp separation between marriage and parenthood—can be linked to gay marriage.[2]

Kurtz also cites Danish social theorist Henning Bech and Norwegian sociologist Rune Halvorsen as having admitted that:

> The goal of the gay marriage movement in both Norway and Denmark . . . was not marriage but social approval of homosexuality. Halvorsen suggests that the low numbers of registered gay couples may be understood as a collective protest against the expectations (presumably, monogamy) embodied in marriage.

The final harm done by same-sex marriage would undoubtedly be a slide down the proverbial "slippery slope." Advocates of same-sex marriage seek to remove the potential for procreation from the definition of marriage, making gender irrelevant in the choice of a spouse, and re-defining marriage only in terms of a loving and committed relationship. If that happens, then it is hard to see how other restrictions upon one's choice of marriage partner can be sustained. These include the traditional restrictions against marrying a child, a close blood relative, or a person who is already married.

While pedophile or incestuous marriages may be further off, polygamous marriages have much stronger precedents in history and culture than do even homosexual ones. Lawsuits have already been filed in American courts—with the support of the American Civil Liberties Union—demanding recognition of plural marriages. And—I am not making this up—news reports in recent weeks have carried stories of an Indian girl being married to a dog, and a French woman who was legally permitted (with the approval of the president of France) to marry her boyfriend—who is already dead.

Lesbian activist Paula Ettelbrick, currently the executive director of the International Gay and Lesbian Human Rights Commission, has said that homosexuality "means pushing the parameters of sex, sexuality, and family, and in the process transforming the very fabric of society." In fact, homosexuality and homosexual civil marriage would rip the fabric of society in ways that may be difficult, if not impossible, to mend.

Notes

1. Theo G. M. Sandfort, Ron de Graaf, Rob V. Bijl, Paul Schnabel, "Same-Sex Sexual Behavior and Psychiatric Disorders: Findings from the Netherlands Mental Health Survey and Incidence Study (NEMESIS)," *Archives of General Psychiatry* 58 (2001): 85–91.
2. Stanley Kurtz, "The End of Marriage in Scandinavia: The 'Conservative Case' for Same-Sex Marriage Collapses," *The Weekly Standard* (February 2, 2004), 27.

Marriage Equality and Some Lessons for the Scary Work of Winning

Evan Wolfson

Founder and executive director, Freedom to Marry, 2003– ; born in Brooklyn, NY, raised in Pittsburgh, PA; graduated Yale College, 1978; worked two years as Peace Corps volunteer in Togo, West Africa; graduated Harvard Law School, 1983; taught political philosophy, Harvard College; assistant district attorney, Kings County (Brooklyn), NY; associate counsel to Lawrence Walsh, Office of Independent Counsel (Iran/Contra); New York State Task Force on Sexual Harassment, 1992; taught at Rutgers University Law School; pro bono cooperating attorney for Lambda, the nation's leading lesbian/gay legal advocacy group, 1984–89; Lambda Legal Defense & Education Fund, 1989–2001; director, Lambda's Marriage Project; coordinator, National Freedom to Marry Coalition; co-counsel, landmark Hawaii marriage case Boehr v. Miike, 1996; adjunct professor of law, Columbia University; senior fellow, New School's Wolfson Center for National Affairs; author, Why Marriage Matters: America, Equality, and Gay People's Right to Marry *(2004); one of the 100 Most Influential Attorneys in America, 2000,* National Law Journal; *one of* Time *magazine's list of the 100 Most Influential People in the World; honored by Kolot Chayeinu (Voices of Our Lives), Jewish congregation in Brooklyn, 2005.*

Editors' introduction: Mr. Wolfson addressed the National Lesbian & Gay Law Association's (NLGLA) Lavender Law Conference. Attending were attorneys, legal academics, and law students. Established in 1988, and an affiliate of the American Bar Association since 1992, NLGLA is a national association of lawyers, judges, and other legal professionals, law students, activists, and affiliated lesbian, gay, bisexual, transgender, and intersex legal organizations. "America is again in a civil rights moment," Mr. Wolfson contended, "as same-sex couples, their loved ones, and non-gay allies struggle to end discrimination in marriage." He maintained, "What is at stake in this struggle is what kind of country we are going to be."

Evan Wolfson's speech:

America in a Civil Rights Moment
One of the good things about my job is I have plenty of time on planes and trains in which to read.

Delivered on September 30, 2004, at Minneapolis, MN. Reprinted with permission of Evan Wolfson.

Right now I'm reading the Library of America's anthology, *Reporting Civil Rights*. In two volumes, they've collected the journalism of the 1940s, '50s, '60s, and '70s, describing the blow by blow, the day to day, of what the struggles of those years felt and looked like . . . before those living through that moment knew how it was going to turn out.

Exhilarating, empowering, appalling, and scary.

That's what a civil rights moment feels like when you are living through it—when it is uncertain and not yet wrapped in mythology or triumphant inevitablism.

This year our nation celebrated the 50th anniversary of *Brown v. Board of Education*.

But what followed *Brown* was not the sincere and insincere embrace it gets today, but—in the words of the time—

- legislators in a swath of states declaring "massive resistance"

- billboards saying "Impeach Earl Warren," the then–Chief Justice who wrote the decision

- members of Congress signing resolutions denouncing "activist judges" (sound familiar?)

- and, of course, the marches, Freedom Rides, organizing summers, engagement, hard work, violence, legislation, transformations . . . pretty much everything we today think of as the civil rights movement—*all after* Brown.

America is again in a civil rights moment, as same-sex couples, their loved ones, and non-gay allies struggle to end discrimination in marriage. A robust debate and numberless conversations are helping our nation (in Lincoln's words) "think anew" about how we are treating a group of families and fellow citizens among us. Today it is gay people, same-sex couples, LGBT individuals, and their loved ones and non-gay allies—we—who are contesting second-class citizenship, fighting for our loved ones and our country, seeking inclusion and equality—and it is scary as well as thrilling to see the changes and feel the movement.

How can we get through this moment of peril and secure the promise?

There are lessons we can learn from those who went before us . . . for we are not the first to have to fight for equality and inclusion. In fact, we are not the first to have to challenge discrimination even in *marriage*.

The Human Rights Battlefield of Marriage

You see, marriage has always been a human rights battleground on which our nation has grappled with larger questions about what kind of country we are going to be—

- questions about the proper boundary between the individual and the government;

- questions about the equality of men and women;
- questions about the separation of church and state;
- questions about who gets to make important personal choices of life, liberty, and the pursuit of happiness.

As a nation, we have made changes in the institution of marriage, and fought over these questions of whether America is committed to both equality and freedom—in at least four major struggles in the past few decades:

- We ended the rules whereby the government, not couples, decided whether they should remain together when their marriages had failed or become abusive. Divorce transformed the so-called "traditional" definition of marriage from a union based on compulsion to what most of us think of marriage today—a union based on love, commitment, and the choice to be together and care for one another

- We ended race restrictions on who could marry whom, based on the traditional "definition" of marriage, defended as part of God's plan, seemingly an intractable part of the social order of how things have to be

- We ended the interference of the government in important personal decisions such as whether or not to procreate, whether or not to have sex without risking a pregnancy, whether or not to use contraceptives—even within marriage

- And we ended the legal subordination of women in marriage— and thereby transforming the institution of marriage from a union based on domination and dynastic arrangement to what most of us think of it as today—a committed partnership of equals.

Yes, our nation has struggled with important questions on the human rights battlefield of marriage, and we are met on that battlefield once again.

Patchwork

As in any period of civil rights struggle, transformation will not come overnight. Rather, the classic American pattern of civil rights history is that our nation goes through a period of what I call in my book, *Why Marriage Matters*, "patchwork."

During such patchwork periods, we see some states move toward equality faster, while others resist and even regress, stampeded by pressure groups and pandering politicians into adding additional layers of discrimination before—eventually—buyer's remorse sets in and a national resolution comes.

So here we are in this civil rights patchwork. On the one hand, as the recent powerful and articulate rulings by courts in Washington and New York states demonstrated in the past few weeks, several states are advancing toward marriage equality, soon to join Massachusetts in ending discrimination and showing non-gay Americans the reality of families helped and no one hurt.

Meanwhile, on the other hand, as many as a dozen states targeted by opponents of equality as part of their own ideological campaign and for their political purposes could enact further discriminatory measures this year, compounding the second-class citizenship gay Americans already endure.

These opponents—anti–marriage-equality, yes, but also, anti-gay, anti–women's equality, anti–civil-rights, anti-choice, and anti–separation-of-church-and-state—are throwing everything they have into this attack campaign because they know that if fair-minded people had a chance to hear the stories of real families and think it through, they would move toward fairness, as young people already have in their overwhelming support for marriage equality.

Most important, as Americans—

- see the faces and hear the voices of couples in San Francisco,

- witness the families helped and no one hurt in Massachusetts and digest the reassuring way in which marriage equality is already finding acceptance there after just a few months,

- engage in conversations in every state and many families, chats with people like us and non-gay allies

—hearts and minds are opening and people are getting ready to accept, if not necessarily yet fully support, an end to discrimination in marriage.

The Union a House Divided

In past chapters of civil rights history unfolding on the battlefield of marriage, this conversation and this patchwork of legal and political struggles would have proceded in the first instance—and over quite some time—in the states, without federal interference or immediate national resolution.

That's because historically, domestic relations, including legal marriage, have under the American system of federalism been understood as principally (and almost entirely) the domain of the states.[1]

States worked out their discrepancies in who could marry whom under the general legal principles of comity, reflecting the value of national unity. The common-sense reality that it makes more sense to honor marriages than to destabilize them was embodied in the relevant specific legal principle, generally followed in all states—indeed, almost all jurisdictions around the world—that a marriage valid where celebrated will be respected elsewhere, even in places that would not themselves have performed that marriage.

States got to this logical result not primarily through legal compulsion, but through common sense—addressing the needs of the families and institutions (banks, businesses, employers, schools, etc.) before them. Eventually a national resolution came, grounded, again, in common sense, actual lived-experience, and the nation's commitment to equality, constitutional guarantees, and expanding the circle of those included in the American dream.

But when it comes to constitutional principles such as equal protection—and, it now appears, even basic American safeguards such as checks-and-balances, the courts, and even federalism—anti-gay forces believe there should be a "gay exception" to the constitutions, to fairness, and to respect for families. Inserting the federal government into marriage for the first time in U.S. history, our opponents federalized the question of marriage, prompting the passage of the so-called "Defense of Marriage Act" (DOMA) in 1996.

> *This federal anti-marriage law creates an un-American caste system of first and second class marriages.*

This federal anti-marriage law creates an un-American caste system of first and second class marriages. If the federal government likes whom you marry, you get a vast array of legal and economic protections and recognition—ranging from Social Security and access to health care, to veterans benefits and immigration rights, to taxation and inheritance, and a myriad of others (in a 2004 report the GAO identified 1,138 ways in which marriage implicates federal law). Under so-called DOMA, if the federal government doesn't like whom you married, this typically automatic federal recognition and protection are withdrawn in all circumstances, no matter what the need.

The federal anti-marriage law also purported to authorize states not to honor the lawful marriages from other states (provided those marriages were of same-sex couples)—in defiance of more than 200 years of history in which, as I said, the states had largely worked out discrepancies in marriage laws among themselves under principles of comity and common sense, as well as the constitutional commitment to full faith and credit.

When this radical law was first proposed, some of us spoke up immediately saying it was unconstitutional—a violation of equal protection, the fundamental right to marry, federalist guarantees such as the full faith and credit clause, and limits on Congress's power. Ignoring our objections, our opponents pressed forward with their election-year attack.

Now they concede the unconstitutionality of the law they stampeded through just eight years ago, and are seeking an even more radical means of assuring gay people's second-class citizenship, this time through an assault on the U.S. Constitution itself, as well as the constitutions of the states.[2]

Because they do not trust the next generation, because they know they have no good arguments, no good reason for the harsh exclusion of same-sex couples from marriage, our opponents are desperate to tie the hands of all future generations, and as many states as possible, now.

This patchwork—and especially the next few weeks and months—will be difficult, painful, even ugly, and we will take hits. Indeed, we stand to take several hits in the states where our opponents have thrown anti-gay measures at us in their effort to deprive our fellow-citizens of the information, the stories of gay couples to dispel stereotypes and refute right-wing lies, and the lived-experience of the reality of marriage equality. While it is especially outrageous that the opponents of equality are using constitutions as the vehicles for this division and wave of attacks on American families, in the longer arc, their discrimination will not stand.

Here are a few basic lessons we can cling to in the difficult moments ahead, to help us keep our eye on the prize of the freedom to marry and full equality nationwide, a prize that shimmers within reach.

Lesson Number One—Wins Trump Losses

While we stand to lose several battles this year, we must remember that wins trump losses.

Wins trump losses because each state that ends marriage discrimination gives fair-minded Americans the opportunity to see and absorb the reality of families helped and no one hurt when the exclusion of same-sex couples from marriage ends. Nothing is more transformative, nothing moves the middle more, than making it real, making it personal—and seeing other states join Canada and Massachusetts will be the engine of our victory.

Losing Forward

Lesson number two—Even where we cannot win a given battle, we can still engage and fight so as to at least lose forward, putting us in a better place for the inevitable next battle.

Now let me say a little more about this idea of "losing forward." After all, as someone most famous for the cases I lost, I've built an entire career on it.

Losing forward is a way that all of us can be part of this national campaign, no matter what our state. Even the more challenged states, the states with the greater uphill climb, the states where we are most outgunned and under attack—even those of us in the so-called "red states" still have a pivotal part in this national movement and can make a vital contribution.

In *every* state—even those where we cannot win the present battle, but fight so as to lose forward—we have the opportunity to enlist more support, build more coalitions, and make it possible for more candidates and non-gay opinion-leaders to move toward fairness. All this contributes to the creation of the national climate of receptivity in which some states may cross the finish-line before others, but everyone can be better positioned to catch the wave that will come back to every state in this national campaign.

> *Beating back as many attacks as possible and enlisting more diverse voices in this conversation, we will win.*

Work on the ground in Georgia, for example, can get us a Bob Barr speaking out against the constitutional amendment, or make districts safe for African-American leaders or "surprising" voices to speak out in support of marriage equality. Work in Michigan—while perhaps not enough to win this round—can still help enlist prominent labor or corporate leaders to our cause.

And, working together, this national chorus will indeed swell, with some states further along and all participating, until all are free.

Wins trump losses. As long as we repel a federal constitutional amendment and continue to see some states move toward equality, beating back as many attacks as possible and enlisting more diverse voices in this conversation, we will win.

Lesson number three—tell the truths.

Now, the principal reason we are going to take hits this year and lose many, if not all of the state attacks in November is because our opponents are cherry-picking their best targets and depriving the reachable middle of the chance to be reached. They have more of a head-start, more money, and more infrastructure through their mega-churches and right-wing partners . . . and fear-mongering at a time of anxiety is easy to do. And, of course, historically, it is difficult to win civil rights votes at the early stage of a struggle.

But, to be honest, there is another reason, too, that we will not do well in most of these votes this year. Quite simply, our engagement, our campaigns in almost all of these states—are "too little, too late." We are starting too late to have enough time to sway people to fairness . . . and we are giving them too little to think about to guide them there. We have to avoid that error in the next wave of battles we face next year, which means, from California to Minnesota, from Wisconsin to Maine, starting not too late, but now, and by saying the word truly on people's minds, doing it right.

Put another way, the country right now is divided roughly in thirds. One third supports equality for gay people, including the freedom to marry. Another third is not just adamantly against marriage for same-sex couples, but, indeed, opposes gay people and homosexuality, period. This group is against any measure of protection or recognition for lesbians and gay men, whether it be marriage or anything else.

And then there is the "middle" third—the reachable-but-not-yet reached middle. These Americans are genuinely wrestling with this civil rights question and have divided impulses and feelings to sort through. How they frame the question for themselves brings them to different outcomes; their thinking is evolving as they grapple with the need for change to end discrimination in America.

What moves that middle?

To appeal to the better angels of their nature, we owe it to these friends, neighbors, and fellow citizens to help them understand the question of marriage equality through two truths:

> **Truth 1**—Ending marriage discrimination is, first and foremost, about couples in love who have made a personal commitment to each other, who are doing the hard work of marriage in their lives, caring for one another and their kids, if any. (Think couples like Del Martin & Phyllis Lyon who've been together more than 50 years.) Now these people, having in truth made a personal commitment to each other, want and deserve a legal commitment.

Once the discussion has a human story, face, and voice, fair-minded people are ready to see through a second frame:

> **Truth 2**—The exclusion of same-sex couples from marriage is discrimination; it is wrong, it is unfair, to deny these couples and families marriage and its important tangible and intangible protections and responsibilities. America has had to make changes before to end discrimination and unfair treatment, and government should not be denying any American equality under the law.

When we see lopsided margins in these votes, it means that under the gun in the first wave of electoral attacks, we have not as yet reached this middle. We can't be surprised not to win when in so many campaigns, and over so many opportunities to date (electoral campaigns and just month-to-month conversations), we have failed to give this middle third what they need to come out right.

When, in the name of "practicality" or advice from pollsters or political operatives, we fail to put forward compelling stories and explain the realities of what marriage equality does and does not mean, it costs us the one chance we have to do the heavy-lifting that moves people. We wind up not just not winning, but not even losing forward.

By contrast, consider how we lost forward in California.

In 2000, we took a hit, when the right-wing pushed the so-called Knight Initiative and forced an early vote on marriage. We lost the vote, but because there had been some, though not enough, education about our families and the wrong and costs of discrimination, polls showed that support for marriage equality actually rose after the election. And the very next year, activists pressed the legislature to enact a partnership law far broader than had been on the table in California before then. Our engagement over marriage continued, and within a couple years, legislators voted again, this time in support of an "all but marriage" bill, which takes effect this coming January. And California organizations and the national legal groups continue to engage for what we fully deserve—pursuing litigation in the California courts and legislation that would end marriage discrimination.

If we do our work right, making room for luck, we may see marriage in California, our largest state, as soon as next year.

To go from a defeat in 2000 to partnership and all-but-marriage in 2004 with the possibility of marriage itself in 2005—that's called winning.

Generational Momentum

Lesson number four—remember, we have a secret weapon: death.

Or to put it more positively, we on the side of justice have generational momentum. Younger people overwhelmingly support ending this discrimination.

Americans are seeing more and more families like the Cheneys, and realizing, with increasing comfort, that we are part of the American family. The power of the marriage debate moves the center toward us, and as young people come into ascendancy, even the voting will change.

This is our opponents' last-ditch chance to pile up as many barricades as possible, but, again, as long as we build that critical mass for equality and move the middle, we win.

The Stakes

Why is it so important that we now all redouble our outreach, our voices, our conversations in the vocabulary of marriage equality?

- In part, because victory is within reach.
- In part, because we can and must move that middle now to make room for that generational momentum and rise to fairness.
- In part, because America is listening and allies are increasing.
- In part, because this is our moment of greatest peril.
- And, in part, because the stakes are so great.

What is at stake in this civil rights and human rights moment?

If this struggle for same-sex couples' freedom to marry were "just" about gay people, it would be important—for gay men and lesbians, like bisexuals, transgendered people, and our non-gay brothers and sisters—are human beings, who share the aspirations for love, companionship, participation, equality, mutual caring and responsibility, protections for loved ones, and choice.

Yes, if this struggle were "just" about gay people, it would be important, but it is not "just" about gay people.

If this struggle were "just" about marriage, it would be important, for marriage is the gateway to a vast and otherwise largely inaccessible array of tangible and intangible protections and responsibilities, the vocabulary in which non-gay people talk about love, clarity, security, respect, family, intimacy, dedication, self-sacrifice, and equality. And the debate over marriage is the engine of other advances and the *inescapable* context in which we will be addressing all LGBT needs, the *inescapable* context in which we will be claiming our birthright of equality and enlarging possibilities for ourselves and others.

Yes, if this struggle were "just" about marriage, it would be important, but it is not "just" about marriage.

What is at stake in this struggle is what kind of country we are going to be.

- Is America indeed to be a nation where we all, minorities as well as majorities, popular as well as unpopular, get to make important choices in our lives, not the government, or a land of liberty and justice only for some?

- Is America indeed to be a nation that respects the separation of church and state, where government does not take sides on religious differences, but rather respects religious freedom while assuring equality under the law, or a land governed by one religious ideology imposed on all?

- Is America to be a nation where two women who build a life together, maybe raise kids or tend to elderly parents, pay taxes, contribute to the community, care for one another, and even fight over who takes out the garbage are free and equal, or a land where they can be told by their government that they are somehow lesser or incomplete or not whole because they do not have a man in their lives?

All of us, gay and non-gay, who share the vision of America as a nation that believes that all people have the right to be both different and equal, and that without real and sufficient justification, government may not compel people to give up their difference in order to be treated equally—all of us committed to holding America to that promise have a stake in this civil rights/human rights struggle for the freedom to marry.

And if we see every state, every methodology, every battle, every victory, and even every defeat as part of a campaign—and if we continue to enlist non-gay allies and voices in this campaign, transforming it into a truly organic movement for equality in the grand American tradition,

- we will move the middle,
- we will lose forward where necessary,

- we will empower the supportive,
- and we will win.

We *are* winning.

There is no marriage without engagement.

Let's vote in November, get others to vote in November, and move forward in our work to win, working together, doing it right.

Notes

1. *Hisquierdo v. Hisquierdo,* 439 U.S. 572, 581 (1979) ("[i]nsofar as marriage is within temporal control, the States lay on the guiding hand"). As the Supreme Court explained in *De Sylva v. Ballentine,* 351 U.S. 570, 580 (1956): The scope of a federal right is, of course, a federal question, but that does not mean its content is not to be determined by state, rather than federal law. . . . This is especially true when a statute deals with a familial relationship; there is no federal law of domestic relations, which is primarily a matter of state concern.

2. The first constitutional amendment to allow Congress to have authority over domestic relations was proposed (and rejected) in 1884. *Scherrer v. Scherrer,* 334 U.S. 343 (1948) (Frankfurter, J., dissenting). Through 1948, 70 similar amendments were proposed, prompted by a national debate (analogous to today's) over whether to allow civil divorce. All such proposals failed, and the states and Americans were properly given an opportunity to work out questions of marriage and interstate respect, while the federal government honored the lawful marriages (and divorces). See, e.g., Edward Stein, "Past and Present Proposed Amendments to the United States Constitution Regarding Marriage" *Issues in Legal Scholarship,* Single-Sex Marriage (2004): Article 1 (2004). And, after a period of conversation and experience, and generational shifts as the institution of marriage evolved, the U.S. Supreme Court clarified that lawful determinations as to marital status, through divorce, must be respected throughout the country. E.g., *Cook v. Cook,* 342 U.S. 126 (1951).

II. Church and State

Separation of Church and State Is Nothing to Sneeze At

Ronald B. Flowers

John F. Weatherly Emeritus Professor of Religion, Texas Christian University (TCU), 2003– ; born Tulsa, OK, January 11, 1935; B.A., TCU, 1957; B.D., Vanderbilt University Divinity School, 1960; S.T.M., Vanderbilt University Divinity School, 1961; Ph.D., School of Religion, University of Iowa, 1967; minister, Crofton (KY) Christian Church, 1961–63; assistant professor, TCU, 1966–73; associate professor, TCU, 1973–84; vice president, Southwestern Commission on Religion Studies, 1981–82; professor, TCU, 1984–2003; president, American Academy of Religion / Southwest, 1988–89; professor and chair of the Department of Religious Studies, TCU, 1990–99; John F. Weatherly Professor of Religion, TCU, 1998–2003; member, American Academy of Religion, Disciples of Christ Historical Society, Supreme Court Historical Society; Danforth Association, 1971; author (with Robert T. Miller), Toward Benevolent Neutrality: Church, State, and the Supreme Court *(1977, revised in two volumes 1996);* Religion in Strange Times: The 1960s and 1970s *(1984), a* Choice *Outstanding Academic Book in Religion, 1985–86;* That Godless Court? Supreme Court Decisions on Church-State Relationships *(1994); Honors Faculty Recognition Award, 1976; third prize winner, national essay contest on religious liberty sponsored by Americans United for Separation of Church and State, 1982; one of three Distinguished Disciples Scholars named by* Disciples Theological Digest, *1988; Chancellor's Award for Distinguished Teaching, TCU, 1998.*

Editors' introduction: Begun in the 1950s, Texas Christian University (TCU) and University Christian Church (Disciples of Christ) jointly sponsor an annual Ministers Week for some 400 clergy and spouses. While held principally for Disciple ministers from the southwest, clergy of other denominations participate as well. During Ministers Week, Dr. Flowers spoke at a dinner for retired ministers at Dee J. Kelley Alumni and Visitors Center on the campus of TCU. Approximately 175 retired clergy and their spouses attended the dinner. "Because I *am* a Christian and an ordained minister," Dr. Flowers explained, "I am . . . an advocate for separation of church and state. . . . For faith to be insulated from the corroding influences of government and politics is a good thing."

Delivered on February 10, 2004, at Fort Worth, Texas. Reprinted by permission of Ronald B. Flowers. An altered form of this speech was published as the featured article in the opinion section of the *Fort Worth Star-Telegram*, Sunday, March 28, 2004, under the title "A Civil Separation."

Ronald B. Flowers's speech: It is common knowledge that in polite conversation, no one is ever supposed to talk about religion and politics. So, that is precisely what I want to discuss and expand to the broader issue of religion and the state.

Recently I received this story by e-mail:

> They walked in tandem, each of the 93 students filing into the already crowded auditorium. With rich maroon gowns flowing and the traditional caps, they looked almost as grown up as they felt. Dads swallowed hard behind broad smiles, and moms freely brushed away tears.
>
> This class would not pray during the commencement—not by choice but because of a recent court ruling prohibiting it. The principal and several students were careful to stay within the guidelines allowed by the ruling, They gave inspirational and challenging speeches, but no one mentioned divine guidance and no one asked for blessings on the graduates or their families.
>
> The speeches were nice, but they were routine—until the final speech received a standing ovation.
>
> A solitary student walked proudly to the microphone. He stood still and silent for just a moment, and then, it happened. The other 92 students, every single one of them, suddenly SNEEZED!!!!
>
> The student on stage simply looked at the audience and said, "GOD BLESS YOU, each and every one of you!" And he walked off stage.
>
> The audience exploded into applause. The graduating class had found a unique way to invoke God's blessing on their future with or without the court's approval!
>
> Isn't this a wonderful story? Pass it on to all your friends.

No, it is not a wonderful story—for at least three reasons:

1. The event described violates the clear teaching of scripture. In Matthew 6:5–6 our Lord said: "And when you pray, you must not be like the hypocrites; for they love to stand and pray in the synagogues and at the street corners, that they may be seen by men, Truly, I say to you, they have their reward. But when you pray, go into your room and shut the door and pray to your Father who is in secret; and your Father who sees in secret will reward you."

2. It glorifies students' disobeying the law, with the encouragement of their parents and other family. The schools of this country, both private and public, ought to teach students to obey the law. The citizens of America are concerned with crime in our cities. No one would want to compare this sneeze episode with the horrendous rape, murder, and pillage in our streets and glorified on TV. They are not at all of the same magnitude, But the story illustrates the inclination of many in our society to break the law in order to impose religion on society by using state-created captive audiences. The schools must teach, at an irreducible minimum, respect for and obedience to the law of the land.

3. The story is correct. The prohibition on commencement prayers in public schools is based on a Supreme Court decision, *Lee v. Weisman*.[1] The opinion was written by Anthony Kennedy, appointed by President Reagan and one of the most conservative justices on the Supreme Court. But the decision was not designed to be hostile to religion. The decision recognized that our society is religiously pluralistic. Not everyone believes in God the same way; some do not believe at all. But they are all Americans. They are all entitled to religious freedom. They are all entitled to *not* have the government or any instrument of government impose religion upon them.

The sneeze story implies that all the members of the graduating class participated in eliciting the blessing of God. Perhaps so. But that would not always be the case. Remember that peer pressure in junior high and high school is enormous. Students who may have objections, religiously based objections, to prayer in classrooms or commencements, may find it very difficult to express those against the majority.

The idea of separation of church and state means one may not use the state as an instrument to practice their religion.

But, you may say, in this country the majority rules, Not in constitutional matters, As Justice Robert Jackson eloquently said in *West Virginia Board of Education v. Barnette*: "One's right to life, liberty, and property, to free speech, a free press, freedom of worship and assembly, and other fundamental rights may not be submitted to vote; they depend on the outcome of no elections."[2]

The precious concept of religious freedom means that every person in this country is free to practice his/her religion. But the idea of separation of church and state means one may not use the state as an instrument to practice their religion. And that means that all Americans, including students in public schools, are entitled to *not* have the government or any agent of government impose religion upon them.

Let us step back from this specific issue to look at a larger principle. I refer to the difference between toleration and freedom, toleration of religion and freedom of religion. We frequently say that the founders of our nation created a system of toleration of religion. But they did not. They created a system of religious freedom. What is the difference?

Toleration means that the government regulates the religious situation in a country. It usually means that a particular religion or religious tradition is favored, but others are allowed to exist. The others may even be allowed wide latitude for religious belief and practice. But the concept of toleration still holds the power in the government to determine the religious situation in a country.

Many countries have this system, In England, for example, the Church of England is the established church. It receives financial and political favors from the government other religious groups do not receive. Although other religious groups may have wide leeway to practice their religion as they please, the government still has the power to limit their religious freedom, or, indeed, to take away their permission to exist.

Religious freedom is different from toleration. Religious freedom means that the government has no say in whether or not a religion may exist in the country. It means that the government has no say in what a religion believes or how it is practiced, with the proviso that religious practice may not harm the public welfare or any part of it.

The founders of America created a Constitution of limited government. In doing so, they gave us religious freedom. So, when they wrote in the First Amendment that "Congress shall make no law respecting an establishment of religion, or prohibiting the free exercise thereof," they meant that religion should be free from government support or control. That is, they also meant government should step back so religious people and groups should be free to practice their religions as they chose. But, again, that means that groups or individuals may not use the machinery of the government to practice their religion. There cannot be any governmentally enforced expression of religion, such as prayer in public school commencements.

Not only does the Constitution contain the First Amendment, but the founders also wrote in Article 6 that "no religious Test shall ever be required as a Qualification to any Office or public Trust under the United States." In this election season, considerable notice has been made of the role of religion in the campaign. The President and all the candidates on the other side have made much of their religious beliefs, sometimes not to their advantage, as when Howard Dean could not remember that the book of Job is not in the New Testament. Religion is very much a part of politics these days. But the cautionary note of the founders in the Constitution is a reminder that one's religious faith, or the lack thereof, ought never to be a part of partisan politics. God does not favor one party over another.

Many argue that they want their leaders to be people of principle and morality. That is certainly a fair enough expectation, The presumption is that the principles and morality will be derived from. religion. That is a logical assumption, also. We consequently want our leaders and candidates for leadership to be religious. But the founders remembered that in colonial America one could not hold public office if he were not a member of the established church. That certainly limited the possibility for a wide range of qualified candidates. So, the founders eliminated the possibility of established religion in the First Amendment and forbade religious tests of qualification for public office in Article 6 of the Constitution.

Obviously both candidates and office holders have the right to be religious and to express their religiosity. But the prohibition against religious tests for public office is a reminder that God does not play partisan politics. And it is a cautionary note that politicians should not use religion as a weapon against their opponents. Religiosity as a political tool can so easily lead to self-righteousness. All good lessons to remember in this election season.

> *For faith to be insulated from the corroding influences of government and politics is a good thing.*

But you may respond to all this by concluding that separation of church and state is hostile to religion. For the Constitution to forbid religious test for public office and to not allow government sponsorship or mandate for religious ceremonies in government institutions like public schools must mean that separation of church and state is hostile to religion.

I talk and write about this subject a lot. People often ask me why, given that I am a Christian and an ordained minister, I am such an advocate for separation of church and state. The answer, of course, is because I *am* a Christian and an ordained minister. I take my faith very seriously. For faith to be insulated from the corroding influences of government and politics is a good thing. Remember that part of the concept of the separation of church and state is the founders' explicit command that government should not prohibit the free exercise of religion. Separation of church and state enables religion to flourish without interference from government power. Separation of church and state has created the condition for religion to be as vibrant, dynamic, and lively as it is in American society. To be sure, government may not use religion as a tool to get its way with the people. It is illegitimate for government to advance or inhibit religion. Separation demands that government get out of the way and let people respond to the divine as they will. The people do that, and in America religion is a major part of the culture. Separation of church and state is not hostile to religion, but rather is the enabler for religions to grow and prosper in America as they do.

But many in our time are fearful of true freedom. They are not willing to trust the people to practice their religion as they choose. Rather they want the government to somehow promote religion. So, we have presidential executive orders to provide government money to charitable programs operated by religious institutions. We have legislatures across the country passing laws and resolutions to post the Ten Commandments in public buildings. We have continual efforts, including bills in Congress to amend the Constitution, to promote prayer and devotionals in public schools. On and on. But there are at least two problems with this trend.

One problem is that in the effort to have government-promoted religion, religion is often trivialized. For example, in many of the Ten Commandments displays, in the effort to avoid being an obvious Establishment Clause violation, other famous sayings are often added. These are sayings from the Declaration of Independence, the Code of Hammurabi, Lincoln's second inaugural address, and other similar passages. They are all fine sayings in and of themselves. But it is clear that they are cover for the Ten Commandments. There is a bit of intellectual dishonesty going on there. What we really have is a kind of theological bait-and-switch operation. Rather than be content with aggressively teaching the Ten Commandments in their churches, synagogues, and homes, many are more interested in playing theological hide-and-seek to sneak the Commandments onto public buildings and monuments.

Another example of the trivialization of religion is the story with which I began. In the attempt to be able to get a prayer into the commencement, albeit ever so brief a prayer, someone went to great lengths to organize all 93 seniors and coordinate the great sneeze. Then, responding to this stimulus like Pavlov's dog, a person was able to say "God bless you, each and every one of you!"

It reminds me of what we junior high kids used to sing at church camp: "Hooray for Jesus. Hooray for Jesus. Someone in the crowd's shouting 'Hooray for Jesus.'" A statement of belief, but bordering on the trite. Hardly profound theology.

Finally, the attempt to get the state to promote religion has great potential to harm the church, I am amazed that some ministers, TV religious personalities and even denominational leaders are so eager to get the government to do the work of the church. In the interest in getting religion more into the public life of the country, they run the risk of marginalizing the church. The more the state does the work of the church, the less relevant the church will become.

Although it probably was unwitting on their part, the founders of this country gave religious people the ideal methodology to have vital, energetic, robust, vigorous religious institutions. They gave us the separation of church and state with its corollary, religious freedom. Free from government dominance or interference, churches could flourish in this country, and they have, But now, in these latter days, in the interest of trying to improve public morality, many believe that the church must utilize the state to get its way with the people. That is a prescription to make the church subservient to the state, to marginalize it and make it less dynamic.

Supreme Court Justice Hugo Black once wrote: "[The separation of church and state] stands as an expression of principle on the part of the Founders of our Constitution that religion is too personal, too sacred, too holy to permit its 'unhallowed perversion' by a civil magistrate."[3]

Isn't that a wonderful concept? Pass it on to all your friends.

Endnotes

1. 505 U.S. 577 (1992)
2. 319 U.S. 624 at 638 (1943)
3. *Engel v. Vitale* 370 U.S. 421 at 431–437 (1962); "unhallowed perversion" from James Madison, "A Memorial and Remonstrance Against Religious Assessments," 1785, ¶ 5.

Annual Religious Liberty Award

Nadine Strossen

Professor of law, New York Law School, 1988– , and president, American Civil Liberties Union (ACLU), 1991– ; born Jersey City, NJ, 1950; A.B., Harvard College, 1972, Phi Beta Kappa; J.D., Harvard Law School, 1975, editor of the Harvard Law Review; *judicial clerk, Minnesota Supreme Court, 1975–76; practiced law in Minneapolis and New York City, 1976–84; associate professor of clinical law, New York University School of Law, 1984–88; adjunct professor, Columbia University Graduate School of Business, 1990; national general counsel, ACLU, 1986–91; appearances on major national news shows; serves on Council on Foreign Relations; has served on the boards of many humans rights organizations; published in numerous university law reviews; co-author,* Speaking of Race, Speaking of Sex: Hate Speech, Civil Rights, and Civil Liberties *(1994), an Outstanding Book, Gustavus Myers Center for the Study of Human Rights in America; author,* Defending Pornography: Free Speech, Sex, and the Fight for Women's Rights *(1995), a Notable Book of 1995, New York Times; awards include: list of 100 Most Influential Lawyers in America (twice), National Law Journal; among the 350 Women Who Changed the World, 1976–1996,* Working Woman *magazine, 1996; America's 200 Most Influential Women,* Vanity Fair, *1998; and 100 Most Important Women in America,* Ladies Home Journal, *1999; several honorary Doctor of Law degrees, including Mount Holyoke College, University of Rhode Island, University of Vermont, and Massachusetts School of Law.*

Editors' introduction: Professor Strossen addressed the Annual Conference of Americans for Religious Liberty and the American Humanist Association. Founded in 1981, Americans for Religious Liberty has as its mission to support "the constitutional principle of separation of church and state." Founded in 1941, the American Humanist Association "educates the public about Humanism," defending Humanists on civil libertarian and constitutional grounds. In accepting the Annual Religious Liberty Award from Americans for Religious Liberty, Professor Strossen cautioned that one should not take the "promises of liberty . . . for granted," reminding the audience that "our work on behalf of religious liberty and tolerance continues to be essential."

Nadine Strossen's speech: Thanks to everyone here for your warm welcome—and, more importantly, for your vital support of freedom of belief and thought! I can't think of an honor that would mean more to me than this award from this organization.

Delivered on May 7, 2004, at Las Vegas, Nevada. Reprinted with permission of Nadine Strossen.

The causes of religious liberty and freedom of conscience have always been at the center of my life, both personally and professionally. On the personal level, both of my parents had all-too-typical backgrounds of emigrating to America to escape religious persecution abroad. My beloved father was born in Berlin in 1922, and under Hitler's infamous Nuremberg laws, he was classified as a "Jew of the Second Degree" and deported to the Buchenwald concentration camp, where he did grueling slave labor in underground salt mines and almost died of pneumonia.

As a remarkable coincidence, about a month ago, I got an extraordinary letter from a very special 93-year-old woman who lives right here in Las Vegas, Beverly Blackford. Thanks to your kind invitation, I had the opportunity to have lunch with her today. After my father was liberated from Buchenwald, he worked with Beverly's late husband, Bob, a U.S. Army intelligence officer, to track down Nazi leaders. Like many Holocaust survivors, my father had not wanted to talk to his children about his harrowing ordeals or his personal heroism. And, alas, he died five years ago. So I'm eternally grateful to Beverly for having reached out to me, taking the trouble to send me old letters and newspaper clippings that documented this horrific chapter in human history, and in my dear father's life.

On my mother's side, my grandfather rebelled against his Catholic upbringing, in angry reaction to the abuses of the Catholic priests in the small Italian village where he grew up before seeking refuge in the U.S. Half a century before sexual abuse by priests became common knowledge, my grandfather told me horrific tales about how the priests in his village preyed—that's "p-r-e-y"—upon the women and children in his village. He also told me that, when his first child was born here in his adopted home country—my mother—he wanted to name her "Liberty," Since my maternal grandmother was more traditionalist, that didn't happen. But certainly the spirit of liberty animated my wonderful mother, as well as my father, and I can never take for granted our Constitution's promises of liberty, especially in light of this family history on both sides.

Nor can any of us take these rights for granted, in light of what is happening all around us now. Of course, we are far from the horrors of the Holocaust. But we are not so far from the anti-Semitism and intolerance that fueled it. All around the world, and right here at home, anti-Semitism and other forms of religious bigotry and even violence are, alas, alive and well. So our work on behalf of religious liberty and tolerance continues to be essential.

The American Civil Liberties Union is working harder than ever to counter the adverse impact that religious zealotry has been exerting not only on our First Amendment freedoms of belief and conscience, but also on so many other rights, all across the ACLU's broad, signature mission: to defend all fundamental freedoms for all people. That whole broad human rights agenda is embattled now, and there is hardly any threat to civil liberties that is not significantly grounded in efforts by some individuals to impose their own religiously-based beliefs on everyone else. That pattern certainly applies to the stepped-up censorship issues we continue to face, against anything that is considered "indecent" or "offensive" to majoritarian religious or moral beliefs. In reaction to the brief broadcast flash of Janet Jackson's breast, government regulators recently have been on an unprecedented, unjustified rampage, cracking down on and chilling any broadcast expression that might offend anyone's religious or moral sensibilities.

Congress and the Federal Communications Commission have issued new regulations that are so vague, and new penalties that are so harsh, that they are causing enormous self-censorship of valuable information and ideas. Let me read you just a couple examples that were set out in the brief that was filed by the ACLU and other free speech and media organizations, as well as artists, calling on the FCC to overturn its recent speech-suppressive rulings:

> An episode of *ER* was edited to eliminate a brief shot of the exposed breast of an 80-year-old woman receiving emergency care. . . . Public broadcaster WBGH edited a hint of cleavage out of its *American Experience* documentary "Emma Goldman." Further, in "The Life and Work of Piri Thomas," . . . PBS felt it must edit [out] certain expletives (including nonsexual . . . epithets) even though they appear in the poetry of subject Piri Thomas, a renowned poet, writer and educator.

As if all of this isn't troubling enough, the FCC also has decreed that broadcasts may not contain "profanity," which it explicitly defines as including "blasphemy." Thus the government is expressly putting its stamp of approval on selected religious views and, correspondingly, suppressing information and ideas that are inconsistent with these government-endorsed views.

Another example of current anti-rights campaigns that are fueled by government sponsorship of particular religious beliefs is the recently renewed effort to entrench discrimination against certain couples, and certain families, on the basis of gender or sexual orientation. The fact that these discriminatory measures reflect particular religious and moral beliefs was underscored by Supreme Court Justice Antonin Scalia, in his dissenting opinion in the Court's landmark 2003 ruling in *Lawrence v. Texas*, striking down a law that criminalized private sexual conduct between two consenting adults only when both were of the same gender. The majority stressed that it was only resolving the issues directly before the Court, but the majority's rationale for that specific holding has the potential for protecting many other human rights, including religious liberty and freedom of conscience.

Justice Kennedy's opinion for the Court included sweeping, inspiring passages that are paeans to individual freedom of choice generally, and I find this especially exciting given who he is: a conservative, Republican, Catholic, who was appointed by a conservative, Republican President, Ronald Reagan. Surely this means that, on at least some key issues, we can reasonably hope for further positive rulings by the current Court.

At the outset of the opinion, Justice Kennedy expressly signaled that the Court's ruling encompassed freedom of thought and belief, among other fundamental freedoms. He declared: "Liberty

Religious intolerance . . . is receiving unprecedented support from the current Administration.

presumes an autonomy of self that includes freedom of thought, belief, expression, and certain intimate conduct," Likewise, Justice Kennedy concluded his opinion for the Court by eloquently endorsing the concept of a living, evolving Constitution that is worthy of the most liberal judicial activists. He gave a completely open-ended reading to the constitutional guarantee that government will not deprive any person of liberty without due process of law—contained in the so-called "Due Process Clauses"—which I find thrilling in its promise of ever-expanding judicial protection of "liberty and justice for all":

> Had those who drew and ratified the Due Process Clauses . . . known the components of liberty in its manifold possibilities, they might have been more specific. They did not presume to have this insight. They knew times can blind us to certain truths and later generations can see that laws once thought necessary and proper in fact serve only to oppress. As the Constitution endures, persons in every generation can invoke its principles in their own search for greater freedom.

One aspect of the *Lawrence* decision is of special significance to our ongoing struggle for religious liberty, and against the religiously-based repression of rights. The Court expressly held that laws cannot constitutionally be based only on predominant community views about morality, including views that reflect religious beliefs. It was this holding in particular that Justice Scalia most strongly decried, rightly recognizing that prevailing religious and moral beliefs constitute the only underpinning not only for laws that discriminate against sexual orientation minorities, but also for many other laws that restrict individual freedom of conscience and intimate conduct. Thus, Justice Scalia correctly reasoned that the majority's rejection of this religious/moral rationale for criminal laws also sounded the death-knell for a whole host of laws, far beyond the Texas law that was directly at issue in *Lawrence* itself. While this sweeping potential of the *Lawrence* ruling was the cause of Justice Scalia's *consternation*, for civil libertarians it is cause for *celebration*! As he wrote:

> State laws against . . . nude dancing, same-sex marriage, prostitution, masturbation, . . . fornication, and obscenity . . . are . . . only . . . based on moral choices. Every single one of these laws is called into question by today's decision. . . . This [decision] effectively decrees the end of all morals legislation.

From a civil libertarian perspective, all of these laws *should* be called into question, since they criminalize private conduct by consenting adults that involves only their own minds and their own bodies. By imposing the moral and religious choices of the majority of the community upon everyone else, all such laws usurp the freedom of all mature individuals to make our own moral and religious choices. Make no mistake about it, it is going to take a long, hard struggle for us to realize fully the liberating, equalizing potential of the *Lawrence* decision, just as it has taken a long, hard struggle to try to realize the liberating, equalizing potential of the Constitution itself! But you can't be an activist without being an optimist, so I always like to stress the positive. As we face increasingly strong assaults on all our freedoms, we must take heart from the fact that we also have increasingly strong tools to combat them, including the broad libertarian, egalitarian rationale of the Supreme Court's *Lawrence* ruling.

To turn back now to the challenges we face, I want to underscore that many civil liberties are endangered by religious intolerance, which is receiving unprecedented support from the current Administration. Two weeks ago (4/24/04), PBS ran a chilling documentary called "The Jesus Factor," which addressed this disturbing question: "Do most Americans realize just how fervent the president's evangelical faith really is?" Actually, consistent with the ACLU's staunch defense of individual religious liberty for everyone—including the President of the United States—it is not inherently problematic for the President to be a fervent believer in his capacity as an individual citizen. To the contrary, that is his First Amendment right, which we fervently defend. But it *is* problematic that George W. Bush's religious zeal has had an overweening influence not only on his personal life, but also on his Presidential policies. As the *New York Times* wrote in its review of the PBS documentary: "The program reminds viewers that this 'faith-based' president has blurred the line between religion and state more than any of his recent predecessors: a vision that affects the Iraq conflict as well as domestic policy." Indeed, on the day of his second inaugural as Texas governor, in a meeting with some close associates, Mr. Bush told them: "I believe that God wants me to be president."

Given the President's belief that he has been divinely chosen for a divine mission, the greatest long-range concern is whether we can continue to count on the kind of judicial safety net for individual rights, including freedom of belief and conscience, that we saw in *Lawrence v. Texas.* As Texas Governor, George W. Bush strongly supported that state's discriminatory, repressive law that the U.S.

Supreme Court struck down in *Lawrence*. As a self-perceived God-anointed President, though, Bush could well do something to prevent such decisions in the future. Throughout his first Presidential campaign, he stressed that the Justices he most admired, and who would serve as models for his appointees, are Scalia and Thomas, who not only both dissented in *Lawrence*, but who also have voted against many personal liberty claims, including freedom of religion and conscience. In 2002, President Bush expressly linked his evangelical faith to his judicial appointments. He said: "We need . . . judges who understand our rights were derived from God. And those are the kind of judges I intend to put on the bench."

This kind of official religiosity, in violation of the First Amendment's bar on government-supported religion, has had an adverse impact even on an area as seemingly distinct from religious freedom as the domestic War on Terrorism and its many unjustified assaults on our freedom and privacy. This connection became clear to me soon after that dreadful date of September 11, 2001. I had been scheduled to do a debate at Harvard's Graduate School of

---

Some of the most stalwart supporters of maintaining separation between government and religion are devout believers and religious leaders.

Education on the Bush Administration's pet project that it calls "faith-based initiatives," but for which a more accurate label is "government-funded religion" or "government-funded religious discrimination," since it pours our tax dollars into religious institutions that are ostensibly providing social services, but that are allowed to discriminate in terms of the individuals they hire and those they serve.

Not surprisingly, in light of the then-recent terrorist attacks, the Harvard audience wanted to hear my thoughts about preserving civil liberties in the context of the counter-terrorism campaign. However, the organizers still wanted me to address the initial topic too. At first I thought it was going to be very hard to find some unifying theme to tie together these seemingly disparate topics. But then I recalled that, just two days after the terrorist attacks, that connection had been made for me by none other than the Reverends Jerry Falwell and Pat Robertson. Falwell was a guest on Robertson's *700 Club* TV show. Robertson of course promptly raised the subject of the terrorist attacks, and here is Falwell's very first comment on this momentous topic: "The ACLU's got to take a lot of blame for this." Let me read the transcript of the ensuing exchange.

ROBERTSON: "Well, yes."

FALWELL: "[T]hrowing God out successfully with the help of the federal court system, throwing God out of the public square, out of the schools. . . . [T]he pagans, and the abortionists, and the feminists, and the gays and the lesbians . . . , the ACLU . . . [a]ll of them who have tried to secularize America. I point the finger in their face and say, 'you helped this happen.'"

ROBERTSON: ". . . I totally concur."

These remarks were widely condemned, including by President Bush. But we have to recognize that they are only a blunter version of the message that we have been hearing constantly since 9/11 from President Bush himself, along with Attorney General John Ashcroft and other proponents of the Administration's unjustified invasions of our freedom in the name of counter-terrorism. They too are scapegoating civil liberties—and those of us who advocate civil liberties—as the purported cause of the attacks. Most notoriously, in December 2001, Attorney General Ashcroft, actually said that his civil libertarian critics "only aid terrorists" and "give ammunition to America's enemies."

ACLU leaders are acutely aware of the danger that government-supported religious zealotry poses to the whole range of civil liberties. Again, I want to stress that the problem here is *not* individuals who zealously believe and practice their own faiths, and who try to persuade others to join them in doing so. Of course, the ACLU zealously defends their rights to do so. But the problem is when private citizens or religious groups go beyond their own zealous advocacy to enlist government support or endorsement, in violation of the First Amendment's non-establishment clause.

I am proud of the important work that the ACLU is doing in this area, in courts and legislatures all over the country, and at all levels of government. However, we must undertake an even more aggressive, strategic public outreach campaign, to counter the myths and misconceptions that too often distort the political and press discussions of these issues. Our opponents too easily get away with their false charges that separation of government and religion reflects hostility toward religion, and that civil libertarians are trying to remove religion from American life. Nothing could be further from the truth!

Some of the most stalwart supporters of maintaining separation between government and religion are devout believers and religious leaders, who understand that government involvement with religion is at least as dangerous to religion as it is to government. Moreover, religious expression by private individuals and groups is strongly protected by the Constitution—and by the ACLU—including when it takes place in public settings that have been opened for diverse private expression, such as public parks, sidewalks, and streets.

I am now coming to the end of my allotted time, and I thought that an appropriate way to close would be with a Humanist invocation. I want to be sure you are all aware of a historic development in this vein: that the City Council in New Orleans opened its very first meeting this year with an invocation by a member of the New Orleans Secular Humanists, Harry Greenberger. I understand that Humanists have given such official invocations on only a couple other occasions, as part of a "public forum"–type approach, in which the government invites private speakers to offer invocations expressing various religious and non-religious beliefs. Such "viewpoint-neutrality" is completely consistent with our First Amendment rights, including our right to be free from government-sponsored religion. When government sponsors such a non-discriminatory, open forum for the expression of diverse private beliefs, it is sponsoring not religion, but rather, liberty of religion and conscience.

In New Orleans in January, the city council members listened respectfully to Harry Greenberger's Secular Humanist invocation, and then issued a proclamation for that date as a "Day of Reason," I think that Harry Greenberger's inspiring words on that noteworthy occasion are a fitting way for me to close now.

> Over 200 years ago when our founding fathers held their constitutional convention to produce the document to establish the rules of governance, for their new country, one of the members of that group, Benjamin Franklin, proposed that a clergyman be invited in to open each session with a prayer. [But] [t]he other authors of the Constitution, including future Presidents of the United States, did not vote to issue such invitations [so] the world's first entirely secular government, instituted by the consent of the governed, came into being without invoking supernatural assistance.
>
> It is therefore appropriate that your first meeting of this new year allow a secular humanist to open this City Council meeting and I thank you for that opportunity.
>
> I don't ask that you close your eyes nor bow your heads, but instead observe your multicultural neighbors who are here for the betterment of this city, in our different ways, sharing a commitment to make the most and the best of this world through which we are passing and to treat our fellow human beings with respect and dignity.
>
> We invoke the Constitution of the United States and ask that this Council's deliberations always take into account the constitutional rights of all minorities, as well as humanist morality, in your decisions.
>
> We ask this, not in the name of the supernatural, but in the name of reason, humanity, the golden rule and the freedoms guaranteed us by the United States Constitution.

The ACLU of Louisiana staff member who circulated that historic Humanist invocation to some friends and colleagues, Heather Hall, added this comment: "To that we should all be able to say 'amen'"! With due respect to Heather, I would amend that slightly to say, "We should all be able to say a-HUMAN"!

Thank you very much.

Faith, Personal Conviction, and Political Life

Donald W. Wuerl

Bishop of Diocese of Pittsburgh, PA, 1988– ; born Pittsburgh, PA, November 12, 1940; graduate degrees, Catholic University of America and Gregorian University, Rome, and doctorate in theology, University of St. Thomas, Rome, 1974; ordained to the priesthood December 17, 1966; ordained a bishop, January 6, 1986, in St. Peter's Basilica, Rome; distinguished service professor, Duquesne University, Pittsburgh; educational and community-service initiatives, including Christian Leaders Fellowship and its many ecumenical enterprises, the Extra Mile Education Foundation for four inner-city parochial schools, the Urban League of Pittsburgh, and the United Way of Allegheny County; chair, United States Conference of Catholic Bishops (USCCB) editorial oversight board for the U.S. Catholic Catechism for Adults; member, USCCB Committee on Catechesis; former chair, USCCB Committee on Education; chair, board of National Catholic Bioethics Center; vice president, executive board, Pope John Paul II Cultural Center; appears on the television program The Teaching of Jesus, *on Pittsburgh's CBS affiliate and in national syndication; author,* The Teachings of Christ *(1976), translated into more than 10 languages;* The Catholic Way *(2001); honored by National Conference of Christians and Jews, American Red Cross, and B'na Zion; Elizabeth Ann Seton award from the National Catholic Education Association.*

Editors' introduction: The Most Reverend Donald W. Wuerl delivered the annual Loebig lecture sponsored by the Saint Thomas More Society of Pittsburgh, a national association of Catholic lawyers "organized to strengthen the religious and charitable commitment of its members and to promote high ethical standards in the legal profession." The bishop gives an annual talk each May to the Pittsburgh chapter. Speaking before approximately 125 society members at the Allegheny County Courthouse in downtown Pittsburgh, Bishop Wuerl advised, "A significant benefit of a democratic society is our ability to fashion the laws that govern how we conduct ourselves as a political community." Maintaining that "this freedom carries with it a serious responsibility," Bishop Wuerl contended, "Each of us is invited to enter into the political process in order to construct a legal structure that represents our most cherished values and articulates a frame of reference for the common good."

Donald W. Wuerl's speech: One of the questions that has received great attention particularly as this presidential election year unfolds is the relationship of a public office holder's deepest held

Delivered on May 25, 2004, at noon, Pittsburgh, PA. Reprinted with permission of Donald W. Wuerl.

personal convictions and the formation of public policy. This is sometimes phrased: Should personal religious, moral, and ethical values impact political positions?

Added to this debate is another more recently articulated question: Should bishops discipline, perhaps even by denying Holy Communion, those members of the Church in public office who do not support essential moral values in public life? Put another way the question is: Should Catholic politicians who do not support the Church's teaching on basic moral values present themselves as if they were in complete good standing within the Church?

The title for this Loebig Lecture is "Faith, Personal Conviction, and Political Life." It is in that frame of reference that I will explore these more specific questions. In the wider context of everyone's obligation in the political order to build a good and just society I will focus on four points:

1. Some actions are intrinsically wrong and can never be justified. Even in politics there are some moral and ethical lines that a Catholic cannot cross.

2. To make such intrinsically bad actions legal is in itself wrong. When dealing with moral absolutes there is never room for separation of our most deeply held values from our politics.

3. Catholics—like all people who recognize the natural moral law—are obliged to oppose all attacks on it. If something is evil, really wrong, it is wrong for everybody.

4. The Church has a responsibility to participate in the process that results in the laws of the land. Traditionally this involves teaching on the part of pastors of souls and the application of it by the faithful.

Our Personal Obligation to a Good and Just Society

A significant benefit of a democratic society is our ability to fashion the laws that govern how we conduct ourselves as a political community. This freedom carries with it a serious responsibility. Each of us is invited to enter into the political process in order to construct a legal structure that represents our most cherished values and articulates a frame of reference for the common good.

The price of citizenship in a democracy involves making choices, weighing consequences, and determining the values that laws nurture and support. While some laws may have very little moral content others are laden with grave implications. It is one thing to determine a speed limit for an open stretch of highway. It is an all-together different matter to vote on the acceptance or rejection of capital punishment.

When we begin to enact laws we recognize that there must be a point of reference. Life does not unfold in a moral vacuum. We have a moral north star that guides our moral compass. Built into God's creation and into human nature is a moral order. Just as there are physical laws that are a part of the created order—such as the laws of physics or the law of gravity—so there is also in human nature, with its ability to reason and make choices, a natural moral order. Philosophers and moralists for millennia have recognized and named it the "natural moral law." Deep within our heart and conscience is the recognition, for example, that you simply cannot kill others anymore than you would want others to feel free to kill you. The injunction: "You shall not kill" rooted in our human nature, proclaimed by our conscience, and confirmed in God's revelation applies to all innocent human life.

Some Actions Are Always Wrong

Civil law in its effort to regulate human activity has always been presumed to be a reflection of, or at least in conformity with, this natural moral order. Thus we can speak of "bad" laws. Slavery was a legal institution recognized by the laws of the land and sanctioned by the Supreme Court of the United States. Yet the laws permitting, fostering, aiding, and abetting slavery were simply wrong. All

---

Elected officials are not asked to deposit their moral and ethical convictions at the door of Congress or the State Assembly where they serve.

---

human beings are created by God and endowed "by nature and nature's God" with the inalienable right to life and liberty.

At the end of World War II when the victorious allies sought to respond in some legal manner and to punish in some justifiable way the leadership of the Nazi Party in Germany what resulted was the Nuremburg Trials. The basis for judgments made in those processes was the natural moral law. The court recognized that there are "crimes against humanity." This principle was articulated at the time by Pope Pius XII. Such crimes remain wrong even when they are approved by a dictator, a ruling party, or the majority of people.

Every citizen must accept some responsibility for the direction of our country. Thus it is that when a person in a democratic society votes that person is called to bring his or her moral values and vision to the process. Otherwise public policy can soon be emptied of moral content or at least a moral reference point. This we see so clearly in the political posture that approves of terribly wrong actions by claiming to support freedom of choice.

"Choice" without an object is really only a slogan. You have to indicate what your choice is. It would be inconceivable today that someone would say that they were personally opposed to slavery but thought that slaveholders should have the choice. Few would accept the logic of the argument that driving under the influence of alcohol is wrong but that each driver should be allowed the choice to drive or not to drive in that condition. The right to choose brings with it the corresponding responsibility to choose the moral and ethical good.

"Freedom of choice" will always resonate with us who place such an enormous value on personal independence and individual freedom. Yet we cannot allow an attractive shorthand statement to be misused. All choice is about some thing. We can only morally support "choice" when we know what is being chosen.

Evil Acts Should Not Be Legal

In making judgments about public policy every Christian, every person, should consider the basic, primary directives of the moral law as the ultimate norm—a norm that cannot be contravened. Thus to take an innocent life should always under all circumstances be prohibited. The right to life is the most fundamental of all human rights. We simply do not have the ultimate sovereignty over creating or terminating life. This is not the theological or denominational dogma of any one specific religious group. The dignity of human life is not just Catholic teaching. The Catholic Church proclaims the value of human life both as revealed wisdom and as the fruit of human reason.

Sometimes a single issue will be so important that it overrides a whole range of lesser issues. Human slavery is one such historic issue. It simply cannot be condoned no matter how much political support it might enjoy. The same could also be said for the classification, discrimination, and even elimination of people for ethnic reasons. The Holocaust is wrong and cannot be justified on any grounds. So also is the taking of the life of an unborn child. The arbitrary destruction of such life cannot be justified on the grounds that one should be free to choose to kill.

The defining issue of our time is respect for human life. One hundred years from now I believe people will look back on this generation and wonder how it was possible that we deluded ourselves into thinking and then enshrining in the law of the land the principle that the right to life is arbitrary and is protected only for those whose lives are deemed convenient. History will not look kindly upon a society that embraced the concept that if a life is inconvenient to you, you can simply kill him or her. Just as we wonder how it had been possible for people to keep human beings as slaves, as chattel, so future generations will look back and wonder how we could so cavalierly kill our unborn children.

Legislation Must Follow the Moral Law

Just as voters are not asked to leave aside their most deeply held moral convictions when they enter a voting booth so elected officials are not asked to deposit their moral and ethical convictions at the door of Congress or the State Assembly where they serve. In fact, we assume that those whom we elect vote their conscience.

In November 2002 the Vatican Congregation for the Doctrine of the Faith published a document entitled "Doctrinal Note on Some Questions Regarding the Participation of Catholics in Political Life." The Doctrinal Note is "directed to the Bishops of the Catholic Church and, in a particular way, to Catholic politicians and all lay members of the faithful called to participate in the political life of democratic societies."

> *Every member of the faithful, including those engaged in political activity, should act out of a well-formed Christian conscience.*

This Vatican document is intended to clarify the teaching of the Church. Its purpose is to help everyone but particularly Catholic politicians understand the relationship between abortion itself and the legislative support of it. The Doctrinal Note reminds us that it is wrong not only to perform an abortion but also to support legislation that enables an abortion. While the Vatican document does not seem to ascribe to both the procuring and performing of an abortion and the voting for abortion legislation the same level of moral turpitude, it does state that the legislator has a "clear and grave obligation to oppose such legislation."

The Doctrinal Note highlights that teachers of the faith now must instruct the faithful that not only is the commission of an abortion an evil action but the support of legislation that permits abortion is in itself wrong. In a way what the Congregation is doing is connecting the dots. If abortion is an intrinsically evil action then legislative support of it is wrong. Thus we come face-to-face with what every Catholic politician must address.

Empowering abortion is not a political action with light or minimal consequences. It participates in a chain of actions that result in the death of an innocent human life. Pro-abortion legislation creates the legal environment that enables huge numbers of unborn children to be deprived of their most basic and fundamental right—the right to life.

What the Congregation is teaching is a clarification about the moral probity of the position "personally I am opposed to abortion but I believe people should have a choice in the killing of unborn human life." The Doctrinal Note says that this position is wrong. It highlights that one cannot take such a position as if there were no linkage between the choice and the object of the choice.

How Should the Church Respond?

Now we come to the question "How should the Church respond? What should the response of bishops be to those who are members of the Church and who at the same time vote for legislation that the Doctrinal Note points out they have a 'clear and grave obligation to oppose.'"

In a way the Church has just responded with the Doctrinal Note. The standard response of the Church, when dealing with grave moral issues, is to teach. Bishops as pastors of souls have the responsibility of instructing the faithful so that they might have a correctly informed conscience out of which to act in that broad spectrum of engagements we call the human enterprise.

Every member of the faithful, including those engaged in political activity, should act out of a well-formed Christian conscience. It is the task of the teaching office in the Church to bring the light of the Gospel message to the circumstances of our day. The role then of the Church as teacher in no way impinges upon the autonomy of the participation of lay Catholics in politics. As the Doctrinal Note reminds us while there is a rightful autonomy of the political or civil sphere from that of religion and the Church it is not from morality. Thus the constant and legitimate task of pastors of souls is to teach.

The Vatican document does not speak of sanctions against those in public life who do not live up to the "grave and clear obligation to oppose any law that attacks human life." The Vatican Note does not speak of disciplinary actions. In fact there seems to be a practice both in Rome and throughout the Diocesan Churches in Europe of refraining from disciplinary actions in such circumstances.

Those who propose some disciplinary action on the part of bishops point to the fact that a Catholic politician who votes to support abortion and offers publicly reasons why he or she can do this and still be considered in conformity with their Catholic faith causes scandal among the Catholic faithful. Because of the publicity given to the voting position of Catholic politicians there is created, some assert, an impression among Catholics that it is acceptable to reject this clear teaching of the Church. Sometimes politicians in defense of their actions present what appears to be "teaching" contrary to the teaching of the Church. So the question arises, "What are bishops doing to counter this scandal?"

The Bishop as Teacher

Bishops continue to teach, as they have so consistently, that abortion is an evil. Abortion takes the life of an unborn human being. For this reason it is intrinsically wrong and is never able to be justified. Perhaps there is no single teaching position articulated by the bishops that is better known throughout our country than this one: "The Catholic Church opposes abortion."

What we must also now teach with greater clarity is that legislative support for abortion is wrong. The Congregation for the Doctrine of the Faith, citing the teaching of Pope John Paul II raises this action—voting on legislation supporting abortion—to the level of moral wrong.

It is questionable whether the wrongness of voting for abortion legislation is understood by Catholics and non-Catholics alike in the United States in the same way that they recognize the Church's teaching that abortion itself is wrong. In fact, with the positioning of voting on abortion legislation within the context of "choice" much has been done to muddy the moral waters and confuse right thinking about what is really at issue.

What the Doctrinal Note calls the Catholic politician to face today is personal accountability in the forum of conscience and to recognize the moral teaching of the Church that to vote for abortion legislation is also wrong. Clearly, far more teaching needs to be done here not only with politicians but also with all the Catholic faithful. For some the question arises, "What in addition to teaching should the bishops do?" In other words, after having taught clearly and consistently that abortion is wrong and that legislative support for abortion is wrong should a bishop take additional steps?

In considering sanctions, which has always been the last response of the Church, other very serious questions arise. Even when we recognize the special level of moral gravity attached to the taking of innocent human life, once we start down the road of disciplinary action where does it lead? Should the same actions be taken against those politicians who support or do not oppose legislation undermining other fundamental human values?

The Doctrinal Note lists a considerable number of issues similar or analogous to or in the same vein as abortion. Among the significant moral issues that the Doctrinal Note cites in the context of political activity are: the defense of unborn human life, the rejection of capital punishment, the definition and meaning of marriage, as well as the freedom of parents regarding the education of their children, society's protection of minors, and freedom from modern forms of slavery such as drug abuse and prostitution as well as the development of an economy that is at the service of human society.

Before taking disciplinary action, if such a route were chosen, there would have to be a clear explanation about what action is being taken, why it is being taken, and how it is justified. The justification for it would have to be convincingly put forth lest Catholic faithful be confused that this is somehow an effort of the Church to force its will on a legislative assembly rather than to convince legislators what they ought to do. This is no small matter. Historically, the people in the United States, including Catholics, react with great disfavor to any effort of a church body that appears to tell people how to vote or to attempt to punish people for the manner in which they vote.

Discipline and Holy Communion

There are some who propose refusing Holy Communion to those Catholics who do not oppose legislation supporting abortion. Another way to focus the issue is on the individual Catholic who approaches the Eucharist. Should people, any and all persons, who are not living in conformity with the Church's moral teaching and/or who reject it come forward to receive Communion?

Before addressing these questions I want to say a word about reception of Holy Communion. It is the ancient teaching and practice of the Church that only those who are properly disposed should present themselves for Holy Communion. The scriptural text that the ecclesial tradition concerning preparedness to receive Communion has always cited is that of Saint Paul: "Therefore whoever eats the bread or drinks the cup of the Lord unworthily will have to answer for the body and blood of the Lord" (1 Cor.11:27).

Today that same scriptural injunction remains in force. Each Catholic has a personal obligation to examine his or her conscience. If individuals are not properly disposed—for whatever reason—they are obliged to refrain from receiving Holy Communion. Again, this is not a new practice in the Church. All of us who grew up with the experience of regular Saturday Confession know the teaching of the Church. It has not changed.

Refusal of Holy Communion implies, according to applicable Church law, that the person who is not admitted to Holy Communion is one who is excommunicated or interdicted, or obstinately persists in manifest grave sin (cf C915).

We should not be surprised by a breadth of interpretation on matters involving the prudential judgment about the application of specific canons in the context of political actions. It is one thing to say that such a conclusion or interpretation can follow from specific Church documents, it is altogether another thing to say that such an interpretation should or must follow.

The statement of the Doctrinal Note that one has a "clear and grave obligation" to vote against abortion legislation is not a declaration of or confirmation that such a person voting in this manner is in personal grave sin. The Catechism of the Catholic Church teaches that "for a sin to be mortal, three conditions must together be met: 'mortal sin' is sin whose object is grave sin and which is also committed with full knowledge and deliberate consent'" (CCC 1859).

Given the long standing practice of not making a public judgment about the state of the soul of those who present themselves for Holy Communion, it does not seem that it is sufficiently clear that in the matter of voting for legislation that supports abortion such a judgment necessarily follows. The pastoral tradition of the Church places the responsibility of such a judgment first on those presenting themselves for Holy Communion.

The pastoral responsibility of a bishop includes making prudential judgments on how best to achieve the spiritual and pastoral goal of conversion of intellect, will, and heart. The first step is to provide adequate and clear teaching on both the nature of abortion and the separate issue of voting in support of abortion legislation. The next step might very well be a private discussion with politicians on the issue. It may eventually become necessary for the bishop to point out publicly that the position or voting record of a politician supporting abortion contradicts the teaching of the Church. Such public declaration would serve to eliminate or at least minimize the scandal of having it appear that a Catholic is free to support "any law that attacks human life."

There may be other means to highlight the discrepancy between a Catholic politician's public profession of faith and his or her public actions. A Catholic politician who supports legislation that clearly violates the right to life of an innocent unborn child should not be surprised if he or she were not welcome on Catholic university or college campuses or were not given honorary degrees, awards, and recognition for fidelity to the Catholic faith. Certainly such politicians would not expect that the doors of Catholic facilities would be open to them in the same way that they would be opened to someone who holds a position that is consistent with the Catholic tradition of faith and morals.

Conclusion

It seems that on the part of the Church's pastors a much greater effort can be made to teach more convincingly why abortion is a primary evil, and more clearly why support of abortion legislation is gravely wrong, and also why our Catholic faithful must not be misled into believing that either abortion or support of it is somehow acceptable simply because some Catholic politicians do not oppose pro-abortion legislation.

In placing so much emphasis on teaching I am persuaded that, at the moment, this approach responds pastorally and adequately to the current situation. The teaching in this Diocesan Church is clear: both abortion and support of abortion are wrong. No informed Catholic can claim that either action is free of moral implications and certainly no one should be led to believe, because of someone else's voting record, that this teaching about abortion is uncertain.

On the part of Catholics who enter political life there must also be a fuller recognition that what the Church teaches about the value and dignity of human life and the evil of supporting abortion legislation are not incidental to their commitment as members of the Church. Public action that contradicts primary moral imperatives compromises a Catholic's proper disposition or preparedness to take a full and complete role in the Church's life.

All of us have an obligation to be informed on how critical the life-death issue of abortion is, and how profoundly and intrinsically evil is the destruction of unborn human life. Our political actions,

out of which come the laws of this country, must be based on the
natural moral law and the most basic of all human rights—the
right to life.

African American Churches and the Changing Nature of Church-State Relations

R. Drew Smith

Scholar-in-residence, Leadership Center, Morehouse College, Atlanta, GA, 1997– , and Baptist clergyman; director, Public Influences of African American Churches Project and the Faith Communities and Urban Families Project; born Indianapolis, IN, October 1, 1956; B.S. in education, Indiana University, 1979; M.Div., Yale Divinity School, 1983; M.A. (1988) and Ph.D. (1990) in political science, Yale University; adjunct professor, New York Theological Seminary, 1988; assistant professor, Indiana University, 1990–94; associate professor, Butler University, 1994–97; served as minister in a number of parish and prison chaplaincy contexts; actively involved in international community development and youth leadership development; Fulbright Professor, University of Pretoria in South Africa, Spring 2005; advisory boards of academic and nongovernmental organizations concerned with religion and public life, including the Pew Partnership for Civic Change, Calvin College's Institute for the Study of Christianity and Politics, and Notre Dame University's Center for the Study of Latino Religion; editor: New Day Begun: African American Churches and Civic Culture in Post–Civil Rights America *(2003);* Long March Ahead: African American Churches and Public Policy in Post–Civil Rights America *(2004); with Fredrick Harris,* Black Churches and Local Politics: Clergy Influence, Organizational Partnerships, and Civic Empowerment *(2005);* Freedom's Distant Shores: American Protestants and Post-Colonial Alliances with Africa *(2006); published numerous articles and book chapters on American and African religion and politics.*

Editors' introduction: Dr. R. Drew Smith addressed faculty, staff, students, and visitors from the public at large in the Ralph Brown Draughon Library auditorium as part of a distinguished public lecture series sponsored by the Auburn University Department of Political Science, University Center for the Arts and Humanities, and the College of Liberal Arts. Concerned that "too close a relationship between religion and government is probably never a good thing," Dr. Smith cautioned, "There is a moral capital black churches acquired through their historic struggles against racial oppression, and a theological capital that derives from their Biblical calling (and their well established practices) of social 'non-conformity' that they run the risk of squandering when clamoring after a seat at the king's table."

Delivered on March 21, 2005, at 3 P.M. at Auburn, AL. Reprinted with permission of R. Drew Smith.

R. Drew Smith's speech: In discussing church-state relations, I'd like to advocate an approach captured in an old saying that went something like this: "He who sups at the King's table, must eat with a long spoon." In other words, you're taking a great risk when you get too close to the king, and for that reason, and for other reasons that I'll outline here today, I hope to convey that too close a relationship between religion and government is probably never a good thing.

Historically, I believe African American churches have largely embraced this principle. They have placed importance on the role of government, but they have maintained a certain caution about embracing the government too tightly or too uncritically. African-American religious leaders—at least through the mid-20th century—have generally attempted to maintain a balance between affirming the best instincts of American government, and denouncing its problematic instincts. It was this way of framing the situation that mobilized the historic movement of change during the 1950s and 1960s that led this country forward in both its political and its religious self-understanding. And it was Martin Luther King, Jr., who did more than anyone to give shape to the Civil Rights Movement, and to the view that black church-based resistance was to serve the dual role of political corrective to American social injustices and theological corrective to Protestantism's tendency toward "identifying the Kingdom of God with a particular social and economic system."[1]

Too close a relationship between religion and government is probably never a good thing.

And while there's always been an element of collaboration between black religious leaders and government, in the years since the Civil Rights Movement the balance within black churches' approach to government and governmental affairs has shifted in a number of ways. Some of these shifts may have helped strengthen the potentially constructive theological and political impact black churches can have on politics and government; some of them may threaten to betray the historic balance black churches have attempted to maintain in their relationship to government. There are many areas where issues of church-state relationships come up, but I will focus almost exclusively on church-state issues within the context of electoral affairs and, specifically on the following two questions:

1. how do black churches approach electoral matters; and

2. how do electoral candidates and political party leaders behave toward black churches?

The 40-year period since the passing of the 1965 Voting Rights Act has clearly been a period of substantial black engagement within electoral affairs. In 1965, there were only about 100 black elected officials within the U.S. There are now approximately

8,000 black elected officials within the country, and the number of blacks serving in appointed public capacities also numbers in the thousands. Black churches have played a significant role within this activity, both as major sources of voters and of organizational capital. In fact, in a national survey conducted by the Public Influences of African American Churches Project, which I direct, 84 percent of the approximately 2,000 black church pastors we surveyed indicated that during the previous 10 years their congregation had been involved with voter registration activities. Nearly two-thirds of the respondents reported congregational efforts to transport people to the polls. And 31 percent said their congregation had been involved in passing out campaign materials. In this regard, black churches reflect a general expansion in black electoral involvement. In the years since the 1965 Voting Rights Act, the national percentage of black voters registered to vote during a presidential election year has remained 60 percent or better, except for 1976 when it dipped to 58 percent.[2]

Just a few years prior to the Voting Rights Act it was a much different picture—especially in the South. In 1959, black voter registration averaged 26 percent among 10 southern states—with none of these states having more than 39 percent of blacks registered to vote and Mississippi having the least at 6 percent. Since 1968, the level of black voter registration in the South has averaged about 60 percent.[3] Black churches, in fact, have been central to the expansion and mobilization of the black electorate, receiving particular attention for their voter mobilization efforts nationally during the 1980 and 1984 presidential elections and receiving attention as well in the 2000 presidential election for contributing to record black voter turnout in Florida and Pennsylvania.

Moreover, significant numbers of black clergy have themselves held elective office. Nearly a tenth (9.2 percent) of the 1,956 BCAP survey respondents indicated that the pastor had served in such a capacity.[4] If the survey sample is truly representative of African American clergy in general, this suggests that hundreds of black clergy have served in elective office over the last 30 years. The most prominent of this group are the seven black clergy elected to the U.S. Congress since 1971: Walter Fauntroy, Andrew Young, William Gray, III, Floyd Flake, John Lewis, J.C. Watts, and (in the 2004 election), Emmanuel Cleaver, who had previously served as Mayor of Kansas City, MO.

There were also black clergy who served in the U.S. Congress in the late 1800s and early 1900s, beginning with Charles Mitchell, who was elected to the Massachusetts legislative assembly in 1866.[5] Among the 22 blacks that served in the U.S. Congress between 1870 and 1901, three were ministers: Hiram Rhodes Revels, who was elected to the U.S. Senate from Mississippi in 1868; Richard Harvey Cane, who was elected to the U.S. House of Representatives from South Carolina; and Jeremiah Haralson, who was elected to the

U.S. House of Representatives from Alabama. Another black clergyman elected to a prominent political office during that period was James D. Lynch, who served as Secretary of State in Mississippi.[6] There were also dozens of blacks that served in State Legislatures in South Carolina, Georgia, Florida, and Mississippi during the Reconstruction period in the South, many of whom were clergymen.[7]

Black clergy have recognized the electoral power of black churches, but this has been true also of politicians, in general, across political party lines. Democratic politicians have routinely interacted closely with black church leaders—especially at election time. Democratic politicians frequently speak at black churches and often enlist prominent black clergy to mobilize black voters on behalf of Democratic candidates. John Kerry, like many Democratic candidates before him, enlisted Jesse Jackson to mobilize black churches on behalf of his candidacy.[8] In fact, it is not unusual for black clergy, individually or in groups, to openly endorse political candidates—with those candidates most often from the Democratic Party.

This pattern of black churches functioning as support bases for Democratic Party candidates goes back at least to Jimmy Carter's 1976 presidential candidacy. Carter's 1976 campaign is viewed as unprecedented among Presidential campaigns in its aggressive outreach to African Americans, including black churches. Despite Carter's style of sending progressive signals on race to black audiences and conservative signals on race to white audiences (a strategy also employed by John F. Kennedy and many other politicians), Carter's campaign had active alliances with prominent black church leaders such as Rev. Andrew Young, "Daddy" King, and Coretta Scott King.[9] Although John Kennedy made what is now a well known call to Coretta King during his 1960 campaign to express his concern about Martin King's trumped up arrest for a traffic violation in Georgia, Kennedy worked assiduously to distance his campaign from open association with black issues. Lyndon Johnson's 1964 Presidential campaign had perhaps a more substantial focus on black issues than any American presidential campaign by a major contender prior to Jesse Jackson's campaigns in the 1980s, nevertheless, Johnson placed no strategic electoral emphasis on black churches in the way Carter did. In fact, the Congressional legislation currently on the books preventing religious groups and tax-exempt organizations from endorsing political candidates is traced back to Johnson's objection to attempts by his opponent in the Texas 1956 Senate race to get conservative Texas clergy to endorse the effort to defeat Johnson.

It was, no doubt, Jesse Jackson's Presidential campaigns in 1984 and 1988 that galvanized a strategic electoral role for black churches within national politics, in particular. The role of black churches was so central to Jackson's campaigns that they functioned, according to an important study of these campaigns, as essentially voting precincts (Hertzke). Jackson's campaigns also set the tone, in many ways, for targeting Sunday worship services at black churches as strategic campaign venues. Bill Clinton certainly built upon this practice in his 1992 and 1996 Presidential campaigns, by making frequent appearances at black worship services during his campaigns. Al Gore did the same in 2000, as did John Kerry in 2004. In fact, Kerry's deputy campaign manager, Bill Lynch, was reported to have stated publicly, "We are going to try to get Kerry into an African-American church every Sunday to deliver his message." George W. Bush is the first Republican presidential candidate to make extensive use of churches, including black churches, as major campaign venues.

As black clergy have functioned in their role as electoral brokers, it has not been unusual to find them making remarks that place a religious importance on electoral matters that seem both theologically and politically inappropriate. For example, during the 1989 mayoral primaries in Chicago, a black Chicago minister informed his congregation that failure to vote for black mayoral candidate, Eugene Sawyer, was tantamount to turning City Hall over to the enemies of black progress (which was itself an arguable claim given that Sawyer's politics were by no means universally viewed by Chicagoans as progressive). Nevertheless, addressing doubters in the audience who might not vote correctly or at all, the minister inquired how they would be able to face Harold Washington once they arrived in heaven; what would their explanation be?[10] The minister was referring, of course, to Chicago's greatly admired first black mayor who had been elected in 1983 and passed away unexpectedly soon after his re-election in 1987. And as important as Washington was to Chicago politics and to African American politics more broadly, it still seems inappropriate for this minister through his remarks to simultaneously confer saintly status on Harold Washington and grant a redemptive importance to the act of voting. In a more recent example, there were press reports of a black pastor in Florida during the 2004 elections proclaiming from his pulpit that John Kerry was "the new Moses."[11] If what the minister meant was that Kerry, like Moses, was a liberator of his people, then that certainly would seem far-fetched—especially to most African-Americans, given how little attention Kerry paid to racial justice issues during his campaign.

Clergy endorsements of political candidates have become so routine that it is not uncommon to find separate groups of black clergy promoting opposing candidates—and sometimes promoting their respective candidates in quite rancorous ways. During the 1995 Chicago mayoral election, approximately 25 Chicago ministers, mostly black, released a statement endorsing Richard Daley's re-election at a prayer vigil they were hosting on his behalf. In response, a group called the Committee Against Plantation Politics, comprised of a handful of organizations including the Council of Black Churches, picketed some of the ministers' churches that endorsed Daley and issued flyers that asked the ministers to justify their claims that "God told them to vote for Daley."

And apparently, Democratic politicians are not the only politicians who recognize the potential political advantage of enlisting black clergy and the religious language, culture, and convictions of black churches into their electoral causes. On the Republican side, President George W. Bush and other Republican Party leaders have hoped to benefit from morally conservative tendencies and affinities among churchgoing blacks. Using the "faith-based initiative" as a primary platform, Republican leaders (including the President) have engaged in an increasingly systematic and intentional targeting of black churches as evidenced by the large number of meetings and interactions they have facilitated with black church leaders in the past four years.

A few weeks after the November 2000 elections, President-elect Bush convened a meeting in Austin with approximately 30 hand-picked religious leaders, many of whom were black, to signal the emphasis his administration would place on partnering with the faith community on social services and other matters. The African American clergy invited to the meeting were in many cases clergy known to emphasize community development involvements more than political rights involvements and who tended to operate independently of the historically black ecclesiastical structures that many would regard as the black religious mainstream and as the backbone of black church-based civic activism. The list of black clergy invitees included a number of black Pentecostal and Charismatic clergy such as Bishop Charles Blake of the Church of God in Christ, Bishop Carlton Pearson of Higher Dimensions Church, and Rev. Eugene Rivers, co-founder of the Ten Point Coalition. Also in attendance were former Democratic Congressman, Floyd Flake, who is an African Methodist Episcopal Church pastor and a prospect at that time for a possible Bush cabinet appointment, Rev. Kirbyjon Caldwell, a United Methodist pastor and strong Bush supporter who gave the invocation prayer at Bush's 2001 inauguration; and Rev. Herbert Lusk, a Baptist pastor and close ally of Bush and his faith-based initiative proposal. Noticeably absent from the meeting were principal denominational leaders from the historically black Baptist and Methodist denominations and Conventions (which account for roughly two-thirds of African American Christians)[12] and activist clergy such as Jesse Jackson or Al Sharpton.

The White House and Republican allies in the U.S. Congress sponsored a series of meetings throughout Bush's first Presidential term to promote Bush's faith-based initiative, particularly among black religious leaders. In April 2001, Congressman J.C. Watts (R-OK), Senator Rick Santorum (R-PA), and Bishop Harold Ray (a

Bush ally and Miami based pastor who heads an ecclesiastical network called the National Center for Faith Based Initiative) convened a meeting in Washington to build support for Bush's faith-based policies. Approximately 400 black ministers were invited and, as was the case in the Austin meeting, few denominational leaders from the historically black denominations were on the invitation list. During 2002, the White House took steps to broaden its support base among black religious leaders for the faith-based initiative by sponsoring a series of seminars around the country aimed at informing clergy about the mechanics of the faith-based initiative. These events attracted hundreds of mainly black clergy, although there were religious leaders in attendance from various faiths, races, and political persuasions.[13]

I raise the issue of the White House Faith-Based Initiative for two reasons. First, the Initiative has provoked a highly charged debate about the Constitutionality of such instances of close collaboration between church and state. I will come back to this issue later in my remarks. Secondly, the Faith-Based Initiative has been used as a means, not just for a kind of programmatic social service collaboration between government and faith groups, but also as a means for strengthening Republican electoral alliances with supporters and potential supporters within various faith communities. With respect to the principle of aggressively competing for electoral support among the faith communities, the Bush administration is simply doing what Democrats and Republicans have done for years. What has been different about the Bush team is how religiously explicit their appeal has been. Some view this as an entirely appropriate electoral strategy (including a cadre of conservative black clergy who have provided electoral support for the President), while others view this as a particularly craven exploitation of the religious factor for electoral purposes (including a number of prominent black pastors and heads of black denominations).

The perspective of the Bush Administration and key Republicans in the U.S Congress has been that their systematic outreach to black churches simply acknowledges the strategic role black churches play in reaching the urban poor. And, as J. C. Watts comments, Republicans want to show black leaders that they are "just as interested as Democrats in helping lift people out of poverty."[14] Black clergy, however, have had varying political interpretations of the Republican Party's outreach to black churches. For example, Rev. C. Mackey Daniels, who was President of the Progressive National Baptist Convention in the early 2000s, issued a press release in 2001 condemning Bush's faith-based initiative and targeting of black churches as "an effort to muffle the prophetic voice of the African American church." Daniels also suggested that support of Bush's initiative was equivalent to accepting "30 pieces of silver."[15]

Interestingly, in a replay of the Austin meeting in 2000, a number of black clergy and civic leaders who supported the President's 2004 re-election were invited to the White House early in 2005 for a meeting with the President—undoubtedly as a way to acknowledge and further solidify Bush's support among conservative black Christians. At about the same time, a historic gathering of black Baptists took place in Nashville between clergy and lay leaders from all four of the historically black Baptist Conventions (Conventions representing a total membership of between 15–20 million people). One purpose of the meeting was to pursue closer collaboration between the four Conventions on social development and public policy matters. With respect to public policy, the Convention leaders concluded the four-day meeting jointly stating their opposition to the war in Iraq, to the confirmation of Alberto Gonzalez as Attorney General, and to cuts in spending to children's health care. The policy positions outlined by these Baptist leaders align neither with President Bush's priorities nor apparently with the policy priorities of many of the black clergy who have been among Bush's supporters. This deepening political division between black clergy has not escaped the attention of the media either, as in the case of a March 2005 *New York Times* article that characterizes these divisions as a "tug of war" between black churches over the role they are to play in politics.[16] Perhaps it's less a tug of war over what role churches are to play—given how widespread black church leaders' commitments to influencing electoral and governance matters have become—and more a competition over the political camps black churches should align themselves with if they are to be seen as representing the best political interests of the black community and the best theological interests of the church. Increasingly, then, the question black church leaders are asking is not whether to become engaged politically, but, rather, which political side to align with.

> *The question black church leaders are asking is not whether to become engaged politically, but, rather, which political side to align with.*

Clearly, black churches have been quite active in electoral affairs, and this is a fitting tribute to the shift away from a context of systematic black exclusion from political participation and toward a context where black participation is legally enforced. But what are the implications for the faith sector of this close relationship between government and black churches—or between government and the faith sector in general (irrespective of race or religion)? And what are the implications for American politics?

There are certainly constitutional implications. Some of this activity appears to violate U.S. constitutional separation of church and state. And while matters of church-state separation have generally not received significant scrutiny by the government (except as a result from law suits brought by citizen groups), the IRS has been closely examining the political activities of dozens of churches and faith groups in the last year to determine whether their activities disqualify them for tax-exempt status. According to the IRS tax guide for churches and other religious organizations, the law prohibiting endorsements of candidates by these groups "is not intended to restrict free expression on political matters by leaders of churches or religious organizations speaking for themselves, as individuals. Nor are leaders prohibited from speaking about important issues of public policy, or inviting candidates to speak at a church, if opposing candidates are also invited." Nevertheless, maintaining tax-exempt status requires that religious leaders not "make partisan comments in official organization publications or at official church functions."[17]

In 1999, IRS enforcement of this policy gained steam in a high-profile case in which it denied tax-exempt status to the Christian Coalition—a leading conservative activist organization. The Coalition's application for tax-exempt status had been pending before the IRS for 10 years. In the end, reportedly, the IRS denied tax-exempt status to the coalition because of its production and circulation of highly partisan voter guides and other materials.[18] Some viewed this as a partisan assault by the Clinton-era IRS on an organization they viewed as one of the chief opponents of President Clinton's administration.

However, charges of partisanship have also been leveled at the Bush-era IRS for its recent scrutiny of the 2004 election-related activities of 60 nonprofit groups, including 20 or more churches. Although details about these cases have not been forthcoming, including the political alignments of most of the groups being investigated, one group whose tax-exempt status is currently being reconsidered by the IRS is the NAACP. Allegedly, an IRS investigation of the NAACP was launched in response to a July 2004 speech by NAACP President, Julian Bond, that was viewed as highly critical of President Bush. Bond's speech made reference to, among other things, his opposition to Bush's judicial appointments and tax reductions for wealthy taxpayers. And while he encouraged blacks to vote, he appears to have approached the matter of who they should vote for only indirectly. He simply stated: "We know that if whites and nonwhites vote in the same percentages as they did in 2000, Bush will be re-defeated by 3 million votes." The NAACP is refusing to cooperate with the IRS investigation and, according to Bond, this will no doubt "invite more scrutiny" by the IRS. It will be interesting to see how the case against the NAACP is decided, and to see the outcome of the cases against the other (as yet unnamed) organizations under scrutiny by the Bush-era IRS.

Even as liberal organizations such as the NAACP (and, perhaps, a number of liberal church leaders) were being investigated by the Bush-era IRS, conservatives (in what is probably a quite unintended bit of irony) were promoting legislation in the U.S. Congress that would allow religious leaders to endorse political candidates from the pulpit. The legislation, which is referred to as "The Houses of Worship Free Speech Restoration Act," is being sponsored by Rep. Walter Jones (R-NC) along with 174 co-sponsors.

All of this has given new energy and urgency to questions about how much formal partisanship religious groups and other tax-exempt groups should be able to embody and still maintain tax-exempt status. This is certainly a thorny issue, and one that I suspect will receive heightened attention as religious leaders from many different camps increasingly lay claim to political processes and activities.

But apart from the legal considerations, there are also philosophical and theological considerations that are raised by collaborations between faith groups and government. And while black churches are certainly not unique among American faith groups in closely aligning themselves with governmental politics, an important question in this instance is whether the political benefits to the black community from these political alignments are worth the loss of moral capital that may result for black churches. There is a moral capital black churches acquired through their historic struggles against racial oppression, and a theological capital that derives from their Biblical calling (and their well established practices) of social "non-conformity" that they run the risk of squandering when clamoring after a seat at the king's table.

Clergy can be supportive of political candidates without risking so much of their own credibility.

And then there is a certain responsibility that comes with being standard bearers of great traditions. Political scientist, Charles Hamilton, offered an analysis of the late Adam Clayton Powell, Jr. that is quite relevant to this point. Commenting on the problems Powell encountered in the 1960s for his refusal to observe a higher standard of conduct than the rest of his Congressional colleagues (especially the tendency by Powell, like his Congressional colleagues, to engage in elaborate travel at taxpayers' expense), Hamilton pointed out that Powell misread the leadership obligations assigned to him by the historical context in which he operated. Says Hamilton, "when you're the leader of a major cause like Civil Rights, you may have to do more."

Clergy can be supportive of political candidates without risking so much of their own credibility by aligning themselves so closely and so uncritically with governmental affairs. It's interesting to note, that Martin Luther King, Jr. did not provide political endorsements for candidates—regarding such practices as inconsistent with his standing as a representative of the church and of the civil rights struggle. When pressured by civil rights activists to endorse John Kennedy's presidential candidacy in 1960, for example, King refused to do so stating that his role "in the emerging social order of the South and America" demanded that he "remain non-partisan."

And while it seems that many black clergy today may not be heeding King's advice on this, ironically, they may be forced to listen to the IRS, through its tax codes, on the matter of whether they will closely align themselves with morally compromising and often short-sighted partisan political matters or with something of greater transcendent significance.

Endnotes

1. Martin Luther King, Jr., *Strive Toward Freedom: The Montgomery Story* (New York: Harper & Row, 1958), 91. King draws on sentiments expressed by Reinhold Niebuhr among others. For a classic articulation of Niebuhr's theological position, see Niebuhr, *Moral Man and Immoral Society* (New York: Charles Scribner's Sons, 1932), especially pp. 22 and 78–82. For King's perspective on Niebuhr, see King, *Stride Toward Freedom*, p. 99. For an additional discussion of the relationship between King's and Niebuhr's perspectives on the church's role as political critic, see Strout, *New Heavens*, chapters 20 and 21.

2. David Bositis, *Blacks and the 1996 Democratic National Convention* (Washington, D.C.: Joint Center for Political and Economic Studies, 1996), 18.

3. Bositis, 18; and Lenneal Henderson, Jr., "Black Politics and American Presidential Election," in *The New Black Politics: The Search for Political Power*, ed. Michael Preston et al (New York: Longman, 1987) 9.

4. The question was specific to the pastor, regardless of whether the respondent may have been an associate minister or, in a few cases, a layperson.

5. Hanes Walton, 1972, 86.

6. Charles Hamilton, 1991, 113; and William Montgomery, 1993, 182.

7. William Montgomery, 1993, 178, 183.

8. David Kirkpatrick, "Black Pastors Backing Bush Are Rare, but Not Alone," *New York Times* (October 5, 2004).

9. Jeremy D. Mayer, *Running on Race: Racial Politics in Presidential Campaigns, 1960–2000* (New York: Random House, 2002), 131.

10. "All Things Considered," National Public Radio (February 23, 1989).

11. Miles Benson, "IRS Takes New Look at Church Political Activities," Newhouse News Service (February 22, 2005).

12. C. Eric Lincoln and Lawrence Mamiya, *The Black Church in the African American Experience* (Durham: Duke University Press, 1990), 407.

13. Thomas Edsall and Alan Cooperman, "GOP Using Faith Initiative to Woo Voters," *New York Times* (September 15, 2002), A5.

14. Rebecca Carr, "GOP Looks for Black Faith-Based Allies," *Atlanta Journal Constitution* (April 25, 2001), A7.

15. Hamil Harris, "Bush Proposal Is Worrisome, Jackson Says," *Washington Post* (February 5, 2001), B3.

16. Neela Banerjee, "Black Churches Struggle Over Their Role in Politics," *New York Times* (March 6, 2005).

17. Miles Benson, "IRS Takes New Look at Church Political Activities," Newhouse News Service (February 22, 2005).

18. Thomas Edsall and Hanna Rosin, "IRS Denies Christian Coalition Tax-Exempt Status," *New York Times* (June 11, 1999), A4.

III. Established and New Media

Interactive Journalism

Drawing in Readers with a High-Tech Approach

Jan Schaffer

Executive director, J-Lab: The Institute for Interactive Journalism, University of Maryland Philip Merrill College of Journalism, 2002– ; born Ashtabula, Ohio, 1950; B.S.J. (1972), M.S.J. (1973), Medill School of Journalism, Northwestern University; journalism fellow, Stanford University, 1983–84; reporter and editor, Philadelphia Inquirer, *1972–94, winning several awards for federal court reporting, including the Pulitzer Prize, 1978, Sigma Delta Chi Distinguished Public Service Award, the Roy W. Howard Medal for Public Service, and the American Bar Association's Silver Gavel; former executive director, the Pew Center for Civic Journalism, 1997–2003; a regular discussion leader at the American Press Institute and has been a speaker and trainer for universities and professional journalism organizations.*

Editors' introduction: Under Director Schaffer's leadership, the J-Lab: The Institute for Interactive Journalism "helps news rooms, educators and communities use innovative information technologies to develop new ways for people to learn about important public issues." In her keynote address to the American Association of Sunday and Features Editors (AASFE), Director Schaffer challenged the audience by asking, "How can we build interactive opportunities . . . that are more than technological gee-whiz stuff?" "Information becomes meaningful," she suggested, "when it is accompanied by attachment or involvement." She concluded, "When people have some participatory stake in a story, you get intelligent interaction." Launched in 1947, AASFE is an organization of more than 200 editors from the U.S. and Canada "dedicated to the quality of features in newspapers and the craft of feature writing." AASFE supports its membership with an annual convention, a writing contest, an annual magazine, and a Web site.

Jan Schaffer's speech: Hello. Thank you for having me today here in New Orleans, which is always a fun city. You are convening at an important moment in the history of journalism and in a troubled year for the practice of journalism.

Delivered on October 1, 2004, at New Orleans, Louisiana. Reprinted with permission of Jan Schaffer.

We've seen more *mea culpas* apologizing for bad coverage than ever before. And we see, daily, how our industry and our definitions of *news* are rapidly changing around us (and not in good ways). We also see how our longstanding journalistic conventions are failing to ensure that we deliver good, accurate reports.

So, today I want to start with an example of news—news commentary—that does not originate from what we classically think of as a news operation: AOL.

AOL News represents two major trends. Increasingly more news and newslike information are coming from non-journalists or quasi-journalists. And increasingly these news producers are using new information technologies to disseminate information.

For the 2004 Presidential Elections, AOL produced a terrific 2004 Election Guide. It offered comprehensive voter information and issues coverage and it was available to all online users, not just AOL subscribers; 30 million people have accessed it since the 2000 elections.

> *Increasingly more news and newslike information are coming from non-journalists or quasi-journalists.*

In 2004, AOL decided to try to reach out to young voters in a new way, using political humor. So it commissioned a number of interactive cartoons. Here's one called **Minister of Fear**.

Now, what would you call this? Do you consider it to be a "news experience?" It informs, it engages, it makes you laugh. I think it's a new kind of news experience.

AOL Elections, by the way, just made it to the top 25 out of 292 entries from 30 countries in PoliticsOnline's contest for 10 Who Are Changing the World of Internet and Politics.

Welcome to digital storytelling. It has arrived with a great deal of promise for making exciting new connections to readers in entirely new ways. Will traditional newsrooms be able to stay in the game? Will we be overtaken by new players: bloggers, nonprofit media, citizen journalists, online service providers?

As important: What can we do with our journalism that adds value—rather than simply adding more noise to an already noisy media environment?

We can stay in the game, but it will require a lot of creative thinking to make it happen. Since most of you at this convention hail from some of the most creative departments in any news organization, I want to share with you observations and examples of what I see happening around the country—and let your fertile brains take it from there.

First, some cosmic observations: Usually when we talk about technology and journalism, we use the word *convergence*. I hate that word.

That's because so much of the emphasis of convergence is on:

- Speed—Who's first?

- Platform—How are we going to deliver it: TV, online, print?

- Mix—International, national, local, entertainment, infotainment?

- Revenue—How can we make money off of this?

- Moving Parts—How many bells and whistles can we add?

When you think about it, this puts the focus not on the *consumer*—our audiences, but on the *supplier*—the news organizations. It becomes an exercise in Us vs. Them. The last people we're converging with are our readers.

In the end, you get a lot of "me-too" news that duplicates what's already out there. It delivers very little added value, but it does deliver more noise.

Our early work in the civic journalism arena when I directed the Pew Center for Civic Journalism tapped into a public appetite for new kinds of news and information. It was distinguished by a higher level of involvement, a more personal stake, and lots of interaction: There were town hall meetings, task forces, and solutions reports. The readers "got" it—they loved participating. They even thanked their news organizations for probing their opinions. These interactions in the mid '90's, of course, tended to happen in real space—a room. Now they are moving into cyberspace.

One example of what you can do with a solutions report online comes from WCPO-TV in Cincinnati, The Purple People Bridge coverage. You not only can read about the problem, in this case revitalizing a run-down side of a bridge connecting Ohio and Kentucky, but you also have 10 different opportunities to contribute to a solution. If you want to pay for a park bench at $750 or a flower planter at $450—just click a button on line. You've just empowered someone to be part of a solution.

How can we build interactive opportunities like this that are more than technological gee-whiz stuff? More than online chats and photo galleries?

Meaningful Information

I suggest that information becomes meaningful when the user develops some kind of attachment to it or involvement with it. Let me repeat: Information becomes meaningful when it is accompanied by attachment or involvement.

So, rather than focus on convergence, we should be focusing on another "C" word: *connections* and how new digital tools can help us build all kinds of innovative, new connections with our audiences. The potential of new media is not simply more noise—but information experiences and meaningful interaction—and even, I would suggest, entirely new kinds of civic participation.

How many of you are familiar with the findings of Northwestern's Readership Institute? You can read all about it at *www.readership.org*. This is major research, millions of pieces of data. Big-time reader surveys. The language of its recommendations is fascinating.

The researchers call for a full-bore "revolution" to forge strong bonds with younger more diverse readers. And they say we have to do more than deliver good "reads." We must deliver good news "experiences" that "purposely play to the feelings and values that readers really care about." They identify eight experiences that are key. Three of these especially resonate with me. They include news that:

- Looks out for my civic and personal interests—makes me feel like a better citizen.
- Makes feel me smarter—I get valuable information.
- Is something to "talk about"—makes me feel at the hub of my social network.

The Readership Institute makes two recommendations:

- Focus on the experiences you want to create in readers and let your news decisions cascade from there.
- Tweak less, innovate more.

An experience is usually something you participate in, right? What if we substituted the words *media participation* for convergence as a goal of journalism? It evokes various levels of interactivity, various experiences. Think of the possibilities—and these are early observations:

- Story making in addition to story telling. And there are two ways to "make" a story:
  - Consuming the stories we make (Content consumption)
  - Making the stories we consume (Content creation)
- Deconstructing in addition to constructing stories
- News exercises in addition to news stories
- Civic participation in addition to news and information

MIT Professor Pablo J. Boczkowski recently published a book, *Digitizing the News* that makes an assertion that resonates with me:

"News in the online environment is what those contributing to its production make of it." He reports that news is moving "from being mostly journalist-centered, communicated as a monologue, and primarily local, to also being increasingly audience-centered, part of multiple conversations and micro-local."

I would add micro-personal.

Digital storytelling allows us to introduce a level of interactivity into our story telling. We can build in entry points for ordinary folks to converse, participate, experience something, and then let that interaction improve the journalism—and also help create it.

Think about the 2004 presidential election cycle: Look at how people used new media tools to create their own news experiences and then shared them with others. All the while, by the way, they were circumventing mainstream journalism.

In addition to AOL's cartoons, we saw:

- Truthsquading at factcheck.org
- People creating ads, like Bush in 30 Seconds, at Moveon.org.
- Full-blown movies, such as *Fahrenheit 9/11* and *Outfoxed.*
- Creative e-mails: We've seen Howard Dean's scream, not only rippling nationwide via e-mail—but it's been mixed and scored to all kinds of music.

Is this journalism? Not as we've defined it. Are these "news experiences?" That's an interesting question.

I think they *are* news experiences.

Opportunities for interactivity really distinguish what journalism can offer in a digital age. Participation gives consumers some attachment—and ultimately some ownership of the information.

It's just like anything—once you get involved in something, you tend to form some attachment, care about it, and want to learn more about it.

These new digital opportunities change the construct a bit from what journalists have traditionally done.

You could think of it this way: Future News might well be less about story telling—the stories we journalists want to write, produce, or tell—and more about story making.

Less about storytelling—and more about story making.

Think about it: People nowadays are able, thanks to new technology, to co-author or co-produce their own stories from various news experiences. In the new media world, I'm seeing two ways to "make a story." One involves consuming the stories we make. One involves creating the stories we consume. One way is internal; the other is external.

Now, how do you get your daily news? Let's see a show of hands. How many of you read you daily paper front to back? Be honest now. Is it a full meal or are you grazing?

Internal Story Making: Individuals as News Aggregators

Daily, most people are constructing their own internal master narratives of that day's events or issues by assembling information from a variety of sources. Each one of us is an individual news aggregator. We find out what's going on from:

- Traditional newspaper stories, headlines, photos
- Drive-time radio
- Internet news sites
- Blogs
- E-mail newsletters and news alerts
- E-mail from friends
- White-noise TV, playing in the background of our offices

- Cell phone news alerts
- Late-night TV comedy from the likes of Jon Stewart, Jay Leno, or David Letterman

As we sift through this onslaught of info-bits, we come up with our sense, or sensibilities, about the day's developments. Because of the explosion of new media sources and the choices people can make in accessing the news, they are much, much more involved as aggregators of information. Sure, Yahoo can do this for you, but, informally, you are really doing this for yourself all day long.

External Story Making: Citizen Participants, Citizen-Created Content

However, another form of storymaking is also going on. Access to easy-to-use publishing software is increasingly making it easier for people to create and publish their own news. This is happening in various ways:

- **Through blogs**. Technorati.com now tracks nearly 16 million weblogs.
    - Blogs as breaking news: Bloggers played big roles in unseating Trent Lott, in exposing the lack of verified documents in CBS reports about President Bush's National Guard duty, and in scooping the national media to report that John Kerry picked John Edwards as his running mate.
    - Beat reporter blogs: Around the country reporters are using blogs to report information that doesn't rise to the level of a full story, to add links to research that relates to their stories, and to tap reader expertise. *The Spokesman Review* in Spokane, WA, is a leader in this arena.
    - Blogs as niche news sites: Whether reporting on the arts, on the media, on politics, on technology, blogs give individuals a way to aggregate news, opinion, or expertise on a particular subject.
- **Through news exercises and games** that allow people to interact with information. I'll talk about these more in a minute.
- **Through citizen journalism efforts**, such as OhmyNews.com in South Korea or NorthwestVoice.com in Bakersfield, CA.
    - Stay tuned: I've just received a $1 million Knight Foundation grant to seed 20 hyperlocal citizen media projects in the next two years.
- **Through e-mail newsletters**, such as the *Washington Post's* Lean Plate Club. The Lean Plate Club e-letter comes out every Tuesday, followed by a Web chat on Wednesdays. It started in August, 2002 with 3,000 subscribers. I recently interviewed its writer, Sally Squires, who'll be here later today, and she told me that when the *Post* required online registration in February,

2004, she feared that would be the end of the newsletter. There were 16,000 subscribers then. Today, there are 122,000. And 75 percent of those who subscribe, open it.

"The biggest surprise to us is the community that has grown up around it," she said.

Deconstructing News Stories

Now, whether the process of story making is internal or external a lot of it involves consuming not so much full stories but often *pieces* of stories—components, such as a headline, a photo, a graphic, a caption, a snatch of TV news, a push e-mail, an online exercise.

Now, here we are journalists and we spend all this time on craftsmanship, right? How can we produce a beautiful story package? And our consumers are sort of grazing and snacking on morsels here and there—what I call *components* of news.

So I'd suggest that future news will, in part, be about building the components that help users co-produce their stories—internal or external.

Future news will, in part, be about building the components that help users co-produce their stories—internal or external.

What are the components that will deliver news and involvement, attachment, connections, experiences? Now the process of assembling components involves deconstructing a story more than constructing—dividing it into its various parts (parts that can, of course, be re-purposed in a multimedia world).

This doesn't mean that we don't produce nice story packages. It's not an Either/Or. It's an AND.

Digital storytelling, as we see around us, is increasingly relying on such components as visual information, interactive databases, games, simulations, news bits, slide shows, streaming audio and video, polls.

These news components open up all kinds of possibilities for creating news experiences in addition to new stories—news experiences are components that accompany, embellish, or add interactivity.

This suggests that a news organization's Web site becomes:

- Not just something you READ.
- But also something you DO.

It provides you with some ways to engage more actively in the news—consuming it, learning more about, reacting to it, creating it. What we see developing around the country is an appetite for a level of interactivity that is very much informing the nature and level of story telling.

The Pew Research Center for People and the Press recently reported that 44 percent of survey respondents had provided online content in various ways.

So, instead of thinking of our audiences as users, readers, viewers, customers, or consumers, we need to think of them as **co-authors, co-producers, active contributors—even active citizens**.

Journalism therefore becomes not just a one-way pipeline for us to disseminate what we think people need to know. Rather it is a two-way conversation—for people to react to what we report, add to it and tell their own stories. People now expect this level of participation—they have gotten used to being part of the conversation simply because they can: They can e-mail, fax, voicemail, instant poll. And they like it.

So how do you involve people?

- By showing as well as telling.
- By providing knowledge as well as news.
- By providing entry points.
- By not just providing space for the stories we want to tell them, but also providing space for them to tell their own stories as well.
- By inviting participation.

When people have some participatory stake in a story, you get intelligent interaction. We are now seeing the creation of entry points that connect with news audiences in new ways.

One of them is the creation of news experiences in addition to news stories. When I think of news experiences, an old, reputedly Chinese proverb comes to mind. It was sent to a *Seattle Times* editor overseeing a news game that engaged people in how to solve Seattle's gridlock woes. The reader told him:

- I hear and I forget
- I see and I remember
- I do and I understand

By playing the *Seattle Times*' gridlock game, he was better able to understand the choices and tradeoffs, the menu of remedies, and the costs involved in transportation planning.

Let's look at some of the various news experiences we're seeing around the country. They take some of the following forms.

- **News organization blogs**, such as the *Virginian-Pilot*'s use of a reporter outside the courtroom to cover the D.C. sniper trial. Or the *Dallas Morning News*' Editorial Page blog, in which the editors add transparency and insight to their decisions.

- **Moblogs**, which involve the use of mobile camera phones to shoot and send news photos and captions, such as this University of South Carolina experiment in covering the state's Democratic primary.

- **Tax and state budget calculators** that allow users to try to close budget deficits or understand the impact of proposed tax bills on their wallets, such as Minnesota Public Radio's Budget Balancer.

- **Clickable maps** that invite users into public decisions. The *Everett* (WA) *Herald* invited readers to participate in rethinking riverfront redevelopment with this exercise

- **Searchable databases**, such as *www.chicagocrime.org*, that invite people to find their own stories in police crime data.

- **Election interactives**, such as candidate matchmakers, Electoral College calculators, and vote-by-issues quizzes.

- **Games**, online exercises that allow for modeling scenarios or playing with planning choices are engaging more readers. The include such things as the GothamGazette.com's Plan your Park game and the *Everett Herald*'s Fix Your Commute exercise.

- **Devil's Advocate exercises**. KQED public radio in San Francisco created its award-winning "You Decide" exercise to educate people about issues by advancing arguments on behalf of multiple positions.

- **Create your own Web sites**. The *Providence* (RI) *Journal*'s Tribute to our Troops invited readers to create Web sites for soldiers serving in Iraq.

- **Explanatory Exercises**. WBUR public radio in Boston covered a Gaugin art exhibit with an interactive exercise in which art experts could be heard explaining various parts of one of his most famous paintings.

- **Multimedia Obits**. Finally, some news organizations, such as *The Spokesman Review*, in Spokane, WA, have offered readers the opportunity to participate in news obituaries, talking about family members who have died.

Several of these early interactive journalism projects—from state budget calculators in Minnesota and California to a downtown revitalization game in Rochester, N.Y., to gridlock exercises in the Pacific Northwest—have impacted public issues. They have served as surrogate public hearings, prompted public officials to alter tax plans, and changed waterfront redevelopment projects. They have created new public spaces for ideas and contributed to the understanding of difficult tradeoffs.

- For instance, 11,000 users wrestled in the spring of 2004 with how to close Minnesota's $4.2 billion funding gap using Minnesota Public Radio's "Budget Balancer" exercise. These people spent as long as 17 minutes on the exercise—then 4,000 came back and tried to balance the budget again. Who were these people? Interestingly, 43 percent were age 30 or younger.

- More than 2,000 people played transit planner last year with *The Seattle Times'* "You Build It." The exercise let people figure out which transit projects they'd like to see built—and how they'd pay for them. Their "vote" was not binding, but it prompted the regional transit board to back off its proposed half-penny sales tax hike and look for other revenue sources to ease the region's gridlock woes.

- After 2,000 people in Everett, Washington, "voted" on waterfront redevelopment options by using the clickable map created by *The Herald* newspaper, there was civic impact: Users strongly signaled they wanted access to their waterfront, so hiking and bike trails were added to the plans.

So we see that one outcome turns out to be not just news to be consumed, but civic/public life to get involved with.

Civic Participation as Media Participation

This leads me to close with the suggestion that we are on the cusp of a new opportunity for media and I think it's very exciting.

It's redefining civic participation.

We've always measured civic engagement by voter turnout. But participation in civic life as measured by voting has been on a downward spiral for nearly four decades. Voter turnout has dropped from about two-thirds of eligible voters to slightly more than half as of the 2000 general elections.

And, of course, news viewership and readership have been on a downward spiral as well.

Yet, citizens' use of media, especially television and the Internet, has steadily risen. All through 2004 we have seen important examples of how civic participation in the presidential elections was becoming a new form of media participation.

People used new media tools to fundraise, fact check, network, mobilize, blog, match issues, follow the money, play a game, design an ad, watch a video clip—and even score it to music. Howard Dean was just the beginning.

The important question for journalists is: Are people not getting what they want from mainstream media and so are using new media tools to create their own information pipelines?

This moment is every bit as redefining as the impact of television on the political landscape of the 1960s.

The difference, though, is dramatic: Then, television empowered a small cadre of the powerful, who broadcast one-way candidate messages to mass audiences. Ordinary people had limited opportunities to respond: They could click the "off" button or cast their ballot. Now, ordinary people have almost unlimited opportunities to participate.

I hope new organizations don't let this creative participation stop with the November election. We should look for opportunities to apply it to other issues—community issues, environmental issues, spending priorities, and legislative proposals. This, and not convergence, is the real promise of a digital democracy.

News media can establish important connections to audiences by developing these participation opportunities. The participation builds attachments. The attachments build relationships. And the relationships build audience.

You can see most of the interactive news games at *www.j-lab.org.* Click on Cool Stuff or Batten entries.

Associated Press Managing Editors

Alan Nelson

Publisher and co-founder, the Command Post, 2003– , and a communication strategist and leadership consultant for a wide range of organizations, including the Carlson Companies, Con Edison, EDS, Korn/Ferry International, McDonald's, Morgan Stanley, State Farm, and PepsiCo; native of Salt Lake City, UT; B.S., political science, B.A., speech communication, University of Utah, 1992; research methodologist, having led over 100 projects examining corporate communication, culture, and performance.

Editors' introduction: On March 20, 2003, Alan Nelson and Michele Catalano began Command Post as a "public service[,] . . . a clearinghouse where multiple bloggers could post news" about the war in Iraq. As of August 15, 2005, the Command Post reported that it had registered over 7,350,000 visitors, posted over 19,000 news items, and registered more than 146,000 reader comments. Command Post was also issued press credentials to the Democratic National Convention in Boston and the Republican National Convention in New York City and has had three of its news pages added to the Library of Congress MINERVA permanent collection. In addressing managing editors of major newspapers who subscribe to the Associated Press news service, publisher Alan Nelson explained, "The fact is that information technology in general, and the Internet in particular, have unleashed a force of economic and social change of great consequence on nearly all of our established institutions." Associated Press Managing Editors (APME) "is an association of editors at newspapers in the U.S. and Canada" that strives to prepare editors to run "multimedia newsrooms in the 21st century."

Alan Nelson's speech: Good morning!

It's an honor to be here today, and I'm delighted to share my reflections on The Command Post, and what I think it means to the newsroom of the future.

But before I get into the meat of it all, I want to say that there's a bit of family history at play here for me today. My grandfather, Ray Nelson, was an AP stringer for the *Herald-Journal* in Logan, Utah. He started as a writer for that paper, and in addition to being a stringer, he ultimately served as editor.

And so it's a bit of a full circle that I stand here today . . . and I think Ray clearly passed some of his passion for journalism along to me.

Let me begin by providing some context about me, blogs, and Command Post.

Delivered on October 16, 2004. Reprinted with permission of Alan Nelson.

As for me, I am not Bill Gates. I'm a management consultant . . . not a technologist . . . and my expertise is in internal communications . . . how communication works inside companies. That's how I became familiar with weblogs . . . we started exploring them as an internal communication tool in late 2001.

For the unfamiliar, a weblog . . . blog for short . . . is a type of Web site with a couple of distinct characteristics . . .

- They are dynamic and frequently updated
- They tend to comprise brief entries that point to other items on the Internet, or to other blogs
- Those entries are in reverse-chronological order, with the most recent content at the top of the page
- People generally have the ability to comment on individual posts
- And finally . . . and this is very important . . . blogs are written in the first person, and the author's personality is very much a part of the posting and the site

Additionally, bloggers tend to create communities of interest . . . even camaraderie . . . among themselves, extending the participation beyond the comments to cross-links and cross-discussions between blogs.

So I was playing with blogs, and posting to a blog of my own, in 2002. The Command Post got its start on March 20th 2003 . . . the morning after the first decapitation strike in Iraq . . . when another blogger, Michele Catalano, and I created the site as a collaborative blog . . . a clearinghouse where multiple bloggers could post news about the war. We welcomed all comers as contributors, and quickly enlisted over 120 bloggers from around the world in the effort.

The site quickly became popular . . . including in the CNN control room . . . and we went from 1,000 visitors a day to 100,000 within about a week.

We ultimately expanded our coverage . . . adding an Op/Ed page, Global War on Terror Page, Global Recon page, and 2004 Election page along the way . . . in each case trying to offer a deep source of global news items on a narrow set of topics . . . deep enough and global enough that readers could "triangulate" a story from a variety of sources.

From the beginning, we've declared that The Command Post is not a professional news service . . . it's just a group of bloggers trying to post the latest professional news that we have seen, heard, or read. In doing so we always cite, and where possible provide a link to, the original source, and we encourage readers to follow those links and see the original sources first-hand.

In fulfilling that mission over the past 18 months, our contributors
. . . there are now 168 people worldwide with posting privileges . . .
have posted over 16,000 items on our four news pages, and our readers have posted over 140,000 individual comments about those
items.

We've had nearly five and a half million visitors in all, and on any
given weekday we average between 13,000 and 100,000 visitors
depending on the news. We were also one of only two blogs creden-
tialed to both the Democratic and Republican national conventions.

All in all, it's not a bad hobby!

But our success begs the question: Why? Why such interest and
demand for citizen journalism?

And that's where the story . . . a story that I think is highly conse-
quential to the newsroom of the future . . . really lies. Not in "what,"
but "why" . . . why so many people would turn to a blatantly
non-professional source during a time in which one would think pro-
fessionally-vetted news items would be of their greatest value.

Is blogging truly a threat to mainstream media?

Yes and no.

I DO think traditional journalism faces a real problem . . . one that
you have to address if you're to maintain not just credibility, but
readership, in the future. And it's not about accessibility or credibility or the appeal of blogger journalists . . . it's about the new economy.

The fact is that information technology in general, and the Internet in particular, have unleashed a force of economic and social
change of great consequence on nearly all of our established institutions.

In his book *Next*, author Michael Lewis noted that the Internet
commercializes and democratizes everything it touches, and it
weakens those who have drawn power from having privileged access
. . . gatekeepers. And over the past decade or so, it's made fundamental changes in how we do business.

Think of it . . .

Just five years ago, did anyone here even imagine that they'd be
able to find and purchase a diamond ring directly from a merchant
in Singapore, after considering equivalent options in Florida and
Germany?

Or think about banking . . . 10 years ago, if you wanted a bank,
you went to the bank down the street. Now you can open an account,
make transfers, pay checks . . . even get cash . . . all without ever
setting a foot in a branch.

Housing . . . cars . . . travel . . . the list goes on. And in each case
the circumstances are the same . . . the ability to compete on price
becomes less important . . . commercialization . . . and the ability to
control the information shifts from seller to buyer . . . democratiza-
tion.

In fact, if there is one general rule for the new economy, it's that information technology has transferred the power of economic exchange from the seller to the consumer . . .

. . . in being able to find what they want, in their ability to negotiate on price, in their ability to demand just what they want, just how they want it.

And so if there's something in our story that can inform the newsroom of the future, we need to see it as a story of economics and social change, rather than just a story of citizen reporters and open-source journalism.

Now, when I think about Command Post within that context, there are four lessons I see for you as editors and journalists as you wrestle with the future of your craft. I call them the Law of the Flow, the Law of the Fast, the Law of the Few, and the Law of the Many.

First, the Law of the Flow . . .

If you've ever taken a class in macroeconomics, you might remember learning about "stocks" and "flows." In economics, a stock is something that is accumulated over time . . . furniture in your house is a stock.

Information in general, and news in particular, is now a flow, and not a stock.

A flow is something that occurs over time, and tends to change the level of a stock. Income and savings are examples of flows.

And one of the conversations you have in macroeconomics is about money, and whether it's a stock or a flow . . . and increasingly, as money has become more ubiquitous with credit cards, checks, cash, PayPal . . . money is more of a flow than a stock. It's not something you ever really have as much as it's something that flows from place to place as a means of accumulating the stocks you DO have.

Here's the lesson from Command Post: information in general, and news in particular, is now a flow, and not a stock.

Before the Internet, information was governed by set distribution channels and gatekeepers . . . brokers . . . who decided who was able to have what. The stock broker had the price. The real estate agent had the prior housing report. The car salesman had your credit report.

And in news, the journalists had the facts, and the editors acted as brokers, making choices about what would be reported and what wouldn't.

Not the case now. The Internet hates brokers. It KILLS brokers. Now, because of the Internet, everyone with a computer, an email address, and a browser is a point of distribution . . . the only thing needed for information to "get out" is an interest on the part of one person to supply it, and a demand on the part of another person to have it.

When you have a billion people connected to each other, there is a supply and a demand for everything . . . and when you have search engines like Google, they actually have the ability to find each other.

This is why technologists like to say that "information wants to be free." In a connected world, it's no longer possible to make discretionary choices about what gets reported and what doesn't.

The Command Post is simply a clearinghouse for news . . . a medium for the flow . . . and our contributors enrich that flow with information from a global network of newspapers, radio, TV, direct observation, and emails sent by readers.

So the lesson from the law of the flow: Your ability to choose when and how something is reported, and the timeline over which you can hold information as you make that choice, are more compressed every day. Anyone can spill the beans, and with the web and email, everyone has access to the beans. The important question to ask about a piece of information . . . and especially highly relevant information . . . is no longer "if," it's "when."

The Law of the Fast

In his book *The Lexus and the Olive Tree, New York Times* writer Thomas Friedman discusses the effects of globalization, and one of his tenets is that in the old economy, the large consumed the small . . . and that in the new economy, the fast consumes the slow.

Information technology and the Internet continually shorten cycle times . . . how long it takes to complete work, evaluate data, plan, share information . . . whatever.

The game now is about being nimble . . . being able to respond first to changing circumstances and opportunities. And as a result consumers have a constantly increasing set of expectations for responsiveness. Once one provider gets it done in 30 seconds, it's awfully difficult to keep getting it done in 45.

And this is one place where the Command Post has a powerful message for the newsroom of the future . . . that newsroom, whatever else happens, needs to be FAST . . . because, remember, with information it's no longer about if, it's about when.

The Command Post is very, very fast.

Any one of our 168 contributors can witness, read, hear, or see a news item, and can have that item online for a global audience in less than 30 seconds.

How fast are we? When U.S. forces captured Saddam, we had the original AP story online at 5:48 A.M. EST . . . before Fox, CNN, CBS, or the rest. Now . . . the AP broke the story. But from there, we were able to distribute it very, very quickly. And from that first post, we were able to update the story very quickly as well . . . in real time.

When Edwards was selected as the Vice Presidential nominee, our first post was up at 7:43 A.M., citing a red banner on FOX-News.com. Then at 7:54 A.M. I posted, from my hotel room, that NPR had made the announcement official, and sent out a breaking news alert, one which preceded the CNN breaking news alert by almost three hours.

If it's going to satisfy consumers, the newsroom of the future MUST be incredibly fast.

And here's the kicker . . . we weren't even first. The story had first broken overnight on an aviation enthusiast web site, where one of the authors had noticed the Kerry campaign jet at Pittsburgh International now read "Kerry/Edwards" . . . a great example of the law of the flow AND the law of the fast.

So the lesson: if it's going to satisfy consumers, the newsroom of the future MUST be incredibly fast. And here's the problem: your editorial structures nearly prohibit you from ever becoming as fast as the bloggers . . . every gatekeeper along the way slows the flow.

Your counter might be that you'll get the facts right . . . but I'll address that in a minute.

The Law of the Few

Another book for you to read: *The Tipping Point* by Malcolm Gladwell, who writes for the *New Yorker*. It's a book about the diffusion of information . . . how ideas spread through social systems.

One of the things he writes about is how not all people are equal in the social network based on how often they communicate, to whom, and how much influence they have . . . and he describes two types of people in particular: connectors and mavens.

Connectors have extremely large communication networks, and what's important about those networks is that they involve people from many different worlds, not just one. They are uber-networkers.

Mavens are information geeks . . . they live on information, love to surface new information, and love to share that information with others. These are the people who are always bringing you new restaurant recommendations, new books to read, new products to use.

Mavens and connectors have always been out there . . . the only problem was that their ability to connect and spread the message was primarily contained to those people with whom they lived or worked.

The Internet, and weblogs in particular, have "lit up" the otherwise latent power of mavens and connected them in a very real way. A weblog is nothing more than a megaphone for a maven . . . and the Internet serves to make mavens instantly connected to the rest of the world . . . and more important . . . to other mavens.

There's a very important lesson here: bloggers should not be underestimated. They are not just average people . . . they are people who, long before blogs came along . . . had the ability to surface information and present it to others in a persuasive and compelling way. They are opinion leaders, and weblogs have only served to exponentially increase their reach and their power.

There's a second lesson here: and it's that weblogs, written by mavens, are also read by mavens. And so there's an accelerant effect for information flowing through the network. When something comes up in the blogosphere it's talked about by a few thousand people who drive opinion for large networks of people around them . . . which is why the mainstream media ultimately has had to recognize issues raised by bloggers . . . they're things people are talking about.

And there's a third lesson: It's that while the network kills brokers, it LOVES editors.

Mavens are editors . . . the people around them trust them to cull the information that's out there and surface what's worth attending to. I don't bother to try every new restaurant in town . . . I rely on my local food maven to try them for me.

I think that in the newsroom of the future the role of the editor will change . . . from someone who works primarily as a gatekeeper of the facts with an interest in quality, to someone who "serves" the reader as a consumer based on an understanding of what readers will consider relevant . . .

. . . and on an understanding that readers will judge the veracity of the content based on comparisons to a much larger and transparent flow of information and ideas.

The Final Law: The Law of the Many

One of the critiques about weblogs is that there is no editorial process . . . in terms of judging the quality of the facts or what readers would consider relevant. This critique was famously leveled during Dan Rather's recent troubles by Jonathan Klein, former EVP of CBS News, who stated: "You couldn't have a starker contrast between the multiple layers of check and balances [at *60 Minutes*] and a guy sitting in his living room in his pajamas writing."

This comment perfectly illustrates a fundamentally wrong premise held by many in mainstream media . . . the fact is that in the long run weblogs will have a better system of checks and balances than will any media outlet, and it's because of the law of the many.

Because information is increasingly transparent, and because many blog readers are mavens passionate about the content, any given blog post doesn't have just one fact-checker . . . it has thousands . . . or in our case, tens of thousands.

Rathergate is a perfect example of this. To recount the history, shortly after *60 Minutes* ran its story about the Guard memos, a reader of the Free Republic weblog posted a comment doubting their authenticity. Other mavens then started to post about that question on their blogs, and some of the more active bloggers started contacting typographers, others were recreating the memos using Microsoft Word . . . and all the time they were linking to each other, developing information in real time . . . remember the law of the fast.

Before long, one blogger even traced the fax number on the memos to the Texas Kinko's from whence it came . . . and learned from the manager that Bill Burkett . . . the ultimate source . . . had an account.

The Rather story illustrates all of these laws . . . the information flowed and CBS couldn't control it . . . it happened very quickly, faster than CBS could keep up . . . and connected mavens drove the process as it developed, and ultimately into the mainstream.

But most of all, it illustrates the Law of the Many . . . that when a marketplace of tens of thousands of people considers a piece of information, the truth inevitably will surface with greater speed and efficiency than when only a few people consider that information . . . just as surely as an Internet-driven global market for diamond rings or interest rates drives price down and quality up.

And it works both ways . . . when a blogger posts something dubious, those same tens of thousands of readers and mavens quickly debunk and dismiss that information as not factual, and it goes nowhere.

And that's one of the things people value about Command Post . . . it allows them a forum to not just receive media, but to participate in it in a real and tangible way . . . not by way of a letter to the editor that likely won't get published . . . but by way of transparent commentary that will be immediately seen by everyone else who traffics the site.

And that's the best editorial and quality process we could ever have.

The lesson: the newsroom of the future is going to have to reconcile itself to the Law of the Many . . . there will be thousands of people who will not only scrutinize your reporting, but they will do so via a network that can tangibly drive public awareness and opinion.

It's like the old joke where the small-town publisher said, "People in our town don't subscribe to the newspaper to read the news, they subscribe to see if we got it right."

Today, the entire world is your small town . . . and we're all reading to see if you got it right.

My advice? Embrace reader participation . . . like the laws of the flow, fast, and few, the law of the many is inevitable, and you're better off engaging bloggers and readers as part of the process . . . it means more openness, and more tolerance for feedback and criticism . . . but when it comes to the mob, I'd rather have them working with me than against me.

In conclusion . . .

. . . as you consider the newsroom of the future do so within the context of the economic and social reality we face.

Journalism and news, like everything else in the marketplace . . . is becoming increasingly commoditized and democratized.

You need to start thinking of your readers not as readers, but as consumers who engage with you in an economic exchange of value, and who do so in a world where the value equation has changed.

And that's the key question: How will you add value in the newsroom of the future?

The value you provided used to reside in your control over distribution . . . now distribution is ubiquitous . . .

It also used to reside in the ability of your reporters to bear witness and do so in a timely fashion . . . and while you still have access to some forums, like the White House press room . . . that the layperson does not, the fact is that people at the White House . . . they blog too. Indeed, now everyone with an Internet connection is a reporter, and they can all report in real time.

Today, the entire world is your small town . . . and we're all reading to see if you got it right.

So where is the value for the newsroom of the future?

It might be in doing little to no national or international coverage . . . coverage that's highly commoditized and democratized . . . and instead offering a deep, detailed level of local coverage that's unrivaled and that readers value highly.

Or it might be that the writing in the newspaper of the future looks more like news magazine writing . . . a level of detail and analysis that the wire services don't provide.

Or it might be that . . . like stock brokers . . . you become more of a consultant, and less of an information broker . . . offering not just news to your readers but expertise and counsel in how to deal with that news.

Regardless, you're absolutely going to have to find a new way to add new value. And while I'm not a technologist . . . nor a journalist, although I play one on TV . . . I think the Command Post is a signpost along the way. People read our site because for them, it adds unique value . . .

. . . it respects the law of the flow, acting as a clearinghouse for global sources of information that allows readers to "triangulate" a story and resolve the "truth" for themselves . . .

. . . it respects the law of the fast, providing information in real time, both through our contributors and those who comment . . .

. . . it respects the law of the few, engaging mavens as contributors and feeding the desire of maven readers with well-selected and relevant content . . .

. . . and it respects the law of the many, both in our large network of contributors, and by allowing our readers to not just read the stories, but to participate in them, discuss them, fact-check them, and inform them.

The balance of power has changed . . . the consumer is now the one in charge. He's increasingly demanding unique and increased value, and however he likes it . . . cars, banks, or news . . . thanks to information technology, is how he expects to get it.

And it's an expectation he increasingly has the power to meet. If papers like the *Herald-Journal* are to remain relevant, it's an expectation their newsroom of the future will have to satisfy . . . or they'll risk losing that consumer forever.

Kaiser Family Foundation, Upon Release of *Generation M: Media in the Lives of Kids 8 to 18*

Hillary Rodham Clinton

U.S. Senator from New York, 2001– ; born Chicago, IL, October 26, 1947, and raised in Park Ridge, IL, attending public schools there; B.A., Wellesley College, 1969; J.D., Yale Law School, 1973; attorney, Children's Defense Fund, 1973–74; assistant professor of law, University of Arkansas, 1974– 77; partner, Rose Law Firm, 1977–92; lecturer, University of Arkansas Law School, 1979–80; in Senate, member of committees on Budget, Environment and Public Works, Health, Education, Labor, and Pension, and Armed Services; author, It Takes a Village and Other Lessons Children Teach Us *(1996) and* Living History *(2004); Claude Pepper Award of the National Association for Home Care, Martin Luther King, Jr., Award of the Progressive National Baptist Convention, and Public Spirit Award of the American Legion Auxiliary.*

Editors' introduction: The report *Generation M: Media in the Lives of Kids 8 to 18*, sponsored by the Kaiser Family Foundation, surveyed "media use among a nationally representative sample of more than 2,000 3rd through 12th graders who completed detailed questionnaires, including nearly 700 self-selected participants who also maintained seven-day media diaries." The study "found children and teens are spending an increasing amount of time using 'new media' like computers, the Internet, and video games, without cutting back on the time they spend with 'old' media like TV, print, and music." This report was released at a forum on March 8, 2005, in Washington, D.C., that included the keynote speech below by Senator Clinton and a roundtable discussion moderated by CNN's Jeff Greenfield. Senator Clinton advised, "Media in kids' lives is a moving target. And we need better, more current research to study the new interactive, digital, and wireless media dominating our kids' lives."

Hillary Rodham Clinton's speech: Thank you so so much and it's such a pleasure to be here, particularly in a space that is named for one of the people I admire so much in our public life, Barbara Jordan, and I thanked [Drew] for that introduction. I'm anxious to hear his daughter's reaction but we'll see how that comes. I want to thank all the panelists for all their work on this very important issue and particularly to thank Professor Roberts and Vicky Rideout for the study that is being unveiled today.

Delivered on March 8, 2005, at Washington, D.C.

It's also very significant that we have an extraordinary range of viewpoints and experiences represented on the Panel, and I thank all of them. Thank you Common for being part of this, it's very important and Mr. Tascan, thank you for coming. And as well, Jordan Levin and Michael Copps. It's very good to see everybody represented here on this Panel. And I also want to thank Jeff Greenfield for moderating.

I come here, somewhat as Drew does, as much a parent as a Senator. You know, I started caring about the environment in which children are raised, including the media environment, before my daughter was born, but then I began to take it very personally and in our own ways, Bill and I tried to implement some strategies, some rules, some regulations but it wasn't quite as difficult 25 years ago as it is today. And although I confess, I still wonder what my daughter's watching as an adult, you know, those days of being involved in a direct and personal way are certainly over in my parenting experience.

But it is probably the single most commonly mentioned issue to me by young parents, almost no matter where I go, when we start talking about raising children. We start talking about the challenges of parenting today, and all of a sudden people are exchanging their deep concerns about losing control over the raising of their own children, ceding the responsibility of implicating values and behaviors to a multi-dimensional media marketplace that they have no control over and most of us don't even really understand because it is moving so fast we can't keep up with it. And so I've spent more than 30 years advocating for children and worrying about the impact of media. I've read a lot of the research over the years about the significant effects that media has on children. And I've talked and advocated about the need to harness the positive impacts that media can have for the good of raising, you know, healthy productive, children who can make their own way in this rather complicated world. And I've particularly advocated for trying to find ways to re-empower parents, to put them back in the driver's seat so they feel they are first knowledgeable and secondly in some sense helping to shape the influences that affect their children.

Almost a decade ago, we hosted the Children's Television Summit at the White House, and we worked for the passage of the Children's Television Act. That law led to the implementation of the V-Chip in every new television over 13 inches, and mandated that broadcasters show at least three hours of educational and informational programming each week. More than five years ago, I urged parents to become more vigilant consumers of media—and I also urged them if they were concerned about the constant exposure to violence or irresponsible sexual activity that there was nothing standing in their way of coming together as parental groups and in effect producing a consumers' boycott against media which offended their values and sensibilities. And particularly, I hear it all the time, many parents feel that way about video games, which were just coming into use in a rather large way and influencing how their children both spent their time and what they thought about. I also appealed to movie, music, and video game producers and broadcasters to come together and develop one uniform ratings system—one that gave parents clear unequivocal information about the media products they and their children were consuming.

I think we've made progress, certainly since I started talking about this and certainly since we began focusing on it in the White House. But I still hear, as I said, from parents all over who just feel overwhelmed. Walking into your child's room, seeing what Drew just showed us, you know, could be a little daunting, especially when you don't know how to use half of the equipment that's in there. But it's especially difficult for parents of young children who are trying to create some barriers to what their children are exposed to. Parents worry that their children will not grow up with the same values that they did or that they believe in because of the overwhelming presence of the media telling them to buy this and that, or conveying negative messages filled with explicit sex content and violence.

And parents who work long hours outside the home and single parents, whose time with their children is squeezed by economic pressures, are worried because they don't even know what their children are watching and listening to and playing. So what's a parent to do when at 2 o'clock in the afternoon, the children may be at home from school but the parents aren't home from work and they can turn on the TV and both on broadcast and cable stations see a lot of things which the parents wish they wouldn't or wish they were sitting there to try to mediate the meaning of for their children. And probably one of the biggest complaints I've heard is about some of the video games, particularly *Grand Theft Auto*, which has so many demeaning messages about women and so encourages violent imagination and activities and it scares parents. I mean, if your child, and in the case of the video games, it's still predominantly boys, but you know, they're playing a game that encourages them to have sex with prostitutes and then murder them, you know, that's kind of hard to digest and to figure out what to say, and even to understand how you can shield your particular child from a media environment where all their peers are doing this.

And it is also now the case that more and more, parents are asking, not only do I wonder about the content and what that's doing to my child's emotional psychological development, but what's the process doing? What's all this stimulation doing that is so hard to understand and keep track of?

So I think if we are going to make the health of children a priority, then we have to pay attention to the activities that children engage in every single day. And of course that includes exposure to and involvement with the media.

And I really commend Kaiser for this report. It paints a picture that I think will surprise a lot of parents across the nation. It reveals the enormous diet of media that children are consuming, and the sheer force of the data in this report demands that we better pay attention and take more effective action on behalf of our children.

Generation M: Media in the Lives of 8- to 18-Year-Olds shows us that media is omnipresent. It is, if not the most, it is certainly one of the most insistent, pervasive influences in a child's life. The study tells us, as you've heard, on average that kids between 8 and 18 are spending 6.5 hours a day absorbed in media. That adds to 45 hours a week, which is more than a full time job. Television alone occupies 3 to 4 hours a day of young people's time. And we all know, that in most homes, media consumption isn't limited to the living room, as it was when many of us were growing up. In two-thirds of kids' bedrooms you'll find a TV; in one-half you will find a VCR and/or video game consol.

We also know from today's study that the incorporation of different types of media into children's lives is growing. And you know, we saw that so clearly in the picture that Drew showed us. In one quarter of the time kids are using media, they are using more than one form at once. So, yes, they are becoming masters at multi-tasking. We know that the amount of time children are spending using media has not increased since the last Kaiser study.

So, today's study suggests that kids are in fact hitting a ceiling in terms of how much time they can spend with media. But they are using media more intensively, experiencing more than one type at the same time. And this creates not only new challenges for parents but also for teachers. I had a veteran teacher say to me one time, I said, "What's the difference between teaching today and teaching 35 years ago when you started?" And she said, "Well, today even the youngest children come in to the classroom and they have a mental remote controller in their heads. And if I don't capture their attention within the first seconds they change the channel. And it's very difficult to get them to focus on a single task that is frustrating or difficult for them to master because there's always the out that they have learned to expect from their daily interaction with media."

You know, no longer is something like the v-chip the "one stop shop" to protect kids, who can expose themselves to all the rest of this media at one time. And so parental responsibility is crucial but we also need to be sure that parents have the tools that they need to keep up with this multi-dimensional problem.

Of course the biggest technological challenge facing parents and children today is the Internet. And today's Kaiser Report goes a long way toward establishing how much media our children are consuming. And one thing we have known for a long time which is absolutely made clear in this report is that the content is overwhelmingly, astoundingly violent.

In the last four decades, the government and the public health community have amassed an impressive body of evidence identifying the impact of media violence on children. Since 1969, when President Johnson formed the National Commission on the Causes and Prevention of Violence, the body of data has grown and grown and it leads to an unambiguous and virtually unanimous conclusion: media violence contributes to anxiety, desensitization, and increased aggression among children. When children are exposed to aggressive films, they behave more aggressively. And when no consequences are associated with the media aggression, children are even more likely to imitate the aggressive behavior.

Violent video games have similar effects. According to testimony by Craig Anderson before the Senate Commerce Committee in 2000, playing violent video games accounts for a 13 to 22 percent increase in teenagers' violent behavior.

Now we know about 92 percent of children and teenagers play some form of video games. And we know that nine out of 10 of the top selling video games contain violence.

And so we know that left to their own devices, you have to keep upping the ante on violence because people do get desensitized and children are going to want more and more stimulation. And unfortunately in a free market like ours, what sells will become even more violent, and the companies will ratchet up the violence in order to increase ratings and sales figures. It is a little frustrating when we have this data that demonstrates there is a clear public health connection between exposure to violence and increased aggression that we have been as a society unable to come up with any adequate public health response.

There are other questions of the impact of the media on our children that we do not know; for example, we have a lot of questions about the effect of the Internet in our children's daily lives.

We know from today's study that in a typical day, 47 percent of children 8 to 18 will go online. And the Internet is a revolutionary tool that offers an infinite world of opportunity for children to learn about the world around them. But when unmonitored kids access the Internet, it can also be an instrument of enormous danger. Online, children are at greatly increased risk of exposure to pornography, identify theft, and of being exploited, if not abused or abducted, by strangers.

According to the Kaiser study, 70 percent of teens between 15 and 17 say they have accidentally come across pornography on the Web, and 23 percent report that this happens often. More disturbing is that close to one-third of teens admit to lying about their age to access a Web site.

Back in 1997, the Clinton Administration hosted an Internet Online Forum: Focus on Children, which called for the development of more sophisticated filtering software—better tools to empower parents to be able to make the best decisions for their children and to prevent their children from intentionally or accidentally straying into areas that are very difficult for the children and the parent to cope with. The Clinton Administration also made a commitment to making the Internet family-friendly by increasing the FBI staff committed to fighting computer-related exploitation of minors by 50 percent, and establishing a task force that specialized in computer child pornography and solicitation cases.

But this problem cannot be solved by law enforcement alone. The Internet is a global online community, one in which it is very difficult to distinguish between children and adults. And let's face it: there is a lot of money at stake. The online adult-entertainment industry generates $1 billion a year in revenue. Plus, about three-quarters of the 400,000 adult-entertainment Web sites are not even located on our shores—making enforcement of our laws impossible. This may be a topic for some kind of international attention, but in lieu of that, parents are going to need and deserve more help in trying to protect their children from the dangers of the Internet. Parental control technology exists, but it is underutilized. Today, only one quarter of children with access to computers

---

When children are more tech-savvy than their parents, as is often the case, it kind of becomes a game and a challenge to get around the filtering.

---

say their parents use parental controls or filters. And these filters, even when used, are imperfect.

Tools that are available to parents can be highly effective in reducing minors' exposure to inappropriate material. But no filter is 100 percent effective; they all allow some amount of inappropriate content to be viewed by children. And when children are more tech-savvy than their parents, as is often the case, it kind of becomes a game and a challenge to get around the filtering.

One of our challenges, therefore, is that technology keeps advancing. Media in kids' lives is a moving target. And we need better, more current research to study the new interactive, digital, and wireless media dominating our kids' lives. While we know a great deal about traditional media platforms and kids, we know very little about multi-user domains, P2P, and wireless technologies. That's why last Congress I worked with my colleagues on a bi-partisan basis, Senators Lieberman, Brownback, and Santorum, to sponsor a bill that created a single, coordinated research program at the National Institute of Child Health and Human Development. This program will study the impact of electronic media on children, particularly very young children and infants' cognitive, social, and physical development. This is another Kaiser report that pointed out the significant effects of media in very young children and that it was not so much the content impact but the progress. You know, I feel like it's back to Marshall McLuhan days, you know, the media is the message, the process has an impact. So we worry about content, but with very young children, we have to worry more about just parking these babies in front of this screen with all of this stimulation without very much adult interaction or supervision.

This bill, which we call the Children and Media Research Advancement Act, will be reintroduced today. I think it is as important a public health issue as any we can worry about with our children. It addresses the links between media consumption and childhood obesity. Since 1980, the proportion of overweight children has doubled, and the rate for adolescents has tripled. An estimated 80 percent of overweight teens continue to [be] obese into adult[hood] and part of the reason is the saturation experience they have in media.

You know, in the 1970s, researchers estimated that children viewed 20,000 commercials a year. Today that number has doubled. And the majority of these ads are for food, for candy, for cereal, for junk food. And they do influence children's behavior or why would the food industry spend you know hundreds of millions of dollars exposing children. Obviously they influence behavior—anybody who says they don't influence behavior should withdraw the ads and not advertise to children because obviously they're wasting their money. And everybody knows that not only do they influence children but in turn they then influence parental buying habits. And so it's a kind of real whammy. You get the child hooked, you know, into these ads and then the child, if you've ever been in a supermarket with a young child, becomes a very effective advocate just to be quieted in the cart. Go ahead and buy it so we can go ahead with the rest of our shopping.

So what can we do to protect children and help parents? I think the most important lesson of today's Report, as with so many earlier reports, is that parents need to understand what their children are exposed to so that they may take corrective action.

You know, if you hear that there is a child with an infectious disease in your school, you're going to be worried and you might not send your child to school and you're going to call and make sure that this child with the infectious disease has been properly treated and can't be contagious. Well in effect, if you think of this from a public health perspective, you know, what we are doing today, exposing our children to so much of this unchecked media, is a kind of contagion. We are conducting an experiment on this generation of children and we have no idea what the outcomes are going to be. You know, stating the problem certainly doesn't answer it because at the very time we've had the increase in media saturation, we've had an increase in working hours with two parents working, with single parents working. The increase in productivity in the economy has made people work harder and harder. They're away from home longer hours. Many parents commute more than an hour each way to go to the jobs that they have. And the media is their constant companion. But what we have to convey to parents is that the price of that companionship can be enormous. And it's necessary for us to try to help parents regain control and to recognize the public health implications of what we are currently experiencing.

First, I would, once again, like to see industry leaders come together to develop a uniform, content-based ratings system that is easy for parents to understand and use. When I proposed this back in 1999, there were some preliminary conversations but it really didn't go anywhere. The ratings should be shown throughout every program or at least after every commercial break, so that parents can jump into a program at any point and learn what's in it and whether it's appropriate for their children to watch.

Second, the television industry should air more public service announcements, particularly about the effect of television on children and the need for parents to help their children utilize media in the best possible way. I think that this is something which would be relatively easy to do and yet would help to reach a very broad audience. Most PSAs, as we know, are not run in primetime. They're often run after midnight. I think we should do much better to use the prime hours of broadcasting to try to educate parents about how to be more literate, effective media users on behalf of themselves and their children.

Third, food advertisers should be more responsible about the effect they are having on future generations and the effect they are going to be having on increasing health care costs. The single biggest driver other than the cost of pharmaceuticals for increases in health care costs right now is the increase in obesity and the projection out over years of what it means to have children who are now suffering from type-2 diabetes, something that was unheard of in previous generations. We've seen examples, such as Kraft, the maker of such attractive foods such as Oreos and Chips Ahoy and Kool-Aid, which agreed not to advertise unhealthy food to children under 12. I would like to see the entire food industry come together to develop voluntary guidelines that take their responsibility to children seriously. I was pleased to see that Governor Schwarzenegger just announced his support for a ban of junk food in schools. I think there are a lot of steps we can take by the private sector and the public [sector] working together to curb marketing and availability of unhealthy products to our children.

Fourth, we need a lot more research on what works best to help parents monitor what their children access on the World Wide Web. Research from the Pew Center on the Internet and the American Life teaches us that the more control parents have in their homes—on their home computers—the more effective they can be at determining what their children can and are accessing. But parents need guidance in using the filtering technologies and understanding the limitations of these technologies.

All of these are voluntary efforts. One could make the argument that with some additional research the case will be conclusive that we are causing long-term public health damage to many, many children and therefore to society. You know, lots of times the response comes back to me, "You know my kid doesn't get all of that, my kid's fine." Well, obviously, certain children are more vulnerable than other children. Children in situations of vulnerability because of family circumstances or neighborhood circumstances may very well be more prey to not only the impact of a multi-media environment but also to individuals who exploit that environment. So yes, we are all of different vulnerabilities, physically and emotionally and psychologically but the evidence is conclusive that on balance the exposure to this much media and particularly to the violent content of it is not good for children and teenagers. And so what I'm hoping is that we can all come together. If there were an epidemic sweeping through our children of some kind of SARS or some other kind of infectious disease, we would all band together and figure out what to do to protect our children.

> *On balance the exposure to this much media and particularly to the violent content of it is not good for children and teenagers.*

Well this is a silent epidemic. We don't necessarily see the results immediately. Sometimes there's a direct correlation but most of the times it's aggregate, it's that desensitization over years and years and years. It's getting in your mind that it's okay to diss people because they're women or they're a different color or from a different place, that it's okay to somehow be part of a youth culture that defines itself as being very aggressive in protecting its turf. And we know that for many children, especially growing up in difficult circumstances, it's hard enough anyway. You know, they're trying to make it against the odds to begin with.

So you know it's not sitting in my home or Drew's home with all the advantages that that brings, with all the work that has been done prior to the age of 16, you know, all of the opportunities that children like ours have had. You know it's so often parents who are at their wits' end. We have a lot of grandparents raising children now. We have a lot of people who are just getting up everyday doing the best that they can. And we're not giving them very much help to make sure that they try to protect and guide the children in their care to become the best of their potential in the future. So I hope we can do more to educate parents on media literacy. I hope the various industries will see that as something that is in the public interest and that they want to participate in. I hope that we can encourage and support the development of technologies of all the great benefits that this media has to offer while minimizing the harm that is done when media fails to recognize that children are not just miniature adults. It is one thing for us to say, that wouldn't affect me. It is hard to imagine whether it would have if you were 8 or 10 or 12 or 16.

So I think we have to begin to be more aware of what our children are experiencing and do what we can to encourage media habits that allow kids to be kids, and that helps them to grow up into healthy adults who someday will be in the position to worry about what comes next in the media universe because we have no idea what parents in 10, 20, 30 years will be coping with. All we can do is to try to set some standards and values now and then fulfill them to the best of our ability.

Broadcast Education Association at the National Association of Broadcasters

Vin Crosbie

Co-founder, president, and managing partner, Digital Deliverance, 1996– , and co-founder and chair, PublishMail LLC, Boulder, CO, 1999– ; born Willimantic, CT, 1955; B.A. in professional photography, Rochester Institute of Technology, 1977; executive, United Press International, 1983–89; executive, Reuters, 1989–93; first director, online publishing for News Corporation, 1993–94; at Freemark Communications, Cambridge, MA, invented the concept of free e-mail, 1994–96; a founder of Paradigm-TSA, 1999–2002; contributing editor, American Press Institute's NewsFuture *newsletter;* Devil's Advocate *columnist for the International Newspaper Marketing Association's Web site; founding contributor, Poynter Institute's* E-Media Tidbits *group weblog; writes* Publishing: Free to Fee *column for Jupiter Media's ClickZ; served on the Interactive Services Association's Ad Hoc Consumer Privacy Task Force; co-author,* Internet World's Guide to Webcasting *(1998); has moderated, presented on panels, or taught workshops for a number of outlets, including Interactive Services, Online News Summits, Interactive Newspapers conference, and NetMedia London.*

Editors' introduction: Vin Crosbie addressed delegates attending a panel at the Broadcast Education Association on the theme "Reinventing the Local TV Station: Ground-Breaking Ideas from Innovative Thinkers." Cautioning that "video news must go online or else," Mr. Crosbie advised broadcast journalism educators and others attending, "Face it, with all these changes, much of the broadcast industry that you've long taught no longer exists." Founded in 1955, the Broadcast Education Association, with more than 1,400 individual and institutional members, is the professional organization for professors, industry professionals, and graduate students who are interested in teaching and research related to electronic media and multimedia enterprises.

Vin Crosbie's speech: Thanks, Max [Grubb of Kent State University's School of Journalism and Mass Communications for his introduction]. The beauty of that is those credentials don't necessarily apply here. Why is a guy with largely newspaper industry credentials here at the world's largest broadcasting conference?

Delivered on April 22, 2005, at Las Vegas, NV. Reprinted with permission of Vin Crosbie.

Because 11 years ago, when I stopped working in the old media and began working full-time in the new medium, print was about all that you could realistically put online. In a world of 300-baud or 1200-baud modems, you couldn't really deliver video online.

How the world has changed since then! According to the latest figure, 56 percent of the American homes that are online now have broadband connections. Most American corporations already do. Video has become as easy to deliver online as is print.

And what a phenomenal latent market for online video news! According to the Pew Internet Study, 83 percent of Americans say that they get most of their news and information from television. They are going to want that news and information online, too.

During the past decade, more than 600 million consumers—including 167 million Americans—migrated online, even though the Internet really gave them only text and still photos. What if they could have just as easily gotten their favorite medium—video—online?

> *To keep what's left of its share of Americans' attention, TV news must be delivered online rather than just on cable or over the airwaves.*

And video news had better get online. According to the investment bank Veronis Shuler, the ratio of time they spent watching TV against the time spent on the Internet, in households that had both, was 8:1 in 2000 but is 4:1 today. To keep what's left of its share of Americans' attention, TV news must be delivered online rather than just on cable or over the airwaves.

The fact is that television, not magazines or newspapers, is the news medium that's lost the most of consumers' spare time and attention to the Internet, according to surveys of consumer media usage.

The conference program says the title of my speech today is *Challenging the News Establishment*. Well, this is the challenge: Video news must go online or else.

Indeed, it's somehow appropriate that this Broadcast Education Association session is held at the end of the NAB conference, when all the exhibits are being torn down. There is a visual metaphor occurring outside: Look outside and you'll see the broadcast industry being disassembled. That's what's actually happening to the broadcast industry.

And I'm glad to be the opening speaker on a panel entitled *Reinventing the Local TV Station; Ground-Breaking Ideas from Innovative Thinkers*. Why? Because it's the local stations that will win or lose the future for the broadcast industry.

We've heard at NAB what the national networks are doing in the face of the major changes the broadcast industry faced. But they've got enough staff and money to do whatever they want (even if they don't know what they're doing). The real challenge in the broadcast industry is what can [a] local TV station do [when] faced [with] the major change in the industry?

And you broadcast journalism educators in the audience have the hardest challenge of all: You've got to teach the future, literally teach the future. Your students are the future, and the future is what you must teach them.

Are there major changes occurring? Of course, there are. Everyone now realizes it. Everybody.

For example, Rupert Murdoch last week gave a speech in which he said about the changes, "as an industry, many of us have been remarkably, unaccountably complacent. Certainly, I didn't do as much as I should have after all the excitement of the late 1990's. I suspect many of you in this room did the same, quietly hoping that this thing called the digital revolution would just limp along.

"Well it hasn't . . . it won't. . . . And it's a fast developing reality we should grasp as a huge opportunity to improve our journalism and expand our reach."

And what's remarkable about that speech isn't what was said but who said it—Rupert, the wizard of old media. He's finally got the new medium religion. In media, that's like the Roman Emperor Justinian converting to Christianity. It's a baptism. What was subversive has now become the accepted status quo.

Broadcast is migrating online. ABC this month launched it's 24-hour news channel only on broadband, not cable or terrestrial broadcast. CNN and CBS have similar broadband channels in the works.

Another example of how the industry is migrating online? The Jon Stewart clip, in which he demolished CNN's *Crossfire* show, got 400,000 viewers on TV but 5 million online. According to Veronis Shuler, the ratio of TV to Internet, in households that had both, was 8:1 in 2000 but is 4:1 today.

And what are these major changes the broadcast industry faces? I'll outline six of them, then we'll let the following speakers suggest ways that local stations can deal with the changes.

Here, in no particular order, are some of the changes that local TV stations face:

- On-Demand. Less and less will programs be viewed only in a program schedule set by the networks or the stations. More and more will people view programs when they want. It's already happening. Look at Tivo users. Look at how cable operators themselves are beginning to install cable boxes that have built-in Digital Video Recorders (DVRs). Although broadcasters might release new programs at specific times, consumers will view those programs more and more whenever they want.

To quote Om Malik: "We can pick and choose what foods we eat, what car we drive, what clothes we wear, but some guy in New York decides when we watch the news?" Or a guy at the local station. Well, no longer.

For an example of a specific effect of this, consider program schedules that have involved lead-ins. If you've had *Oprah* scheduled just before your evening news program, it's been a good lead-in that drives more viewers into your evening news. But now when consumers' digital devices will be recording shows and later playing them whenever those consumers want, they'll be recording just *Oprah* and not your following local news show. The "art" of program scheduling ceases to exist.

- Another major change, and related to on-demand, is Customized Programming. Indeed, no more network.

For example, a consumer named Wilma will no longer watch the ABC network shows or the Channel 11 shows. She'll be creating and watching the Wilma network, a network just for herself. She'll pick her favorite shows, favorite actors, and favorite genres, and then have her digital TV device find those shows from among all networks and assemble those shows into a customized network just for her. Even if some of those shows otherwise run at the same time on competing networks.

A TV network or a local TV channel will no longer necessarily be a network or channel, but just pieces for assembly into almost as many networks as there are viewers themselves. Particularly when TV migrates online into IP TV.

No mass, no more. TV networks and local TV channels will no longer be mass media, but ingredients for a massive number of very personal TV networks.

- Another change is Pervasive Mobility. You'll no longer need a TV to get TV.

Part of this change is that every digital device will accept video. For example, Korean TV next month will begin satellite broadcasting of 13 channels of digital TV directly into Koreans' cell phones. Of course, they've got the Third-Generation (3G) broadband cell phones there. Likewise soon, iPods and similar digital music devices will begin playing video as well as audio.

Another part of this change is that every surface can become a display. All e-paper—the flexible electronic paper—under development can accept video, not just text. The printing industry has developed electronic displays that don't require screen-printing in a computer "clean room." In seven to 10 years, your local print shop will be able to go out and screenprint a computer display onto anything. Walls, trucks, refrigerators. You've seen giant electronic displays here in Las Vegas, but you'll soon be seeing them on the sides of delivery trucks in your local town. And those will be displaying video.

- Another change is that Bandwidth and Memory are No Longer Problems. Broadband consumers have hundreds of thousands of kilobytes per second of download capacity, if not already megabytes. And it's hard to find a hard drive of less than 10 or 20 gigabytes nowadays, except digital still cameras.

- That everyone can webcast is another change. Thank broadband and inexpensive, even free, video apps. And that webcasting is taking three forms:

Individuals are webcasting or video blogging. That can range from 11 year-old Dylan Verdi, whose videos are seen by thousands of people per day, to 50-something Jeff Jarvis, whose office webcast was seen here during the Radio and Television News Directors Association.

Non-video media is now webcasting. Newspapers are clamoring to add video to their online offerings. Even radio is. Last week, the Clear Channel company announced that 200 of its radio stations will start offering live video online.

Everyone is becoming a broadcaster online. And many of them are beginning to trade videos online. Peer-to-peer video networks are beginning to form. Or sites like OurMedia.org, which provides free storage and free bandwidth for trading people's own videos, audio files, photos, text, or software.

Face it, with all these changes, much of the broadcast industry that you've long taught no longer exists. It's being disassembled almost as quickly as the teamsters and carpenters outside can disassemble the NAB display floor.

Now, the bad news. As Rupert said, the broadcast industry didn't do as much as it should to deal with these changes. Still largely isn't doing what it should. Five years ago, many broadcasters dismissed these changes when the dot.com boom ended. But it was simply a case that they could no longer see the forest because of all the trees.

Many pundits nowadays are fond of quoting Harvard Business School Professors Clayton Christensen, of *The Innovator's Dilemma*, or Clark Gilbert. I instead prefer to cite Professor Donald Sull, who studies how legacy companies or legacy industries react to major changes. He found that the reaction isn't paralysis but what he calls "active inertia." Companies or industries tend to react to change by doing what they've always done, only more feverishly, even though doing so no longer makes sense.

Don't do that in broadcast education.

Many, such as *Ad Age* magazine columnist Bob Garfield, are predicting a meltdown of the broadcast industry, predicting that the transition won't be happy or pretty but will be chaos and disaster. I agree.

- The advertising industry won't be subsidizing traditional broadcasting much longer. For example, Proctor & Gamble is now advertising most of its new products off the airwaves. Seventy-five percent of ad spending to launch Prilosec OTC was off the airwaves. American Express now does 80 percent of its advertising off airwaves. Pepsi One won't use TV advertising.

- Likewise, 70 percent of Digital Video Recorder users skip commercials.

- And more and more advertising revenues are going to new competitors that didn't exist a decade ago. For example, Google earned $3 billion in ad revenues last year. That's more than The New York Times Company or Dow Jones & Co. earned. Google earned as much in advertising as not just *The New York Times* newspaper, but that paper plus *The Boston Globe* plus 23 regional daily newspapers plus the NYT TV and radio stations, all combined. Google did that just with text search. What happens when it also gets video search?

- As for paid subscription broadcasting, remember that more efficient technologies more efficiently reduce what consumers are willing to pay.

- Similarly, the economies of scale, all built atop the mass medium business model, are going to disappear.

- And here's a final, dark note for you broadcast educators: The 17th-century English author John Donne sermonized that "No man is an island." But Customized Programming in which viewers can see only what they want to see will create large numbers of insular viewers.

That some may want to see only Britney Spears news may be their democratic right, empowered by new medium technology. But how do you responsibly inform the public without contravening that right?

I don't think this insularity will create a new Dark Age, but it could very well create a Gray Age of ignorance. Some say that is already happening.

What can you do to make it otherwise?

In the interest of time, I'll yield to my fellow panelists. Among them, Jerry Condra, who helped organize this panel, had asked me to talk about what broadcasters can do now to make great Web sites. If anyone is interested in that, we can talk about it in the question and answer period.

Thank you.

IV. Seniors and Social Security

Redefining Aging

Mariah Burton Nelson

National expert and keynote speaker on sports, success, and leadership, 1987– ; born Springfield, PA, April 14, 1956; B.A. in psychology, Stanford University, 1978; M.S. in public health, San Jose State University, 1983; worked at hospices for several years; star basketball player, Stanford University, 1974–78; professional basketball in Europe, 1978–79, and in the first U.S. women's pro league (Women's Basketball League), 1979; former president, National Speakers Association, Washington, D.C., 2000–01; author: Are We Winning Yet? How Women Are Changing Sports and Sports Are Changing Women *(1991), Amateur Athletic Foundation's Book Award, 1992;* The Stronger Women Get, the More Men Love Football: Sexism and the American Culture of Sports *(1994);* Embracing Victory: Life Lessons in Competition and Compassion *(1998);* The Unburdened Heart: Five Keys to Forgiveness and Freedom *(2000);* We Are All Athletes: Bringing Courage, Confidence, and Peak Performances into Our Everyday Lives *(2002); articles in* Newsweek, Fitness, Glamour, Cosmopolitan, Redbook, *and other periodicals; appears on major broadcast and cable news programs; gives some 50 keynote speeches on leadership to association, corporate, government, and college audiences each year; coaches her mother, Sarah, who holds two Arizona State breaststroke records for women aged 75–79; numerous awards for women in sports, journalism, and public speaking, including: Women's Sports Foundation's Magazine Journalism Award, 1988; National Women in Sports Hall of Fame, 1996; Communications and Leadership Award 2002, District 27 Toastmasters; and Capital Outstanding Speaker Award, 2003, from the National Speakers Association.*

Editors' introduction: Ms. Mariah Burton Nelson gave the closing keynote address to the AARP National Leadership Conference. AARP is a "nonprofit, nonpartisan membership organization for people age 50 and over . . . dedicated to enhancing quality of life for all as we age." In her speech about "aging, identity, and pride," Ms. Nelson informed delegates to the AARP conference that our present definition of aging is "inaccurate, disrespectful, and discriminatory." "We need," she concluded, "to celebrate and honor old people for their experience, wisdom, and contributions . . . with heartfelt respect for who old people are and what they have accomplished."

Mariah Burton Nelson's speech: After this presentation, we'll have time for Q and A.

Delivered on April 30, 2004, at Washington, D.C. Reprinted with permission of Mariah Burton Nelson.

But there's one question people always ask me, and I have to answer it early on, or you'll just sit there wondering. That question is not, "How did you get to be a successful author and speaker?" or, "What was it like playing professional basketball?" When you see me standing here, you wonder . . ."

Audience: "How tall are you?"

Yes. This is a burning question, apparently. People actually chase me down the street: "How tall are you, anyway?" So I tell them— What do I tell them?

Audience: "Six-two."

Right. Or, as I used to say in high school, "Five-fourteen." Then they say, "You don't LOOK that tall!" Well then: "Why are you chasing me down the street?" They also ask other questions. My favorite is, "Have you always been that tall?"

It was my mother who taught me to be proud of my height—as if it were a personal accomplishment. Mom's five-ten and a half. She never leaves off that half inch. Dad's six-three, my brother's six-four. My sister's only five-nine—but we let her stay in the family anyway.

We didn't have a strong ethnic or national identity. We're English, French, Irish, Scottish, Dutch, German, Norwegian, and Swedish. Mom wanted us to have some identity, so she decided we should be the Tall Family. She taught us to have Tall Pride, to do Tall Bonding, and to say, "Tall is beautiful."

Mom taught us to identify with other tall people. She would point out tall people wherever we went, as if we couldn't see for ourselves who was tall. "There's a tall woman, Mariah," she would say. "Go ask her where she buys big shoes."

I realized recently that Mom wasn't really talking about height. She was giving me permission to be outstanding, to be myself, and to take pride in an identity that could otherwise ("Stringbean, Beanpole, Jolly Green Giant, Stretch") be used against me. She knew that, in a society that still wants girls to be dainty, delicate, decorative, and deferential, I'd need encouragement to take pride in my height.

Today I'm going to talk about aging, identity, and pride. I'm going to encourage you, as AARP leaders, to take a leadership role in redefining aging.

The Gerontophobe

But first I have a confession: My name is Mariah, and I'm a recovering gerontophobe. Gerontophobia, of course, is ageism: the irrational fear of old people or aging. I like the term "gerontophobe" better. It's more fun to say. It sounds more like a . . .

Audience: "Dinosaur."

Yes. And, like a dinosaur, a gerontophobe is a huge scary mythic outdated creature that still has a certain power over us. It whispers things in our ears like, "Old is ugly." And, "Old is shameful." And, "Whatever you do, don't look or act old!"

I didn't expect to become a gerontophobe. As child, I spent a lot of time with four grandparents and two great-aunts, one of whom lived with us for several years. I loved these people.

But I don't want to LOOK like them. Yet now, when I examine my hands, I see Aunt Minnie and Aunt Ollie.

When I look at my face in the mirror, I see my grandmothers.

And if I put on my glasses, THEN look in the mirror . . . I see [peering at a mustache] my grandfathers.

And I'm only 48!

My grandparents and great-aunts were beautiful people. As a child, I could see that very clearly. Isn't it amazing how vision really does deteriorate with age?

Acknowledging Your Age and Honoring Your Elders

Now let me ask you to do something. If you are 50 or older, please stand, if you're able. (If you need to stay seated, please raise your hand.)

Now, if you're 60 or older, stay standing.

Now, if you're 70 or older, please stay standing.

These are our elders.

Audience: Spontaneous applause.

These are volunteers and staff who, like you, are dedicating their time and energy to a cause we all believe in. As our elders, they have contributed more than the rest of us, not only to AARP but to their families and society and, in many cases, the nation. They have gained a perspective that we can't have. They know things we don't know. They deserve our respect: for their experience, their contributions, and their wisdom. Let's give them another round of applause.

Audience: Rousing applause.

What did I just do? Two things.

First, I asked you to acknowledge your age. Was that difficult? I could tell from the nervous laughter that for many of you, it was. And yet: You're AARP. If you're going to play a leadership role in helping the country eradicate ageism, wouldn't it be a good idea to be honest about your own age?

If admitting your age made you uncomfortable, you're not alone. There's good reason for it. Whose fault is it?

Audience: "Ours."

Not really. I like to blame it on that old dinosaur, the gerontophobe. It's helpful to externalize it, to realize that our ageist attitudes are not inborn; they're acquired by living in an ageist society. Yes, we all have a gerontophobe within—but we're not, at our core, fundamentally ageist people. It's just our conditioning, and we can successfully overcome it.

Second, I asked you to acknowledge and show respect for our elders. If you come from a family or culture that habitually demonstrates respect for older people, that may not have felt new for you. But for many of you, that did feel new. I think your spontaneous applause arose not from any ritual you've grown accustomed to, but rather from a deep need to acknowledge and publicly thank your elders. From the expressions on the faces of the people over 70, I can tell that your heartfelt gratitude felt new to them as well, and very welcome.

As you know, as a society, we don't applaud our elders. We don't even talk to them. We don't visit them. We don't make sure they have adequate food and shelter and health care.

The Power to Make It Better

Bill Novelli has asked us: What's one powerful thing AARP should do to "make it better"?

One powerful thing AARP could do to make it better is to redefine aging. As I prepared for this presentation, the phrase "redefine aging" came up over and over again in conversations with Mary Foerster, Lee White, Joe DeMattos, Hugh Delehanty, and Cathy Ventura-Merkel. This concept is described in the Member Value Agenda that was approved just this week by your board of directors.

The way [aging is] currently defined is so inaccurate, disrespectful, and discriminatory. Because ageism hurts all of us.

Goal #5 states, "AARP makes a significant contribution to shifting the perception of aging in this country toward a vision of creativity, wisdom, and empowerment."

This is what I want to talk about today: redefining aging. Why? Because the way it's currently defined is so inaccurate, disrespectful, and discriminatory. Because ageism hurts all of us.

Hugh Delehanty, Editor-in-Chief of Publications for AARP, told me recently, "America is already redefining aging. It's happening. The question is, Will AARP lead in that effort, or try to catch up? I'd like to see us play a leadership role." I would too.

My Background

I'm not an expert on aging (though I'm getting more experience every day). I know that you've already given a great deal of thought to aging, and have a vast network of programs, plans, and policies in place, along with legislation, litigation, and more.

I do have a psychology degree, and master's in public health, and I worked at hospices for several years, as a volunteer and as a volunteer coordinator. But my expertise really lies in sports, success, leadership, and language. I'm interested in identity and terminology, and how those influence self-esteem. I'm interested in social change movements, and have been involved in a few, most notably the women's sports movement.

In a way, I'm in the business of redefining things. I've written about how sports participation is changing women; how women are changing sports; and how relationships between women and men change as they play and work together on teams. I like to think I've played a role in redefining "athlete," and even redefining "woman."

Now I'd like to redefine aging. But I can't do it alone. I need your help.

An Athletic Identity

I believe we are who we are because of the stories we tell ourselves about ourselves. As I'm telling you some of my stories today, I hope you think about your own stories: sports stories, but also the kinds of things you say to yourself about your body, your age, your aging process, and what it means to you to grow old. (Nice phrase, isn't it? You can't grow young. You can only grow old.) I hope that, as an outsider (and an aspiring member), my perspective will help you think about some things in new ways.

I brought my Stanford basketball uniform to show you. I played five different sports in my two high schools in Pennsylvania and Arizona, then arrived at Stanford in 1974, and this is what they gave us for a basketball uniform. What's it called?

Audience: "A pinney."

Right. It goes on like this, like an apron, and is symbolic of those days when women were "supposed" to stay in the kitchen. Fortunately, it was not the WHOLE uniform.

How do you think my teammates and I felt?

Audience: "Like second-class citizens; angry."

Yes: Angry, naturally, like anyone who is treated as a second-class citizen. The men had real uniforms. The men played in Maples Pavilion, which seats 8,000. The men had paid coaches and 12 scholarships. We had volunteer coaches and no scholarships and played in the dinky "women's gym," where the walls are so close to the court you have to put your foot up after you do a layup so you don't smash into the wall.

We staged sit-ins in the athletic director's office. This was 1974, but we had HEARD about the sixties, so we spent all our free time sitting in the athletic director's office, demanding real uniforms, paid coaches, scholarships, and access to the "big gym." We demanded that he implement Title IX—the federal law prohibiting sex discrimination in educational institutions—which had just passed in 1972.

Finally, in my junior year, we received real uniforms and access to the big gym. The year after I graduated, Stanford gave women 12 full scholarships. In 1990 and 1992, Stanford won national basketball championships. I like to think that through my activism as well as my athleticism, I helped "build the program."

After graduating from Stanford, I was recruited to play for a French professional team, and also drafted onto the New Jersey Gems of the WBL, the first U.S. women's pro basketball league. (I now think of that league as the LNEH: The League Nobody's Ever Heard of.)

So I had a choice: France or New Jersey? Paris or Piscataway? No offense to those of you who are from New Jersey, but having grown up in Pennsylvania, I'd already been to New Jersey. I had never been to France. So I went to France. The following year, I did play for the Gems.

So I'm a former professional basketball player, but more importantly, I'm an athlete. Being an athlete is still very much a part of my identity. Everywhere I go, I encourage others to think of themselves as athletes. I guarantee you: If you think of yourself as an athlete, it will change the way you walk, the way you work, and the decisions you make about leadership, teamwork, and success.

My athletic identity is changing as I age. At six-two, people have always asked me about basketball, but the questions have changed. People used to ask, "Do you play basketball?" Now they ask, "DID you play basketball?"

I don't play basketball anymore. But I swim two miles most mornings, or lift weights. I've got a resting pulse rate of 44. I can hit a golf ball 240 yards. (Golfers will understand that I use that statistic because it's more impressive than my handicap, which is more relevant.) Every day, I draw on my athletic experience and identity to bring courage, confidence, and commitment to excellence in my work as an author and speaker.

What If We Reclaimed the Word "Old"?

Identity matters. It shapes our sense of self and our interactions with the world. So what about that identity, "old"? What shall we do about that little three-letter word? Must we distance ourselves from it, protesting that we are not old?

Can we lobby effectively for people over 50 if we're pretending we're not over 50, or pretending we're younger than we are, or accepting the belief that there's something feeble and embarrassing about the word "old"? Seems to me it could be empowering to claim it, to own it.

If we don't do this—if our social change movement on behalf of people 50-plus is based on the premise that we are not old, or that only people 90-plus are old—then aren't we sending a mixed message?

Women do not consider it a compliment when told, "You're one of the guys." People of African heritage do not consider it a compliment when told, "You don't look black." Yet we still offer these as compliments: "You don't act your age." "You don't look your age." "You're young at heart." And, "You look pretty good, considering your age."

From Martin Luther King to Gloria Steinem to Ellen DeGeneres, social change leaders have urged us to eradicate internalized shame—the sense that, because others don't like us, there must be something wrong with us—by claiming the words that have been used against us.

We have adopted the words "black" and "woman" and "lesbian" and "gay." Some of these words sounded odd at first. The words "black" and "African-American" sounded odd, as opposed to "Negro" or "colored." The word "woman" sounded odd, as opposed to "lady" or "girl." The words "lesbian" and "gay" still sound odd, even shameful and accusatory, in some circles. Social change takes time.

> *Maybe the reason old people can't agree on a term is that they don't want to be defined by age.*

But gradually, language influences people's beliefs. Maybe the word "old" could be rehabilitated, and put to good use.

Old People Don't Want to Be Defined by Age

Studies show that even old people can't agree on a term. They don't like "senior" or "elderly" or "older." Naturally, they're not crazy about "old folks," "old bags," "old hags," "old biddies," "old birds," "old fangled," "old fashioned," "old and decrepit," "over the hill," "blue hairs," "golden oldies," "vulnerable," "frail," "declining," "dowdy," "doddering," "not getting any younger," and responsible for a "mountain of debt" that will become an "intolerable burden on society."

No wonder AARP came up with "people over 50." I think you're onto something.

Maybe the reason old people can't agree on a term is that they don't want to be defined by age. Nor do young people. To "define" can mean "to limit," and no one wants to be limited. I know I don't. I want to accept my age, and listen to my body, and resist age discrimination, but I don't want to be defined by my age any more than I want to be defined by my femaleness or the color of my skin or my height. I'm just a "person over six feet." (Many old people say they feel invisible. Somehow, I think this is not going to be my problem.)

But to avoid being defined by our age, and to avoid joining that club called Old Age, we tend to deny that we're old—or even in the Middle Ages. We lie about our age, and we try hard not to look as old as we are.

Greeting card image: Psychologists say we go through seven stages of adjustment when we turn 30: Denial, Denial, Denial, Denial, Denial, Denial, Denial.

Greeting card image: Turning 40 is like peeing in the pool . . . If you're lucky, no one will notice.

Greeting card image: The Dwarves at 50: Touchy, Baldy, Squinty, Gassy, Chubby, Cranky, Drafty

What If We Stopped Trying to Pass as Young?

Last week I went to the drugstore and bought some lotion. When I brought it home, I put on my glasses and saw that it said, Oil of Olay's Age-Defying Daily Renewal Cream. Oh! I had thought it said Age-DENYING.

But maybe that's the same thing. Age-defying, age-denying, what's the difference? And why are we all trying so hard not to look the age we are? Whose fault is that?

Audience: "The gerontophobe."

Right. Who else would decide that wrinkles are ugly? They're not INHERENTLY ugly. This is just an outdated IDEA we have about wrinkles.

There are economic reasons why this dinosaur rears its ugly head. Know how much money the anti-aging products industry brought in last year? More than $17 billion, with a projected growth of 11 percent over the next four years.

My mother's about to turn 80, and most of her friends are in their sixties. "They talk all the time about their ugly wrinkles," she tells me. "That's the word they use: ugly. Or they say they could never let their hair go gray, because they would look SO OLD. Well, I look old. I have wrinkles. And I know they love me. They're very ageist, but it's unconscious. They have no idea how much their words hurt me."

I know another woman who's 93. She rarely tells people her age. Why? "Once you're over 90," she says, "no one takes you seriously." Here's the kicker: She lives in a retirement home. She's trying to have serious conversations with 70- and 80-year-olds, and they keep patting her on the head and saying, "You're doing so well, dear."

At various points in history, Jews have passed as Gentiles and black people have passed as white. There was a good reason for this: survival. Old people's desire to pass as young may feel like a matter of survival now. But I don't think it's helping our cause, and I know it's not helping our self-esteem.

Secrecy always leads to shame. Even if you have a very good reason for keeping a secret, when you pretend to be something or someone you're not, you inevitably feel bad about who you are.

We need new ways to think about and talk about aging. Not talking about it isn't working—any more than my "age-defying" daily renewal cream is working.

An Experiment in Reclaiming the Word "Old"

What if, just as an experiment, we reclaimed the word "old"? Maybe if we try it on, it won't have so much power over us.

In a moment I'm going to ask you to say it with me: I'm old. I know it's a word with a bad, boring, shameful, scary, grumpy reputation. But it's just a word. If you've never said the word "old" out loud, and want to warm up to it, you can say "cold." "I'm cold." That's easier.

Or, "I'm bold." Seems to me that if we are going to take a leadership role in redefining aging, we're going to have to get comfortable with this simple three-letter word.

Even if it's not true for you—even if you're young, or somewhere in the Middle Ages—what the heck, let's practice saying "I'm old." It will be true soon enough.

Okay, here we go.

Audience: "I'm old."

There. How did that feel?

Would it be possible to say that sentence with pride, head held high?

New Language

Some new language is emerging:

- Middlescence: the turbulent, rebellious middle age of baby boomers (Gail Sheehy)

- Elder as a verb: to share wisdom with people who are younger (Rabbi Zalman Schlachter-Shalomi, who based this usage on an ancient Jewish tradition of elders making decisions and resolving conflicts)

- Elderweds: an older version of newlyweds

- Grandboomer: boomers with grandkids

- Boomeritis: injuries older athletes suffer when trying to do things their bodies can no longer do

- Silver ceiling: attitudes and policies that prevent older employees from rising in the work place

- Longevity bonus: the 30 years longer we live now (an AARP phrase); and

- Senior moments: we all know what those are, unless we've forgotten

A Name for This Movement?

We need more language. We need a name for this movement, don't we? It's a civil rights movement, but it's not THE Civil Rights movement. What shall we call it? Here's one suggestion:

All of us
Aging with
Respect and
Purpose

I've heard the question at this conference; Is AARP an association or a movement? I believe it could be both. You could effectively brand the movement to be synonymous with AARP.

We also need a rallying cry. Imagine a million of us marching on the Washington Mall. What would we say? How about this:

We're old.
We're bold.

We're always too hot
Or too cold.
Not quite there yet? You have the power to make it better.

Midlife Astonishment

Gerontophobia rears its ugly head during a transition called Midlife Astonishment. A Boston psychologist named Sarah Pearlman came up with this term. Basically, it's that shock you get when you look in the mirror and say, "What the heck happened?"

Pearlman calls Midlife Astonishment a "developmental crisis marked by sudden awareness of the acceleration and stigmatization of aging, and characterized by feelings of amazement and despair at the convergence of diminished physical and sexual attractiveness and the multiple losses and changes related to age." It can "initiate a disruption of one's sense of self of identity and result in feelings of heightened vulnerability, shame, and loss of self-esteem."

> *It's probably fair to say that midlife astonishment precedes most facelifts.*

It's probably fair to say that midlife astonishment precedes most facelifts.

I've identified two phases of Midlife Astonishment.

The first is, "I'm going to die!"

It's been said, "Anyone who's over 50 and not thinking about death is not paying attention."

But as we begin to deal with creaking joints, faulty vision, and assorted other indignities and challenges, from bunions to bursitis to backaches; and as our parents die; and as we face the death of dreams and attractiveness as defined by this culture, we tend to become acutely aware of our own mortality. We tend to feel victimized by our own bodies, or by life. Some people never get past this phase. Depression, bitterness, anger, and withdrawal are widespread in old people.

Fortunately there's a second phase of Midlife Astonishment: "I'm going to live!" This is when you transition from a sense of victimization to a sense of freedom, choice, and clarity. There are two keys to shifting into this second, empowered phase of Midlife Astonishment.

The first is what I call Physical Intelligence. This is the ability to listen to one's body and respond wisely to it. It's not the same as knowing a lot about nutrition, exercise, or rest. We've all got access to that kind of information. Physical Intelligence is based on the kind of information our bodies give us each moment of each day. Your body talks to you, telling you what it needs. In fact, I bet your body is trying to tell you something right now. Take a moment to practice your Physical Intelligence. Tune in, and listen to what your body is saying.

The way it works is, if we respond wisely to these signals we get, our bodies tend to function pretty well. If not, our bodies go tell someone else—usually a doctor or emergency room technician. At that point, it's much more difficult to give the body what it needs.

AARP has already taken a leadership role in sponsoring Tri-Umph, the sprint triathlon series. Now you're developing a national walking program. AARP was quoted just last week in an article about older athletes on the cover of the *Washington Post's* Weekend section.

Research has shown that nursing home residents who start lifting weights experience incredible improvements in strength and mobility, sometimes even discarding the walkers or canes that they had come to think of as inevitable accessories of old age. Often, old people are not weak or frail due to old age. They're weak or frail due to poor Physical Intelligence and insufficient conditioning. I recommend that Physical Intelligence become an integral part of how we redefine aging.

The second major key to an empowered, "I'm going to live" approach to midlife (and later life) is what AARP President Marie Smith called "ohana," or family. Research has shown that people who have the support of their families or extended families suffer fewer physical and emotional maladies than people who are isolated. Pearlman agrees that social support, affiliation, and a sense of belonging are keys to a healthy acceptance of aging. AARP already plays a major role in providing people over 50 with a sense of belonging.

Pearlman also recommends: meaningful work or other interests; positive role models; spirituality; political understanding of the oppression of older people; and engaging in social or political activism on behalf of older people. AARP plays a leadership role in all of those ways as well.

Diving Into the Unfamiliar Waters of Old Age

Before we close, let me tell you some more about Mom. This is a story about identity, leadership, and confidence.

My mother's very athletic, and very competitive. But like many women of her generation, she didn't have anyone to compete against. I remember watching her swim laps at the Y. Some poor unsuspecting person in the next lane would finish a lap, and Mom would say, "Ha! Beat you!" She was not very popular at the Y.

I realized recently that's why my mother had children: to create some rivals. But my older sister had no interest in sports. My older brother loved baseball, but he had ear infections that kept him out of the water. So I got to be born.

Our first race took place in our neighbor's pool. I remember it clearly. Mom was so happy. She had waited for this her whole life. I was five years old. She was 37. If you want to picture us, Mom looked like I do now, tall and thin. At five, I was already . . . five-eight or so. I was wearing a suit with a little skirt, like a ballerina's tutu. Mom had bought that for me. Know why?

Audience: "To slow you down."

Right! To increase drag in the water, slowing me down. Mom won that first race ("Ha! Beat you!"), but I joined a swimming team, and ditched the ballerina tutu, and each summer I'd challenge Mom to a rematch. She won when I was six, and seven, and eight, and nine, but each year I got a little closer, and finally, the year I was 10, I beat Mom. She disputes this, maintaining I was 11.

We also teamed up—as many rivals ultimately do—competing in the mother-daughter relay at our swim club's year-end championships. The daughters would swim the first lap, then the mothers would swim the final lap. I was never the fastest daughter but Mom was always the fastest mom, so we won that trophy for about 10 years in a row.

Mom and I still compete. I give her a head start, because I'm a lot faster now—and also a lot nicer than she was. But I never let her win.

But for years, I've been telling her about masters swimming, where you compete against people your own age and gender, in five-year increments: 40–44; 45–49; 50–54. She was reluctant, though, as so many of us are afraid to dive into unfamiliar waters.

All of us are reluctant to dive into the unfamiliar waters of old age. Those waters are deep and scary.

Finally, about 10 years ago, when she was visiting me in Arlington, Virginia, I took her to my masters swimming practice. I sent her over to the far left lane, where my friends Helen, Lorraine, and Frank train. At that point they were all in their sixties or seventies. After practice, Mom was thrilled. Know why?

Audience: "She won."

Right! It was just practice, but she felt like she won. She gained confidence. When she returned home, she joined the Phoenix Masters swim team. That was the year she was 69. But she waited until she turned 70 before entering her first meet . . . so she'd be in the bottom of her age group, not competing against all those fast 65-year-olds. That's one of the many benefits of masters sports programs: People are glad to enter a new decade.

And now Mom holds three Arizona state breaststroke records for women aged 75–79.

I tell you this story because you, too, probably know people who are reluctant to dive into the unfamiliar waters of physical fitness, or AARP leadership, or other challenges. You could take them by the hand, introduce them to a new environment, and help them gain the confidence they need to succeed.

All of us are reluctant to dive into the unfamiliar waters of old age. Those waters are deep and scary. We've never been old before. We have few role models who are proud of their age. How in the world can we grow old gracefully, when surrounded by such ageist beliefs and behaviors?

You can help us. You're AARP. We look to you for leadership. You can play an important role in taking us by the hand, and leading us, and helping us feel less confused and afraid.

Now, how exactly can you play a leadership role in redefining aging? I don't know. You're smart people. You figure it out.

Seriously, I'd be honored to be a part of your team. Just let me know if I can help. You've already done so much. Meanwhile, here are a few suggestions:

- Honor your elders.
- Redefine "old": Creative, Wise, Empowered (AARP terms).
- Name this social change movement.
- Develop your physical intelligence.
- Tame the gerontophobe within.
- Hold a member contest to "Draw a gerontophobe"—or otherwise involve members in playful and effective ways of redefining aging, resisting age discrimination, and eradicating their own gerontophobia.

Emily Dickinson wrote,

> By a departing light
> we see acuter, quite,
> than by a wick that stays.
> There's something in the flight
> that clarifies the sight
> and decks the rays.

We all have a gerontophobe within. We all hear that big dinosaur's voice: "Old is ugly." "Old is shameful." And, "Whatever you do, don't look or act old!"

But old age—or whatever we choose to call this time of departing light—can be full of understanding, excitement, opportunity, creativity, wisdom, and growth, a time when "we see acuter." It can be a time when we feel gratefully awake and alive.

We need to celebrate and honor old people for their experience, wisdom, and contributions—not in a phony, patronizing way, but with heartfelt respect for who old people are, and what they have accomplished. We need to help them when they need our help. We need to redefine aging so it's no longer associated with ugliness or shame. This is already part of AARP's mission, message, and Member Value Agenda, and I commend ALL of you, no matter how old you are, for your work in this amazing association. You also have the power to make it even better.

A Little Song for AARP

Let's close with a song. I'm not a singer—as you'll hear in a minute—but I like to write songs, and I sing as a way to demonstrate courage. That's my mission statement—to demonstrate courage, compassion, creativity, excellence, and athleticism as I write and speak the truth as I understand it—so this is the "demonstrating courage" part. I invite some of you to demonstrate courage with me, and take this small public risk. AARP depends upon and honors its volunteers. In that spirit, may I ask for a few volunteers?

As they're coming up here, let me sincerely thank the people who were tremendously helpful as I planned this speech: Mary Foerster, Lee White, Joe DeMattos, Hugh Delehanty, Cathy Ventura-Merkel, Kristin Dillon, Carlos Rojas-Moncriff.

"You've Been Working Hard for AARP"

Sung to the tune of "I've Been Working on the Railroad"

> You've been working hard for AARP
> all the livelong day
> You've been working so creatively
> Why oh why do you work this way?
>
> Why do you serve your members in each state
> Rise up so early in the morn?
> Complaints and problems keep filling your plate
> Why oh why were all these boomers born?
>
> Is it for the dough?
> Is it all e-go?
> Is it 'cause you like the strain and stress?
> Sometimes days are long
> Sometimes things go wrong
> What if you goof up and make a mess?
>
> People 50-plus are smilin'
> People with old relatives are feeling good now
> Even younger people are smilin'
> Saying, "I can't wait to be old too."
>
> You like to help people be strong and smart and safe and free
> and bold
> Promoting independence and empowerment and purpose too
> You are redefining what it means to grow old!
> That's why we appreciate you.

Budget Deficits, Social Security, and Younger Generations

Peter R. Orszag

Joseph A. Pechman Fellow in tax and fiscal policy and senior fellow in economic studies, Brookings Institution, 2001– ; co-director, Tax Policy Center, 2003– ; director, Retirement Security Project, 2004– ; A.B. in economics, Phi Beta Kappa, Princeton University, 1991; M.Sc. (1992) and Ph.D. (1997), London School of Economics, attending as a Marshall Scholar; economic adviser to Russian government, 1993; staff economist, Council of Economic Advisers, 1993–94; professional research staff, Centre for Economic Performance (London School of Economics), 1994–95; senior economist and senior adviser, Council of Economic Advisers, 1995–96; special assistant to the president for Economic Policy, 1997–98; founder, president, and currently senior director, Sebago Associates, Inc., public policy consulting firm, 1998– ; lecturer, University of California at Berkeley, 1999–2000, 2002; co-editor, American Economic Policy in the 1990s (2002); co-author, Protecting the American Homeland: A Preliminary Analysis (2002); co-author, Saving Social Security: A Balanced Approach (2004); has testified on numerous occasions before Congress and is a regular commentator on economic policy in the national press; John Glover Wilson Memorial Prize in Economics, Princeton University, 1991; M.Sc. Economics Prize, London School of Economics, 1992; member, National Academy of Social Insurance and Pacific Council on International Policy.

Editors' introduction: John Spratt (D-SC), ranking member of the U.S. House of Representatives Budget Committee, and other Democratic members of the committee organized the forum "Reality Bites: Why Young People Should Be Concerned About the Deficit." A Democratic staff report by that same title was released at this meeting, chaired by Congressman Harold Ford (D-TN). Conflicting points of view were presented to some 20 interns, students, and reporters. In discussing "the effect of budget deficits on young adults," Dr. Orszag counseled that "it is disproportionately younger generations who will inherit the consequences of our fiscal policies."

Peter R. Orszag's testimony: Thank you for inviting me to discuss the effect of budget deficits on young adults. Debates over the federal budget may seem quite removed from the hectic lives of adults below the age of 35, who are struggling to finish school, decide upon a career and find a job, and in some cases to start a family.

Delivered on September 13, 2004, in the Rayburn House Office Building, Washington D.C.
Reprinted with permission of Peter R. Orszag.

The reality, though, is that policy-makers in Washington are making decisions with substantial implications for these young adults, for it is disproportionately younger generations who will inherit the consequences of our fiscal policies. In other words, we have become used to thinking about how environmental policy leaves a legacy for younger generations. But fiscal policy also leaves a legacy. And on our current fiscal path, policy-makers are simply not doing right by today's young adults.

Young adults deserve a better future than the one implied by today's national saving rate of less than 2 percent of national income, which is the lowest since 1934. That low saving rate, which reflects our elevated budget deficit, necessarily carries one of two possible implications: Either we reduce the amount we invest at home to 2 percent of income, which would starve young Americans of the computers, buildings, and other productive capital they will need to enjoy better standards of living in the future. Or if we do invest more than 2 percent of our income, we must borrow the difference from foreigners—which would leave younger generations increasingly indebted to other nations. Either way, today's young Americans are the ones who will pay the price for our current unwillingness to pay our way.

> *On our current fiscal path, policy-makers are simply not doing right by today's young adults.*

Let me illustrate the point. Under reasonable projections, the budget deficit over the next decade will amount to about $5 trillion. Compared to a balanced budget, these deficits will reduce national income in 2015 by $2,000 or more annually per household, on average.

Budget deficits have another adverse effect on younger Americans, who disproportionately tend to be in debt. Data from the Survey of Consumer Finances suggest that almost a fifth of households headed by young adults have negative net worth—for example, because their student loan and credit card debts exceed their assets. Standard estimates suggest that the budget deficits projected over the next decade will raise interest rates by about one percentage point, which will impose additional costs on young households in debt.

The 2001 and 2003 Tax Cuts

A key factor in this inauspicious budget outlook is the effect of extending the 2001 and 2003 tax cuts. Young adults should be demanding that policy-makers explain precisely how the tax cuts will be financed, since continuing to borrow to pay for them will just shift the costs to the future—when today's young adults will bear a significant share of the burden. The less older generations pay toward the government's bills, the more younger generations will have to pay, and vice versa.

The choices for financing the tax cuts are not attractive—which is perhaps why no one has put forward a credible proposal to do so. For example, just to finance the revenue losses in 2014—and not even cover the interest costs on the tax cuts before then—requires an 11 percent cut in all non-interest spending; a 49 percent cut in all spending other than interest, defense, homeland security, Social Security, Medicare and Medicaid; or an 80 percent cut in all domestic discretionary spending, such as for environmental protection, education, and homeland security.

If we're not willing to pay for the tax cuts through the types of changes I just described, we shouldn't keep charging them to the nation's credit card and leaving young Americans with the bill.

Social Security

I'd like to close with a short discussion of Social Security. Social Security faces a long-term deficit. Restoring long-term financial balance to Social Security is therefore necessary, but it is not necessary to destroy the program in order to save it—especially since the Social Security deficit is not the primary explanation for the nation's long-term budget imbalance. The tax cuts and particularly the projected increases in Medicare and Medicaid are much more important factors.

I would emphasize two key aspects of the Social Security debate to younger Americans. First, despite the misleading claims of some Washington charlatans, there are no free lunches—someone has to pay. So younger Americans should be asking how we should finance the necessary changes across different generations, and across different people within generations.

These questions are particularly important because many of the Social Security reforms that are advanced as benefiting today's young Americans would actually impose the greatest costs on them. For example, replacing the current Social Security system with a fully-funded individual account program requires someone to pay. One possible financing scheme is to cut off our parents and grandparents from the benefits they are already receiving or are planning to receive in the near future, but that seems neither likely nor desirable. The most plausible alternative, at least within an honestly funded plan, would require today's young workers to pay twice: Once to make sure that their parents and grandparents are protected, and again to build up their own retirement funds.

In other words, it is precisely today's young workers who would bear the brunt of the so-called transition costs in moving to an individual account system. Such proposals are often misleadingly presented as benefiting today's young workers, whereas in reality they would impose substantial additional costs on today's young workers in exchange for generating significant benefits to far-distant generations. A recent reform plan that Professor Peter Diamond and I have put forward is aimed at a more even distribution of the necessary costs across different generations in the future while also eliminating the projected deficit in Social Security.

A second point is equally important. The image of Social Security solely as a retirement program is inaccurate: The program provides a key layer of financial security during other particular times of need, such as disability or the death of a family member, and about one-seventh of beneficiaries are younger than 62. Social Security thus provides not only benefits to our parents and grandparents, but also insurance to today's younger workers. This is valuable, since today's 20-year-olds have more than a one-in-five probability of receiving disability benefits before age 67. And the benefits that are paid out from Social Security are protected against inflation and the risk of stock market collapses. Many individual account reform proposals reduce disability and young survivor benefits. Individual accounts do little to offset such reductions, since workers becoming disabled or dying young have typically not had time to build up their accounts—and some proposals do not give disabled workers access to whatever modest balances they have accumulated in the accounts. Especially as the private retirement system on top of Social Security shifts from a defined benefit to a defined contribution one, it makes little sense to engineer a shift to individual accounts within the core layer of financial security provided by Social Security.

Thank you once again for inviting me to testify this afternoon, and I look forward to your questions.

Radio Address on Social Security

George W. Bush

President of the United States, 2001– ; born New Haven, CT, July 6, 1946, and raised in Midland and Houston, TX; attended Phillips Academy, Andover, MA; B.A., Yale University; M.B.A., Harvard Business School, 1975; F-102 pilot, Texas Air National Guard, 1968–73; oil and gas business, Midland, TX, 1975–86; senior adviser in father's presidential campaign, 1987–88; one of the partners who purchased the Texas Rangers baseball franchise, 1989, and managing general partner of the team, 1989–94; governor of Texas, 1995–2000.

Editors' introduction: During his second term in office, President Bush mounted a prolonged campaign to reform Social Security, provoking a national debate. In one recommendation that caused the most disagreement among Republicans, Democrats, and others, the president advocated that "younger workers" be given "the option to save some of their payroll taxes in a personal retirement account." Maintaining that, "for young workers, Social Security is on the road to bankruptcy," President Bush concluded, "Every year we put off the coming crisis, the higher the price our children and grandchildren will have to pay."

George W. Bush's speech: Good morning. This week, I met with some of our fellow citizens from across the country to discuss one of the great responsibilities of our nation: strengthening Social Security for our children and grandchildren.

For 70 years, the Social Security system has fulfilled the promise made by President Franklin Roosevelt, keeping our elderly citizens out of poverty, while assuring younger Americans a more secure future. Along with employer-funded pensions and personal savings, Social Security is for millions of Americans a critical element to their plans for a stable retirement. And for today's senior citizens and those nearing retirement, the system is sound. But for younger workers, Social Security is on the road to bankruptcy. And if we do not fix it now, the system will not be able to pay the benefits promised to our children and grandchildren.

When President Roosevelt signed the Social Security Act in 1935, the average life expectancy was about 60 years, which meant that most Americans would not live to become eligible for benefits, then set at age 65.

Today, most Americans enjoy longer lives and longer retirements. And that presents a looming challenge. Because Social Security was created as a pay-as-you-go system, current retirees

---

Delivered nationally on January 15, 2005, by radio.

are supported by the taxes paid by current workers. Unfortunately, the ratio of workers to retirees is falling steadily. In the 1950s, there were about 16 workers paying in for each person drawing out. Today, it's about three workers for every beneficiary. And by the time today's workers in their mid 20s begin to retire, there will be just over two.

> *Every year we put off the coming crisis, the higher the price our children and grandchildren will have to pay.*

What this means is that in the year 2018, the system will go into the red—paying out more in benefits each year than it receives in payroll taxes. After that, the shortfalls will grow larger until 2042, when the whole system will be bankrupt. The total projected shortfall is $10.4 trillion. To put that number in perspective, $10.4 trillion is nearly twice the combined wages of every single working American in 2004.

Every year we put off the coming crisis, the higher the price our children and grandchildren will have to pay. According to the Social Security trustees, waiting just one year adds $600 billion to the cost of fixing Social Security. If we do not act now, government will eventually be left with two choices: dramatically reduce benefits, or impose a massive economically ruinous tax increase. Leaving our children with such a mess would be a generational betrayal.

We owe it to the American worker to fix Social Security now. And our reforms begin with three essential commitments. First, if you're receiving your Social Security check, or nearing retirement, nothing will change for you. Your benefits are secure. Second, we must not increase payroll taxes on American workers because raising taxes will slow economic growth. Third, we must give younger workers— on a voluntary basis—the option to save some of their payroll taxes in a personal retirement account.

Unlike Social Security benefits, which can be taken away by politicians, the money in a personal account would be yours. And unlike the money you put into Social Security today, the money in personal accounts would grow. A child born today can expect less than a 2 percent return after inflation on the money they pay into Social Security. A conservative mix of bonds and stocks would over time produce a larger return. Personal accounts would give every younger worker, regardless of income, the chance to save a nest egg for their later years and pass something on to their children.

Saving Social Security is an economic challenge. But it is also a profound moral obligation. Today's young Americans deserve the same security their parents and grandparents enjoyed. Because the system is broken and promises are being made that Social Security cannot keep, we need to act now to strengthen and preserve Social Security.

I look forward to working with members of Congress from both parties to keep the promise of Social Security.

Thank you for listening.

The Urgency for Social Security Reform in the United States

Mark Warshawsky

Assistant secretary for Economic Policy, U.S. Department of the Treasury, 2004– ; born 1958; has lived primarily in Chicago, IL; B.A., Northwestern University, 1979; Ph.D. in economics, Harvard University, 1984; senior economist, Federal Reserve Board (Capital Markets Section), 1984–92; supervised a study of underfunded defined benefit plans for the IRS (Employee Plans Division), 1992–95 (Assistant Commissioner's Award); manager of pension research, TIAA-CREF, 1995–98; deputy assistant secretary for Economic Policy, Microeconomic Analysis, U.S. Department of the Treasury, 2002–04; author, The Uncertain Promise of Retiree Health Benefits *(1992); co-author with Jeff Brown, Olivia Mitchell, and Jim Poterba,* The Role of Annuity Markets in Financing Retirement *(2001); co-author with William Gale and John Shoven,* Private Pensions and Public Policies *(2004); author of over 50 professional articles, including "In Sickness and in Health: An Annuity Approach to Financing Long-term Care and Retirement Income,"* Journal of Risk and Insurance, *2001 (with Brenda Spillman and Chris Murtaugh), which won a prize competition sponsored by the British Institute of Actuaries, 2001.*

Editors' introduction: For many years in the United States, elected officials and others have debated what should be done to sustain the Social Security system begun by President Franklin D. Roosevelt. During his second term in office, President George W. Bush launched a prolonged campaign to reform Social Security, provoking a national debate. In his speech to the National Newspaper Association, Assistant Secretary Warshawsky called for a "reform plan that modernizes the program, is fair, and puts Social Security on a sound and sustainable financial footing." Established in 1885, the National Newspaper Association (NNA) "is the national voice" of some 3,200 owners, publishers, and editors of America's community newspapers.

Mark Warshawsky's speech: Thank you for the kind introduction. In his State of the Union address the President said, "One of America's most important institutions—a symbol of the trust between generations—is also in need of wise and effective reform."

He was of course referring to Social Security. As you are aware, President Bush has made Social Security reform a major priority of his second term. Accordingly, we in the Administration want to formulate a reform plan that modernizes the program, is fair, and puts Social Security on a sound and sustainable financial footing.

Delivered on March 11, 2005, at Washington D.C. Reprinted with permission of Mark Warshawsky.

Today I'll explain why it is so important that responsible Social Security reform occur now, and why one element of a successful reform plan must be personal retirement accounts [PRAs] that give individuals more control over their financial futures. There is a great new Web site that all Americans can use to learn more about what I will be talking about today: *StrengtheningSocial-Security.gov*.

> *Delaying reform only reduces the options for fairly distributing the benefits of Social Security across generations.*

I have been in the economics field for 25 years researching retirement security policies and if you had told me at any point that the solvency and reform of Social Security would be discussed around the kitchen table, the water cooler, or in the news everyday, I never would have believed you. Now the fact that Social Security cash flows will start going into the red in 2018 and the trust fund will be exhausted by 2042 is on the minds of Americans. And they want a solution. The debate has come much further than anyone could have imagined. Now we need ideas, more rather than less, to produce real results.

It is imperative that Social Security be reformed now well in advance of the exhaustion of the trust fund. Why? As I'll explain in this speech, delaying reform only reduces the options for fairly distributing the benefits of Social Security across generations. As reform is delayed fewer generations are able to participate in a reformed entitlement system that will close Social Security's funding gap, and, therefore, the more severe those reforms will need to be.

It is also imperative that PRAs be part of the Social Security solution. Why? PRAs provide individual control, ownership, and offer individuals the opportunity to build a nest-egg that the government cannot take away. They allow individuals to partake in the benefits of investing in the financial markets. Individual control and ownership means that people would be free to pass any unused portion of accounts to their heirs. But most importantly, PRAs allow effective pre-funding of Social Security benefits. I like to characterize PRAs as individual "lockboxes" for Social Security surpluses. PRAs are effective because the government can never take that money away.

The Size of Social Security's Financing Shortfall

According to the Social Security actuary's current projections, Social Security cash surpluses (payroll and benefit taxes less benefit payments) that last year amounted to 1.6 percent of taxable payroll will get ever smaller after the extraordinarily large baby boom generation begins to retire in 2008, and will ultimately turn to deficits beginning in 2018. Starting at that time, benefits payments will have to be at least partially financed from general revenues that initially correspond to interest payments earned by the Trust Fund and later by redemptions of Trust Fund balances. Under current projections, the drawdown of trust fund securities will be complete in 2042, at which time only about three-quarters of benefits will be payable.

Of course, full benefits could continue to be paid after 2042 if the payroll tax rate, now 12.4 percent, were to be increased. If, for example, the system were to operate on a pay-as-you-go basis in every year beginning in 2042, current projections indicate that the payroll tax rate would have to rise gradually, but steadily, to more than 19 percent at the end of the current 75-year projection period.

Alternatively, Social Security which has a $3.7 trillion deficit calculated over 75 years could be made solvent over the next 75 years if the payroll tax rate were immediately increased by 1.9 percentage points (to 14.3 percent), or if all current and future benefits were reduced by 13 percent. In either case, a large Trust Fund would accumulate that would be exactly dissipated at the end of the 75-year projection period. This type of reform would therefore not make the system permanently solvent. With each passing year, the Trustees would report an ever larger financial imbalance as the 75-year scoring window is moved forward to include years with ever larger gaps between expected system costs and income.

This last observation—that reforms that make the system appear solvent when calculated over 75 years do not make the system permanently solvent—shows that a 75-year horizon does not fully capture the financial status of the Social Security program. In fact, no finite period will completely embody the financial status of the program because people pay taxes in advance of receiving benefits; at any arbitrary cutoff date, people will have accrued benefits that have not yet been paid. For example, the current 75-year projections include nearly all of the 2010 birth cohort's taxes but virtually none of their benefits. In order to get a complete picture of Social Security's permanent financial problem, the time horizon for calculating income and costs must be extended to the indefinite future. Such a calculation is provided in the 2004 Trustees Report; it is estimated there that for the entire past and future of the program, the present value of scheduled benefits exceeds the present value of scheduled tax income by $10.4 trillion. This is the financing gap that program reforms must ultimately close. To put this in perspective, eliminating the permanent deficit could be accomplished with an immediate and permanent 3.5 percentage point increase in the payroll tax rate (to 15.9 percent), or with a 22 percent reduction in all current and future benefits. In both cases, there would be massive near-term Trust Fund accumulations.

Intergenerational Equity: Why Social Security Must Be Reformed Now

These results make clear that the Social Security system is not financially viable and must be fixed. How to close the permanent financing gap raises difficult questions over how the net benefits of Social Security should be shared across generations. In this context, it is important to recognize that the large unfunded obligations in the system are primarily the consequence of the past system generosity to generations that are now either dead or retired. Of course, those early generations are beyond reform's reach, so the entitlement reforms needed to close the financing gap must fall entirely on later generations.

Viewing Social Security from the perspective of how it affects generations and individuals explains why it is imperative that Social Security be reformed now. Delaying reform only reduces the options for fairly distributing the benefits of Social Security across generations. Most people agree that it would not be fair to alter Social Security's promises to retirees and near retirees. The longer reform is delayed, the fewer generations that are left to participate in a reformed entitlement system so as to close Social Security's funding gap, and the more severe those reforms will be.

There is no doubt that fairness to future generations requires that action be taken now.

To make this point more concretely, consider a policy of closing Social Security's permanent financing gap by immediately increasing the payroll tax rate by 3.5 percentage points. If the tax increase were instead delayed until 2042 when the trust fund is depleted, the requisite tax increase would be 6.5 percentage points. Clearly, I do not advocate any of these policies. My point is that there is no doubt that fairness to future generations requires that action be taken now.

Fixing the System

Fortunately, this untenable situation is fixable. President Bush has said that "Social Security is one of the greatest achievements of the American government, and one of the deepest commitments to the American people." The President supports Social Security reform that increases the power of the individual, does not increase the tax burden, and provides economic opportunity for more Americans. The President has issued guiding principles for reforming Social Security.

One very important principle is that the benefits of seniors at or near retirement should be protected, and that payroll taxes should not be increased.

Another principle is that personal retirement accounts (PRAs) should be made available for younger workers to build a nest egg for retirement that they own and control, and which they can pass on to their children and grandchildren.

Additionally, we must pursue the goal of a permanently sustainable system, eschewing halfway measures that would necessitate further reforms in the future.

Personal Retirement Accounts. I would like to focus on the advantages of PRAs. PRAs provide individual control, ownership, and offer individuals the opportunity to partake in the benefits of investing in private-sector markets. Individual control and ownership means that people would be free to pass the value of accounts to their heirs (bequests).

Personal accounts will provide Americans who choose to participate with an opportunity to share in the benefits of economic growth by participating in markets through sound investments. Personal retirement accounts will be voluntary. At any time a worker can "opt in" by making a one-time election to put a portion of his or her payroll taxes into a personal retirement account. A worker who chooses not to opt in will receive traditional Social Security benefits, reformed to be permanently sustainable.

Perhaps most importantly, the retirement security of our current young and future workers depends on PRAs. They allow individuals to save now to help fund their retirement incomes. In principle, that could be done with reforms that save tax revenues in the Social Security Trust Fund. But such "saving" would almost certainly be undone by political pressures to increase government spending and hence produce larger deficits outside of Social Security. The only way to truly save for our retirement and give our children and grandchildren a fair deal is with personal accounts. Personal accounts serve as private and therefore effective "lock boxes." When prefunding is done using a personal account, there is no pressure to increase government spending, because this pre-funding belongs to individuals and does not appear on the government balance sheet as budget surpluses.

As proposed by the President, PRAs are designed to hold down administrative costs, encourage careful and cautious investing, and provide a reliable income for the full length of retirement.

Centralized administration and a trim menu of investment choices will hold down administrative costs. The PRA administration and investment options will be modeled on the federal Thrift Savings Plan (TSP), the voluntary retirement savings plan offered to members of Congress and other federal employees. TSP offers benefits and features comparable to those available to private sector employees in 401(k) retirement plans. The Social Security Administration's actuaries project that the ongoing administrative costs for a TSP-style personal account structure would be roughly 0.3 percentage points—that is $3 for every $1,000 invested.

PRA investors will have access to low-risk, low-cost broad index funds like those currently available to TSP participants. Workers will also be able to choose a "life-cycle" fund. The asset composition of a life-cycle fund changes automatically to adjust investment risk downward as the fund's owner ages. To protect near-retirees from sudden market swings on the eve of retirement, the President's plan specifies that a life-cycle fund be the default fund for workers age 47 and older. The worker can opt out of this default if the worker and his or her spouse sign a waiver form stating they are aware of the risks involved.

Conclusion

To conclude, let me say that I am encouraged that Social Security reform is finally being earnestly debated, and that all parties are motivated to make Social Security fair and permanently solvent. Today, my small contribution to this debate consists of four major points:

- Social Security as currently designed cannot be sustained. We know with absolute certainty that Social Security will ultimately be reformed. The only question is when and how.

- Social Security reform is urgent. The longer reform is delayed, the more unfair reform will be to future generations, and the more difficult it will be for individuals to plan their financial futures.

- Social Security reform must make Social Security permanently solvent. Half measures ensure that further reforms will be necessary, and amount to a delay of reform that would be unfair to future generations.

- Making Social Security permanently solvent requires that retirement incomes be pre-funded in PRAs rather than the Social Security Trust Fund. Any attempt to pre-fund retirement incomes in the Trust Fund would be undone by excessive government spending outside of Social Security.

Social Security and American Values

William E. Spriggs

Senior fellow, Economic Policy Institute (EPI), 1990–93 and 2004– ; born Washington, D.C., 1955; B.A., Williams College, 1977; Ph.D. in economics, University of Wisconsin-Madison, 1984; taught at North Carolina A & T State University (Greensboro), 1981–83, and Norfolk State University, 1984–90; head of staff, National Commission for Employment Policy, 1993– 94; senior economist, Joint Economic Committee of Congress, 1994–97; Department of Commerce, 1997–98; Small Business Administration, 1998; executive director, National Urban League's (NUL) Institute for Opportunity and Equality, 1998–2004—editor, State of Black America 1999, and research on pay equity (for NUL, 2001 Winn Newman Award from National Committee on Pay Equity); board member, 1993–99, and president, 2000, National Economic Association, professional organization of black economists; member: National Academy of Social Insurance (NASI), 1999– , Black Enterprise magazine Board of Economists, 2000– , and board of the Congressional Black Caucus Political Education and Leadership Institute, 2001– ; participant, UN World Conference Against Racism, Xenophobia, and Related Forms of Intolerance, 2001; Time magazine Board of Economists, 2002; co-chair, 2003 NASI conference that produced Strengthening Community: Social Insurance in a Diverse America; policy board, Association for Public Policy Analysis and Management, 2005– ; published in popular and academic journals; appearances on several television and radio news programs; among those awarded Congressional Black Caucus Chairman's Award, 2004; congressional testimony on effects of government policies on black and low-income communities.

Editors' introduction: Dr. Spriggs spoke as a panelist at a seminar on "Values Matter in the Social Security Debate: Faith-Based Insights," sponsored by the National Academy of Social Insurance (NASI), a "nonprofit, nonpartisan organization" whose "mission is to promote sound policy making on social insurance." Other participants were members of gerontological and public policy organizations, and the seminar's purpose was "to help illuminate issues in the Social Security debate." Contending that "values have been missing from the official debate about Social Security," Dr. Spriggs concluded that, "if we face the facts of what working families need, . . . recognize the realities of what Social Security has provided, . . . and . . . rededicate ourselves to the values of work, family, responsibility, and community, then we will have a different kind of debate."

William E. Spriggs's speech: Let me begin by admitting a shameful fact. I am an economist.

Delivered on June 17, 2005, at the First Amendment Lounge of the National Press Club in Washington, D.C. Reprinted with permission of William E. Spriggs. David Kusnet of EPI helped edit the transcript.

But, in my work about Social Security, I don't just think about federal budgets and trust funds and actuarial tables. I think about values—values like work, family, responsibility, and community. And I believe that most Americans think that way, too. This is why President Bush's plan to privatize Social Security is in big trouble.

> *I believe most Americans think about Social Security in terms of values.*

Now, it's true that values have been missing from the official debate about Social Security. President Bush and the other members of his Administration usually quote the Bible as much as most preachers. But they haven't talked about their Social Security plan in terms of values; instead, they've used slick phrases like "Personal Retirement Accounts," which sound like advertising copy. And most Democrats also have talked about Social Security in terms of dollars and cents—not right and wrong.

But I believe most Americans think about Social Security in terms of values. And Americans are rejecting the President's privatization plan—not because they don't understand it—but because they've figured out that it violates their values.

Social Security appeals to Americans because it embodies our most basic beliefs.

First, there's the fundamental American value of work.

To put it bluntly, Americans believe that, if you're able to work, you're supposed to get up and go to work.

That's America. You're not supposed to be on the dole.

That's why Americans ended up rejecting welfare as we used to know it—Aid to Families with Dependent Children. It was possible to depict that program as encouraging people to go on the dole and stay there.

But, in a society that says you have to work, there is the question: What happens when, one day, you wake up and you can't work anymore?

Maybe you're too old. Maybe you've been injured. Maybe you've become disabled.

That is what Social Security is. It honors the value of work. And it answers that moral question of what happens when we can't work anymore.

Social Security is based on contributions we make when we are working.

And it provides for the day when we are no longer able to work and to provide for ourselves and our families.

Now, Social Security doesn't only honor the value of work; it honors the values of family and responsibility.

When the day comes when wage-earners are unable to get up and go to work, the problem isn't only how can they support themselves, the problem is how can they provide for those who depend upon them.

Social Security provides for breadwinners' spouses and their children through its disability and survivors' benefits.

I'll say more about both benefits a little later.

But, for now, I'll say that Social Security honors the values of family and responsibility because, when wage-earners pay into the program over the course of their working lives, they are providing for their families when the day comes that they can't work anymore.

That is what Social Security is. It is the guarantee to American workers that the people who depend on their paychecks will not become destitute if they can't live up to their responsibility to go to work.

And that leads to another value that Americans tend to practice more than we preach—the value of community.

Americans are more likely to talk about our responsibilities to ourselves and our families than our responsibilities to the strangers who are our fellow citizens.

Social Security is not a retirement plan—it's a social insurance plan.

But, given the opportunity and the necessity, as with the hurricanes in Louisiana and in Florida before that, we help each other out. There are some virtues we preach more than we practice; but there are other values that we practice more than we preach—and community is one of those values.

It's that way with Social Security. There is no way that most American workers could afford an insurance policy that provided them with retirement income and their families with disability coverage and survivors benefits. But, by pooling our contributions, we can help each other provide for our retirements and protect our families against the risks that we will become disabled or die before our time.

That's what social insurance means—all of us, together, protecting each other against the risks that we and our families face.

So it's important to understand: Social Security is not a retirement plan—it's a social insurance plan.

Only 45 percent of people getting a Social Security check are workers who have [worked] their whole lives and then retired.

So who are the other 55 percent?

Some are disabled workers, some of whom lived long enough to now be old and now are classified as getting a retirement benefit but they initially got a disability benefit.

Then the bulk are family members. Children and wives and husbands and parents and adult disabled children of workers. And the children and wives and husbands of workers who have died before they retired.

That is why President Bush's rhetoric about Social Security doesn't reflect the realities of Americans' lives—or resonate with our values of work, family, responsibility, and community.

So when President Bush talks to people about Social Security as only a retirement program, while over half the people who have gotten a check didn't get it that way—they feel uncomfortable with what he's saying.

The people who talk about individual accounts have still never answered the question of how they tie back the individual account to this covenant that is in Social Security—that it will take care of your family if you die or become disabled before you retire.

The National Academy of Social Insurance put out a whole book filled with questions about how do you go from the private account to what we currently have? How do you say to a man, "You know, you married a wife who is four years younger so when you go to get your joint survivors annuity from your private account, you are going to get a lower retirement benefit because she's four years younger than you, while your neighbor, with the exact same earnings history, gets more because his wife is his age."

When they do the annuity and figure it out, the guy with the younger wife gets punished because she's four years younger. Answer this question: "What are you going to do? What are you going to do with the example of the 73-year-old man who already annuitized his private account [and] marries a 71-year-old who has annuitized or is benefiting from some annuitized account? What do you do?"

Under Social Security, they still get their Social Security benefits so there is nothing that keeps them from marrying and keeping their Social Security benefits. They will draw whichever is the best benefit. Of course, they can't triple dip because it's an insurance program. I cannot burn down my house and then go to the insurance company and say, "It burned down three times." Right?

The insurance company is only going to give me a replacement for one house, so you can't claim three Social Security benefits. A wife can't say, "I'm divorced, I'm married, and I had my work record." She can't do that. Under a private account, how do I now get back to get the benefit that I would have under current law?

Understand that Social Security balances risk. It's an insurance program so it balances being a survivor, being disabled, and dying, and getting to old age. From a family's perspective, all they really have to do is care about loving you.

If you have a massive stroke at 59 today, or at 61 today, from the family's perspective the benefit is going to be the same whether you're disabled, you die, or you make it to old age. The President says, "Well, I'm cutting benefits through my proposal to index benefits differently for survivors and for those who get the old age benefit." He hasn't said what he's going to do about disability. Suddenly you can have the family going to the stroke victim, "Live but don't be able to go to work because if you're disabled, we're better off." That's weird. What value is that?

Turning a family insurance program into a personal retirement account—to use the President's phrasing—runs counter to the family values he preaches.

The President hasn't answered what happens under a private account when a spouse leaves and then gets remarried. The children under Social Security still get a survivor's benefit regardless. But under most state laws, that private account becomes the property of the new wife. How do the kids get back to that money? Those who talk about privatization have had years to answer these questions.

The fact is that they have no answers to the questions. None. Even the President in his State of the Union speech laid out his ideas and didn't mention disability, didn't mention survivor's benefits. This is why people get nervous when they hear him talk about it. Privaters have had years to answer these questions. They have had years to think them through. They have had years to tell how they would treat families.

This has a special importance for African-Americans.

In the African-American community we get very nervous because the average age of an African-American getting a Social Security check is 58. In the African-American community we get very nervous, extremely nervous, when people start talking about Social Security and they don't want to talk about survivor's benefits or disability benefits.

From 1935 through 1983 every time we went to revise Social Security it was always to answer what's wrong with the program and how do we make it better. And those solutions made Social Security more expensive.

We did not have the President saying, as in Eisenhower's case, "Oh, disabled people, we can't cover them. That's too expensive. That can't be done. We want to figure out how we can keep the program small."

We understood that, just as the individual has the obligation to work, society has the responsibility to cover you if you can't.

So, Eisenhower signed an expansion in the program so disabled people get covered. It costs more money but that's what you have to do as a moral society. That is our moral obligation.

We have improved the program and this is the first time we've had a debate where the debate isn't about correcting gaps in coverage, as we did in the 1950s when we corrected the fact that blacks had been cut out in the original act by excluding domestic and agricultural workers.

Then, we said, "No, all workers must be covered."

We undid that in 1993 over a Nanny Gate issue and we now have "uncovered" a lot of Hispanic workers because we went back on the promise to domestic and agricultural workers; so, we can improve the program.

In fact, adding covered workers makes the program more solvent. It doesn't actually add cost to it. It makes some rich people uncomfortable to pay for nannies. But this is the first time we've had the debate where people are saying, "We can't afford our moral obligation."

Now, our leaders don't want to hear about improvements. They don't want to hear about why we stop at age 19, instead of age 21 as we did before, in terms of the student benefit, when today, of course, it's even more needed that children know that their parent's absence from the work force will not deny them a college education.

But, when we exclude people from opportunity, there is a cost. The drop in college attendance that took place when we took away the benefit to age 21 for students was dramatic for those who had

---

The only way you are really making caring for those who can't work cheaper is if you say, "I ain't doing it."

---

been eligible for survivors and disability benefits. We are not talking about that because it adds more money and everybody wants to talk about how we can cheat on our moral obligation.

Somehow or another, people have presented the problem as there are more people we have to take care of. That's how it's presented, you know? The President says, "Look in the future. There are going to be more old people. This is a bad thing." It doesn't make it a bad thing, does it? I'm going to be old. I hope it doesn't become a bad thing. I got my invitation to join AARP on my birthday this year so I hope it's not a bad thing to be older.

People say the program is going to double in size in terms of the GDP. But somebody is going to pay for that older person. If we are going to keep our parents at the same lifestyle, it means that it's going to cost us the same amount anyway.

If we are going to fulfill our promise to our parents in their old age, if we are going to fulfill our promise to our nieces and nephews who have lost their parents, if we are going to keep our promise to our brothers and cousins who have become disabled, if we individually do that, it's going to cost all of us the same amount anyway.

It's going to be the same share of the GDP. The only way you are really making caring for those who can't work cheaper is if you say, "I ain't doing it." That's the only way you can make the program cheaper. Then the question becomes: Who administers making this promise? Is it the Government who channels what we think is our obligation, or is it us as individuals?

Do we leave it to chance as we do now with most poor people when it comes to raising their children and we tell them, "Well, you know, you don't have any money. That's tough. Your kid will just have to be poor."

This is the one program where we don't answer it in that cold-hearted way. This is the one program where we don't, where we honor our pledge to our families and to each other, so privatizing it doesn't meet the way that Americans think of their covenant.

That's why the President is failing in his message. That is why we can succeed in keeping the promise of Social Security; preserving and improving it for future generations; and reaffirming the American values of work, family, responsibility, and community.

In conclusion, if we face the facts of what working families need, if we recognize the realities of what Social Security has provided generations of Americans for 70 years, and if we rededicate ourselves to the values of work, family, responsibility, and community, then we will have a different kind of debate.

V. America and the New Europe

Enlarged European Union

The Financial Strength and Weakness from a Global Perspective

Stephen J. Dannhauser

Executive partner, Weil, Gotshal & Manges, 1989– ; chair, Weil, Gotshal & Manges, 2002– ; born New York City, 1950; B.A., State University of New York at Stony Brook, 1972; J.D., Brooklyn Law School, 1975; member and decisions editor, Brooklyn Law Review, *1973–75; admitted to the Bar of New York, 1976; joined Weil, Gotshal & Manges, 1975, and has spent the past 30 years with the firm, 22 as a partner; areas of practice are capital markets, corporate, mergers and acquisitions, finance, and restructurings; member, American Bar Association; awards: New York City Police Department Bomb Squad honoree; Ellis Island Medal of Honor; Founder's Medal of Boys & Girls Harbor, Inc.; Chairman's Award of the National Minority Business Council; Honorary Assistant Chief, Fire Department of The City of New York; Michael Bolton Charities' Lifetime Achievement Award.*

Editors' introduction: Mr. Dannhauser spoke to leading economists, policy makers, representatives of international financial and educational institutions, and other experts attending the 12th European Banking and Financial Forum. In a speech to this same forum one year earlier, Mr. Dannhauser had expressed his trepidation about the prospect of "rapid European unification and a rise to superpower status." One year later, in the 2004 address below, Mr. Dannhauser said he was "encouraged by the enlargement of the European Union." "When I walk the streets or meet with business leaders in Warsaw, Budapest, and Prague," he concluded, "I am amazed at the transformation that has taken place in the 13 years since we opened our first European offices there."

Stephen J. Dannhauser's speech: I am honored to be back in Prague to participate in this distinguished panel on a topic of great importance—not only to Europe, but also to the world.

Let me give you a little context for my remarks. I am chairman of Weil, Gotshal & Manges, an international law firm headquartered in New York, with clients and offices all over the world.

As the leader of an international firm that provides legal services to other international businesses, I am encouraged by the enlargement of the European Union. While my firm has an extensive presence in Europe—with offices in London, Paris, Frankfurt, Munich, Brussels, Budapest, Warsaw, and here in Prague—we identify

Delivered on March 23, 2004, at Prague, Czech Republic. Reprinted by permission of Stephen J. Dannhauser.

most closely with the spirit and drive personifying the will of the newest member countries. When we opened our first office outside of the United States in 1991—not long after the fall of what Winston Churchill named the Iron Curtain—my firm did not initially seek the well-trod path of Western Europe. Instead, we began our European expansion in Hungary, working side by side with the Hungarian-American Enterprise Fund, an investment fund established by the U.S. government to promote the Hungarian private business sector. Later that same year, we opened in Poland to promote the development of the private sector there, teaming with the Polish-American Enterprise Fund. Shortly thereafter, we established roots here in the Czech Republic. So we know a little bit about this region and about many of the issues—particularly the legal issues—that admission of 10 new member states to the EU implies.

The issues aren't simple—if they were we wouldn't be here talking about them today. Nonetheless, I am cautiously optimistic that an expanded EU will afford the clients of my firm—as well as the firm itself—with increased economic opportunities in a larger, more stable, and more cohesive marketplace.

But this isn't only about economic opportunity; it is also about economic risks—and, of course, political risks. The world is interconnected, economically and politically, as never before. To paraphrase an old adage—when Europe catches a fever, the U.S. sneezes, and Asia sneezes and so on, and so on. So a strong and healthy European Union helps immunize the rest of the world.

Since we expanded into Central and Eastern Europe in 1991, I've had the opportunity to see first-hand how Poland, Hungary, and the Czech Republic, and the business and legal communities within these nations, are working to adjust to new regulatory and legal requirements necessary for accession into the EU. We have applauded (and sometimes assisted) as the prospect of EU membership—together with the national will to achieve—has helped these newly democratic nations develop their market economies, adjust their administrative structures, and create more stable economic and monetary environments, as required by the Madrid European Council in 1995.

For these nations, the very prospect of unity with the larger community of Europe has already provided considerable benefits. It has helped them focus on concrete and achievable objectives, for example, building and fine-tuning the legal and regulatory infrastructure necessary for an efficient and enduring market system.

As a lawyer, I tend to view things through the lens of legal developments. I see law as the framework—the expression of the parameters—of Europe's "ever closer union." It is through law that the political decisions of this union, and the rights and responsibilities of its member states and its citizen are expressed. It is law that gives effect to the free flow of goods, peoples, and capital across EU borders.

And it is through the harmonization of law among a broader range of nations that EU enlargement will provide the efficiencies through which European businesses across the continent—and all those doing business in the region—will benefit. We've already seen how harmonization of trade rules, tariffs, and administrative procedures throughout the EU—and a common currency—helps simplify transactions for those operating within and outside of Europe. The move to common audit and international accounting standards will also enhance the ability to carry out transactions efficiently. And all of this efficiency should increase with enlargement. Of course, removing protectionist barriers also increases competition, which by definition brings a change in the status quo, and some businesses may fail as a result. But if you believe in market systems, as I do, you believe that competition—with its failures and pressures for rebirth—is beneficial in the long run.

We know from a new body of economic literature that clear, transparent, and fairly enforced laws are essential for attracting investment capital and for operating markets in which entrepreneurship, efficiency, and growth thrive. A country's inclusion in the EU signifies to investors, among other things, that certain legal protections are in place. Therefore, the increased pace of transactions between both the U.S. and EU member states with acceding nations is not surprising. More corporations and investors, including private equity-backed investors, are willing to undertake complex transactions in these markets. My firm recently surveyed the major U.S. and European private equity-backed investors on this subject, and the overwhelming majority of respondents viewed Central and Eastern Europe as being increasingly more attractive as a source of investment opportunities over the next 12 months—interestingly, with U.S. respondents in particular even keener to invest there.

In 2003 alone, the Czech Republic attracted more than $5 billion in foreign investment. Poland has also been a major beneficiary of foreign invested capital. Last year in Poland, we represented a consortium of private equity funds on their 110 million* acquisition of its leading cable television and Internet operator. We also represented a Dutch retail company in the first commercial mortgage-backed transaction executed in Poland, which was the first euro market term securitization there. In Hungary, we represented a consortium, including Intel and the EBRD, on their combined funding of a telecoms equipment manufacturer.

These are just a few examples. I am convinced that the emergence of these kinds of opportunities and the heightened level of interest in such investment transactions arise from increased investor confidence—a confidence which I believe is strongly correlated to the prospect of membership in an enlarged EU.

---

* *Editors' note:* Text does not specify dollars or euros.

In my judgment, the potential positives from EU expansion—particularly from a commercial and economic perspective—far outweigh any perceived negatives. The difficulty, of course, lies in the ability to set aside immediate short-term national protectionist interests for the good of the whole—and this may require a leap of faith. Cultural and political differences, which are often embedded in the law, are complex. The laws among European nations—corporate laws, labor and social benefit codes, bankruptcy rules, securities regulation, competition, environmental, tax, and on and on—vary widely. EU efforts to achieve greater uniformity have at times posed real challenges. Without a doubt, the inclusion of 10 new nations in the mix will strain further the ability to achieve consensus. That may have the effect of weakening to some degree the commercial, economic, and financial underpinnings of a broader unified market. Yet, while achieving consensus within a larger group of diverse nations may be more difficult, more diverse voices may result in better, more fully developed ideas. The key is to move slowly—harmonization cannot and should not happen overnight. Nor can it—or should it—be absolute.

> *The potential positives from EU expansion—particularly from a commercial and economic perspective—far outweigh any perceived negatives.*

Then, of course, there is the issue of the euro. As an American accustomed to traveling 3,000 miles from coast to coast in the United States without having to concern myself with a diversity of currencies, enjoying a similar experience across much of Western Europe is welcome. Obviously this sentiment is not shared uniformly across Europe, however. Not even the entire roster of the current member states has adopted the euro and, among some of those that have, there may now exist a new cynicism about the uniformity of enforcement of the financial disciplines that were intended to be the bedrock of the currency's strength and acceptance across the EU—particularly the discipline of deficit management among the larger countries. What has become a seemingly dual standard—on the one hand the requirement to maintain solid economic fundamentals among the existing member states (and to similarly position the economies of the new member states) and, on the other hand, the recent relaxation of those requirements at the convenience of a handful of larger, more dominant countries—can only exacerbate the cynicism of those who remain skeptical of a common currency. Notwithstanding what is hopefully an aberrational lapse, I think it is clear to most that implementing the fiscal disciplines and economic restructuring required for universal adoption of the euro across all of Europe continues to be the right goal. It remains to be seen whether what many view as a crass—but now officially endorsed—violation of consistent application of the criteria, undermines the achievement of an ultimately worthy objective.

As you know, the subsidiary principle guides much of the EU's decision-making by serving to ensure that decisions are made on as local a level as possible. Under this principle, the EU cannot take action (except in the areas which fall within its exclusive competence) unless doing so would be more effective than action taken at national, regional, or local level. Such a principle can be viewed as both a strength and a weakness, depending on one's perspective—not unlike the age-old debate between the "Federalists" and the states-rights advocates in the U.S. It serves as a check on EU power—a desirable intention to many, anathema to others. Irrespective of one's views on the merits of the principle, the result is that companies doing business will continue to face differences in rules across a broad spectrum, including tax, bankruptcy, social welfare, employment, and corporate governance.

This is not unique to the EU. We in the U.S. have a somewhat similar doctrine embedded in an amendment to our Constitution that results in 50 state statutes governing, among other things, incorporation and the organic structure of corporations, capitalization, securities offerings, shareholder rights, and various tax schemes. Fifty different state courts enforce and interpret these laws. All of this is in addition to a whole set of federal securities, tax and other laws, enforced by the Securities and Exchange Commission, the Internal Revenue Service, and the federal courts.

In certain respects, the EU is confronting the fundamental issue the U.S. faced in devising its own federal system: to what extent do laws and regulations among member states need to be the same? The solution requires finding a balance that provides a common framework but allows diversity.

Two years ago, my firm was retained by the European Commission to deliver a comparative study of European corporate governance codes. We were asked to offer an opinion on whether the variety of these largely voluntary codes cause impediments to a single European market and whether a European-wide code should be adopted. In short, the Commission wanted to know how and to what extent the governance codes of various European countries should be harmonized.

Ultimately, our study concluded that the Commission should avoid expending effort to develop a single EU-wide corporate governance code—which, given the variation in the laws concerning investor rights, would at best address only general principles (an area of guidance already provided by the OECD's Principles of Corporate Governance). Rather, we recommended that the Commission focus its efforts on: (1.) reducing the information and participation barriers faced by investors throughout the various EU member states; (2.) encouraging listed companies to provide more information about internal governance, including information about corporate ownership structure, board composition, and governance processes; and (3.) creating a forum in which policy makers for member states could share ideas and approaches.

I'm pleased that the European Commission's Action Plan on Corporate Governance reflects our recommendations and I believe that the plan promises to strengthen the position of the member states as safe harbors for capital inflows and investment. Although each element of the proposal will require further development, the plan focuses on steps to reduce the cross-border obstacles for investors and increase the level of protection for their assets. While the plan would harmonize certain requirements relating to disclosures and shareholder protections, it would allow for diversity among member states as relates to other governance practices. And this is key: variety itself is a significant asset, for it encourages, over time, the adaptation, experimentation, and convergence of practices that emanate from different legal systems.

> *EU expansion brings with it the inevitable tensions of adjustment —but it also promises tremendous opportunities for prosperity, democracy, and peace.*

The circumstances and forms of our unions remain distinct. However, there exist sufficient commonalities between the U.S. and the EU experiences to warrant an examination into how the U.S. has, through trial and lots of error, coped with the complexity of 50 distinct sets of local law, while developing a federal regulatory system that provides the investor protections required to encourage capital formation yet still allowing room for the corporate flexibility needed for entrepreneurial activity.

Of course, the European experience is different from the U.S. experience in many ways, and there exists within Europe impediments to convergence and harmonization that the U.S. system has not had to face. It is much easier, for example, to talk about different state rules on takeovers and shareholder rights, and different state court interpretations of these rules, when a consensus already exists on the objective of the corporation and to whom it is held accountable. And ultimately, in the U.S., the political will to achieve harmonization can be found when the circumstances are right, as demonstrated by the very quick adoption in 2002 of the Sarbanes-Oxley Act, the first broad federal law passed to regulate corporate governance since the 1930s.

I hope that Europe will find the political will to achieve consensus in these turbulent times, including agreement on foreign policy. As I pointed out in my remarks at this conference last year, the lack of foreign policy consensus has economic ramifications. I noted that the threat of terrorism is not just an American issue, but it is a European issue, as well. As an American living in post–9/11 New York City, my heart goes out to the Spanish people and the families and loved ones who were the recent victims of terrorism. But the effects are felt far beyond Madrid. The tension across the continent is evident as governments become more introspective as they reexamine their own security measures and attempt to insure safety for their citizenry. None of this, of course, stimulates international trade or promotes commerce.

Putting aside the political considerations which, in my view, are themselves compelling, extending the zone of stability in Europe through EU enlargement offers the promise to increase the financial and economic strength of the entire region and, by extension, the world. The financial and economic considerations notwithstanding, inclusion is also necessary to realize the purpose of the EU—to heal European divisions through an "even closer union" of peoples. I know that EU expansion brings with it the inevitable tensions of adjustment—but it also promises tremendous opportunities for prosperity, democracy, and peace.

When I walk the streets or meet with business leaders in Warsaw, Budapest, and Prague, I am amazed at the transformation that has taken place in the 13 years since we opened our first European offices there. So much has progressed in such a short period of time. It is truly an economic miracle and is a remarkable testament to the vision and determination of these peoples. While there is still a long way to go, and there is no shortage of challenges along the way, I am convinced that their accession to the EU, as well as the accession of the other member-elect states, will advance that transformation further—and perhaps provide a lesson or two for the original member states and even the rest of the world.

Thank you.

The United States of Europe

The New Superpower and the End of American Supremacy

T. R. Reid

Washington Post's *Rocky Mountain bureau chief; majored in classics, Princeton University, subsequently working as a teacher, naval officer during the Vietnam War, and lawyer; Tokyo bureau chief,* Washington Post, *1990–95; head of* Washington Post's *London Bureau; columnist, Japanese newsweekly* Shukan Shincho; *has hosted films for* National Geographic TV *and for the A&E network; regular commentator, National Public Radio's "Morning Edition"; visiting professor, Colorado College and the University of Michigan; board member of several community organizations and schools; author,* The Chip: How Two Americans Invented the Microchip and Launched a Revolution *(1984);* Confucius Lives Next Door: What Living in the East Teaches Us about Living in the West *(1999);* The United States of Europe: The New Superpower and the End of American Supremacy *(2004); translated one book from Japanese.*

Editors' introduction: Mr. Reid spoke to persons attending the "Books for Breakfast" program sponsored by the Carnegie Council on Ethics and International Affairs. He talked about his new book, *The United States of Europe: The New Superpower and the End of American Supremacy*, which had made the *New York Times* best seller list the week of his presentation. A "big crowd" attended the session, including the EU ambassador to the United Nations and several other European diplomats. Mr. Reid reported, "I think the Americans in the audience were interested in the changes that have swept Europe since the end of World War II; the Europeans in the audience were interested to hear what an American reporter had to say about those changes. . . . I write these books and give these speeches to get a dialogue going." The discussion took place at the upper east side townhouse called the Merrill House, which houses the Carnegie Council on Ethics.

T. R. Reid's speech: Good morning, everybody. Thanks for coming. My publisher paid for this trip, so I feel obliged to point out that my book makes great Christmas giving. Solve all your problems right there.

It's really fantastic for me to come to this lovely house, Carnegie Council in New York City. I'm from Colorado. This is quite exciting for me. I'm just delighted about two things. I'm delighted that so many people came out on a December morning in New York to hear

---

Delivered on December 8, 2004, at Merrill House in New York City. Reprinted by permission of T. R. Reid.

a talk about the European Union; and I'm delighted that the Carnegie Council exists, that this organization is here, because just your existence disproves one of the, I think, vicious stereotypes about our country in Europe, and this is the sense, the very strong sense, in Europe that Americans are insular, that we're ignorant of and indifferent to the rest of the world.

You know, they constantly think we don't know languages, we only care about the United States—I was on the BBC once and the guy said, "Oh yeah, you Americans with your World Series, where only two countries are allowed to play," that kind of thing—you know, the way Americans speak French is they say it in English only louder. You've heard all this kind of thing.

I dealt with this kind of notion—I think it's baloney myself—that America is insular, all over Europe in debates, TV shows, radio shows, and academic forums. One day I went to the Oxford Union, this great debating society at Oxford University, where the two sides make the argument and then the students vote.

The resolution was: "Resolved, this house condemns the ignorance of the United States of America." Gwynn Davies from the State Department and I were asked to come in and argue—what do you argue? "No, we're not ignorant," that's what I wanted to say.

We walked into the Oxford Union and were met by this kid who's the president of the Oxford Union, which means in about 25 years he'll be Prime Minister, if you look at their history. He was a very nice kid. He said, "Thank you so much for coming. I just want to tell you your side is going to lose." The kids at Oxford knew we were ignorant.

How do you deal with this? You know, that's a pretty bawdy, raucous organization. "Resolved, this house condemns the ignorance of the United States of America." We're insular, we don't know any languages, we don't know anything about the rest of the world.

Well, there are two arguments. To me the most tempting one is: "Oh yeah? Well, if we're so stupid, how come we're the richest, most powerful country in history?" The kids didn't like that. So then I tried facts—you know, "What do you mean we don't know languages? Do you know there are 125,000 American citizens whose first language in the home is Cambodian; there are three newspapers in the United States published in Polish with a circulation of half-a-million apiece? I don't think there are 500 people in all of Britain who speak Polish and not 25 who speak Cambodian," says I.

My opponent was George Galloway, a leftie member of Parliament. He was not impressed. He stood up and said, "Yeah, they have Cambodian speakers, but they imported them. That's cheating."

As a reporter, I thought my job was to tell Americans we should see ourselves as other see us. We need to know this, so I spent a lot of time when we lived in Europe tracing this America bashing. It's a great national pastime. They really like it. So I watched a lot of TV, I read a lot of crummy books and articles, I went to many academic seminars where they bashed our country.

A lot of it was drek, let's face it. But occasionally I saw some very good theater, including the hottest play for the last two years on the West End in London. Perhaps some of you have seen it. This is *Jerry Springer, the Opera.* Do you know this? I think it's coming to New York. This is kind of an acid test of our will to laugh at ourselves.

Jerry Springer, the Opera started in the National Theater on the South Bank. It's about as establishment as you can get. Like many successful plays there, it then moved to the West End. If you go to London, you have to tell the concierge the first minute you arrive that you want this ticket. It's a very tough ticket to get.

I scored this ticket. *Jerry Springer, the Opera* has two jokes basically. First of all, the poster for this thing explains it all. It says: "All the elements of grand opera—triumph, tragedy, trailer park trash." That's what they're doing. They're doing a *Jerry Springer Show* with all the paraphernalia of grand opera. They have a chorus, they have septets, they have duets, they have big arias.

At one point, the lead soprano, who is an American named Peaches, steps to the front of the stage, and the orchestra is going "oom pah pah, oom pah," and you can see this is going to be the big aria of the night, and her aria is "My stepbrother's girlfriend used to be my dad," which is right out of *Springer* if you think about it. You get this joke. It gets old fairly quick, but it's pretty good for a while.

And then the second joke in *Jerry Springer, the Opera,* is they have gathered every stereotype that Europeans love about our country. So every American in this play is incredibly fat; everybody is hauling a gun, and they tend to pull it out when they get mad; everybody has a lawyer standing behind them who's taking down notes and hoping somebody spills coffee. That's the big joke, "Spill coffee on me, I'll get rich" kind of thing. And if this isn't bad enough, at the end of the first act, the Ku Klux Klan dances on the stage, with their pointed hats and their white robes, and they burn a cross right on the stage—you know, this "typical day in America" kind of thing.

It's funny, but it's debilitating, it's wearing, for an American to watch this. I was sitting next to this very nice British woman who got the ticket that morning from her next-door neighbor. I think she thought she was coming to a real opera, and she was kind of dumbfounded. I was kind of dumbfounded. I turned to her and said, "You know, our country really isn't like that." And she said, "Oh don't worry, dahling. Look on the bright side. At least it's providing employment for a lot of really fat opera singers."

Anyway, my point is they think we're insular, they think we don't know the rest of the world. Everybody loves stereotypes. We have stereotypes about the French, the Irish, the Poles, and they have their stereotypes about us, which I think are largely wrong.

On the other hand, I do want to point out that I think the Europeans understand—even the most lefty America-bashing Frenchman understands—the large virtues of our country. I think they really sense our openness to innovation, the way we've opened our arms to new ideas, new products—we love them—and new people from all over the world. I think they really get that. I think they really admire the youthful vigor of our country and our willingness to take on any challenge, the sense that "we can do it." I think they like that. I think those virtues are not as strong in Europe. They're there, but not as strong as they are here.

And when you talk to everybody in Europe—particularly in the eastern half of Europe—everybody has a cousin or a grandson or a neighbor who has emigrated to Tallahassee or Portland or Denver or something. One thing they really like is (a) we take these people in, we let them become American citizens; and then when they do become American citizens, we have a big ceremony with a judge or a senator to give a speech and say, "Hey, welcome to the family."

I think it's fair to say that Europe is more united today than at any time since the Roman Empire.

This doesn't happen in Europe. You know, you can become a citizen of a European country, and here's how you do it, at least in Britain here's how you do it: you go up to the ninth floor of the municipal building, you hand over 50 Euros as your tax, a guy stamps a piece of paper, and you're in. That's it. So they really don't have the notion of the grandeur of becoming a member of the national family that we have.

May I just say the Europeans also feel dissed by us. They don't feel that we understand one very important fact of Europe, which is why I wrote my book really, and that is that they have pulled off in the last half-century, and particularly in the last 10 years or so, a crucially important geopolitical revolution; they really have come together. I think it's fair to say that Europe is more united today than at any time since the Roman Empire.

You know this. Usually I can astonish American audiences by telling them this. I've got this group here today that already knows that Europe has a president, it has a parliament, it has a constitution, it has a Bill of Rights that applies to every citizen, every person on the continent. It has a court system that can overrule the highest courts of any member court. It can overrule the legislature.

While I was in Britain, the European Court of Human Rights ordered the British to allow homosexuals in their military, which the Brits had been arguing about for 30 years and had never been able to do. What really astonished me was the next morning the Brits did it—"Okay, a court in France told us we have to do it, we'll do it," because they signed up to the European Convention on Human Rights and they're going to live by it. Well, actually it's the Brits who wrote the European Convention on Human Rights, so they should.

Europe has a flag, it has a national anthem, it has a pretty much standardized passport. Border controls are basically gone. Last fall I drove from the Arctic Circle to the Mediterranean, going through eight countries. I never changed currency, I never got anything stamped in my passport. This kind of ticked me off. I always liked getting all those visas stamped in my passport. It's like driving from New York to North Carolina, very similar.

I had teen-agers in Europe so I pay a lot of attention to pop culture. I argue in the book quite strenuously that I think there's a single European culture emerging. It's very strong. They have a single sport and single hero—that's of course David Beckham of Real Madrid, who is huge all over the world, bigger than Michael Jordan, bigger than Tiger Woods I'd say.

I think there is clearly emerging a common language of Europe. The French don't like this, but it's English. The language of European T-shirts, baseball caps, brand names, bumper stickers, posters, is English.

You know, Belgium is a country with three official languages, French, German, and Flemish, depending on what part you're in. But you go into a post office in Belgium and they have the slogan of the Belgian Postal Service on the wall. You know what it is? "Belgian Stamps Are Cool." My argument is that a common language is emerging.

And this common culture is strongest among the younger cohort. These are people aged 15 to 40, who are known as "Generation E." Generation E are young professionals, college graduates, who are workers. They may live in Edinburgh or Toledo or Tallinn, and they are Scots and Spaniards and Estonians, but they're Europeans. You talk to a Scot and say, "What are you? Are you British?" "Oh no, mate. A Scot today is a European who lives in Scotland or a Scot who lives in Europe." That's what they'll tell you. I think this feeling is very strong.

And I think that sense, sometimes called "a single European home," reflects the reason that Europe came together, which of course, as we said, is they decided that they had no choice but to reorganize their ancient continent. In my book I say this is fairly inspiring. It's a noble motivation.

You know, they had three brutal wars, from the Franco-Prussian War through World War II. It depends on which historian you ask: 60 or 70 million Europeans were killed in these three wars. Every 30 years they had a brutal war on the continent. In the total rubble after World War II, a group of visionaries decided they'd better do something or they would do it again. Many of these people were Catholics driven by a moral imperative to end war, because you could look at Europe, with the Iron Curtain coming down, the countries were rebuilding their military before they rebuilt their cities, and you could see another brutal, lethal war coming to Europe. A group of visionaries said, "No. We've got to reorganize. We've got to find some new way."

One of the leaders of this movement was Winston Churchill. I'm sure you know this, that Churchill single-handedly galvanized the British and the British Empire to fight Hitler at a time when all of Europe had fallen to the Nazis. You know, the Nazis were bombing civilian neighborhoods in London every night while we still had an Ambassador in Berlin sipping champagne with Goebbels and Hitler. We were neutral. Churchill galvanized the world to fight. He was 70 years old. He had three or four hours' sleep for seven years. This was the hardest-working man in the world. On May 8th of 1945, VE Day, he won, the Nazis surrendered, and the war was over in Europe.

You all know how the British people thanked him. Three weeks later, there was a national election and they dumped him. His wife Winnifred looked at him, and he was just a shell, he was 70 years old, he was sick as a dog, he hadn't slept in years. She said, "Well, Win, maybe it's a blessing in disguise." Churchill of course said, "Well, at the moment it's bloody well disguised."

I became friendly in London with a wonderful guy, a Conservative Member of Parliament, Nicholas Soames, and Nick Soames is Winston Churchill's grandson. In 1946, when he was a young kid, Nick Soames was living in Chartwell, Winston Churchill's home, and he had been ordered never go in granddad's study because granddad was in there thinking big thoughts. You know, he wasn't running the country anymore so he had big thoughts.

One day Nick Soames was playing with his toys on the floor and on the radio, he heard the BBC announcer say something totally astonishing: "Winston Churchill is the greatest man in the world." It totally blew him away.

So he broke the rule. He ran into his granddad's study and said, "Grandpapa, is it true? Are you the greatest man in the world?" Churchill said, "Of course. Now bugger off," because he was thinking, as he described it, about the future of Europe.

We know that in 1946 Churchill gave two famous speeches about the state of Europe. One was in Fulton, Missouri: "An iron curtain has fallen across the continent." But the speech that the Europeans know better is one he gave in Zurich three months later in which he said, "I want to speak to you today about the tragedy of Europe," and he said, "We've had these three brutal wars and we're going to do it again. Anybody can look and see we're going to do it again unless we reorganize our ancient continent, and the model is going to be the great republic across the shining sea."

You know how Churchill talked; he was quite eloquent. He said, "We have to build a sort of United States of Europe." In a war-torn, ravaged, fearful continent, that notion just caught on like wildfire. It caught on with me too, as you can see; that's what I named my book "The United States of Europe."

I argue in the book one of the amazing things about this is that it worked. They have had internal civil wars in Europe, they've had some problems with internal terrorism, but in 60 years there hasn't been a war between European nations, and there is not going to be. I think anybody can see that. You go to the continent, you drive through eight countries without a border guard, you talk English to everybody, you see the same songs on the same European MTV everywhere you go. There is not going to be another war. This continent is now too organized and too unified. It really worked. So that to me is a noble motivation for forming a new kind of union in Europe and an admirable result.

But I argue in my book there was also a somewhat less noble motivation for this—you know, the basics: power, greed, money, or other reasons—because if it's 1946 or 1947 and you're a Spaniard or a Hollander or French or British, the world has kind of caved in on you. Until then, these countries ran the world. They had global empires. They had the biggest economies. Now the age of empire is coming to an end, their economy and their infrastructure is total rubble, and suddenly these great world leaders are kind of minor planets orbiting around a very bright American sun, and they had to do something.

> ### *There is not going to be another war. This continent is now too organized and too unified.*

I think any intelligent person could see that Britain, Italy, even Germany and France, none of those countries was ever going to be able to challenge the political and financial power of the United States. But Britain, Italy, Germany, Hungary, Sweden, Spain, Portugal, Greece together, yes they could. I think this is a key motivator for the Europeans coming together. In European academic thought this is known as the "counterweight theory." They were going to build a counterweight to American power.

If you go to European summits—I made a big mistake when I was based in Europe for the *Washington Post*. I stupidly told my editors I was really interested in the European Union, I saw it as a great historic development. So they said, "Great, you can go to all the summits," because nobody else wanted to.

You know, the European summits are pretty boring. There's a bunch of prime ministers and every one of them comes up and says, "We're building a superpower. Look out, United States." I heard it over and over.

But I finally concluded it's true, they are doing this, they are building a force that can stand up to us. They have more money. They have more trade, as we said. Europeans now have so much trade they make most of the rules that govern world commerce. This goes from the fact that the Europeans forced Microsoft to rewrite Windows. Our own Justice Department failed at that, but they had the clout to do it.

Simple things. I personally drink Kentucky bourbon. I like bourbon. I think it's the quintessential American drink. I've drunk it everywhere I lived in the world. You go into a liquor store today to buy a bottle of bourbon, and it doesn't come in a pint or a quart. Have you noticed this? It's a 70-centiliter bottle. Now I ask you: do you think Americans stormed the liquor stores and demanded to drink their bourbon by the centiliter? No. The Europeans told them to do it, and Europe has that kind of power in the world.

You remember the last big legislation that passed Congress before the members went home for the election this fall was this new tax bill in which they repealed a 25-year-old tax subsidy that we had for American exporters. This is a very popular tax among American exporters. It probably helped with our balance of trade deficit, and nobody wanted to repeal it, except for Pascal Lamy, a Frenchman who's the European Commissioner for Trade.

Here's what he did. He went to the WTO, where Europe is a controlling force now because of its trade clout, and said that this tax subsidy for American exporting companies is illegal, it's a violation of WTO rules. He basically forced the WTO to impose tariffs on the United States, billions of dollars a month in tariffs.

Lamy was asked what he was doing. He said, "This is simple. The name of the game is to change U.S. law." This is a Frenchman telling us to change our law.

The Speaker of the House, Dennis Hastert, responded I think exactly correctly. Here's what he said, quote: "My gut feeling about this is that we fought a revolution 230 years ago to stop Europeans from telling us what taxes to pass in this [country]." And then Hastert goes on in this same speech on the floor, the House floor, and I'm quoting: "But the fact is we have to do it. The EU and the WTO have a sword to our heads. We don't like it, but we have to do what the Europeans are telling us to do."

And they did it; they eliminated this tax subsidy. Now, it seems to me if Europe has the clout in the world to make us make expensive changes at great cost that we don't want to do to our laws, that's power. That's my argument.

Now, I've been traveling the country talking about this. Fortunately for me, people are buying my book. I called my friends in Europe and said, "See, we're not insular. People are buying books about the EU. That's pretty good." They still say, "No, no, you're ignorant." They don't buy my argument.

But Americans have said to me, "What do I care? It's nice if they found an alternative to war. It's good that they filled a big market over there. It's a bigger market than the United States or Japan. This is a very good thing for American companies. If you make your product or get your product into any of the 25 EU countries, it can go everywhere without any tariff, any border control. I think it's a good thing for American tourists. Don't you feel traveling in Europe is just easier today? No border controls. You really don't have to worry."

In my house I've got a house full of junk that I have picked up at airports because I'm leaving Lisbon and I'm going to use the last of my escudos. When am I going to use them again? You know, I've got a house full of junk from the Lisbon airport and Schiphol in Amsterdam. Now when you leave Lisbon you're going to take those Euros to Berlin with you, or Helsinki, and use them. So I think in many ways it's a better deal.

But I always say to Americans: "Look, if you don't think this matters, here's what I want you to do. Place a call to Boston to a guy named Jack Welch." Jack Welch is the legendary CEO of General Electric, a great corporate leader, brilliant, studied in business schools all over the world. After 20 years of running GE very successfully, Welch announced just before his retirement that he had one more great achievement to do, one more great contribution to American industry and to GE's stockholders, and that was he was going to buy Honeywell, another great industrial titan. This was the biggest industrial merger in history, a $45 billion merger. Nobody tried something this big. There had been financial mergers this size, but nothing on this scale in the industrial world.

Jack Welch is so persuasive and his timing is so good, he just happened to do this two months after a Republican administration took over in Washington, and that merger just sailed through our Justice Department. The Antitrust Division stamped it clean, just like that.

And while they were popping the corks up at GE headquarters, somebody said, "By the way, Jack, you have to go to Brussels and meet an Italian named Mario Monti."

"Oh, what's an Italian doing in Brussels?" "Well, he happens to be the antitrust czar for 25 European countries, the biggest market in the world."

So Welch goes over, he gets on the plane with his phalanx of high-paid antitrust lawyers—maybe some of them are in this room, I don't know—and they're thinking strategy, and they decide that their strongest weapon is Jack Welch himself. He's so smart and so persuasive and so likeable, the best thing is to send him in alone to make the pitch to Mario Monti.

So they go to a restaurant in Brussels, and Welch—charming guy, very American, charming, casual—walks in and he says, "Mario, call me Jack." Monti says, "Mr. Welch, we have a regulatory proceeding underway. I feel it would be more appropriate if you referred to me as Signor Monti." Right then he knew he had a problem.

In my book I describe in great detail how GE and the Bush Administration totally botched the negotiations with the EU. They never understood the ambitions, the drive, of the EU, Mario Monti's need to be an antitrust power independent of Washington, to make his own rules, and to impose those rules on the world.

In the end, Mario Monti called Welch one day in his suite in Brussels and said, "Jack, you can now call me Mario, because the transaction's over. In two weeks at the European Commission meeting"—that's their cabinet, the European Commission—"I'm going to recommend that we reject this merger."

Okay, so it's over. So Welch lost. But no, Jack Welch is not a quitter. He has never been a quitter. That's why he was so successful. So he hangs up the phone and immediately calls the White House Chief of Staff, Andrew Card, and says, "They can't do this. This is a company in Connecticut buying a company in New Jersey and some Italian in Belgium is telling us no."

And sure enough, George W. Bush got on the phone to several European prime ministers and said, "This is wrong. You can't do this." Completely wrong thing to do, the worst blunder of the whole deal, because the last thing this proud, strong, rich European Union wants is to have some swaggering guy in Washington telling them what to do. It's not going to work.

In my book I list many other occasions where the Bush Administration and the Clinton Administration failed to figure this out. They just didn't understand how to deal with Europe because they don't understand the drive there, the counterweight theory.

Anyway, when the thing did come up for vote, they didn't even debate it. That merger went down 20-to-0 in the cabinet, and it was easy. I mean the European cabinet ministers were showing backbone, which is quite easy. If you're sticking it to two American companies, why not?

So Jack Welch had to come home to his Board and say, "I'm sorry, we spent a year's time on this, a lot of money and effort, and we have nothing to show for it." It ended his career with a humiliating failure.

I argue in the book that this completely turned around the business press, which had always been great cheerleaders for Jack Welch. That's how we reporters are—you know, we switch on a moment. And then Jack Welch became the poster child for corporate excess. As you know, his marriage fell apart. None of which has a lot to do with the EU, but it's so interesting I threw it all in the book anyway.

And here's my key point—are you ready? So he spent, according to members of the GE Board, about $50 million on antitrust lawyers working on this merger, maybe $30 million on investment bankers. They would have paid more, but the bankers tend to charge you when the deal is done and the deal was never done. So he spent $75 or $80 million to learn the lesson about the drive and strength of the new Europe. For 25 bucks you can learn it from my book. We're talking a big bargain here.

So that's the short take. I feel that this audience knew all this, or knew much of it, but I've been traveling America talking about this, and it's very interesting to see the reaction. "You're kidding me" is usually the reaction. People don't know. Anyway, thank you so much.

Institut d'Études Politiques de Paris

Condoleezza Rice

U.S. Secretary of State, 2005– ; born Birmingham, AL, November 14, 1954; B.A. cum laude and Phi Beta Kappa, University of Denver, 1974; M.A. in political science, University of Notre Dame, 1975; Ph.D. in political science, University of Denver's Graduate School of International Studies, 1981; fellow in the arms control and disarmament program, Stanford University, 1981; assistant, associate, and professor of political science, Stanford University, 1981–99; national fellow, Hoover Institution, 1985–86; international affairs fellow of the Council on Foreign Relations and special assistant to the director of the Joint Chiefs of Staff, 1986; director and senior director of Soviet and East European Affairs in the National Security Council, 1989–91; senior fellow, Hoover Institution, 1991–93; provost, Stanford University, 1993–99; assistant to the president of the United States for National Security Affairs, 2001–05; National Endowment for the Humanities trustee; fellow of the American Academy of Arts and Sciences; honorary degrees from Morehouse College, 1991, University of Alabama, 1994, and University of Notre Dame, 1995; has written numerous articles and several books on international relations and foreign affairs, including Germany Unified and Europe Transformed: A Study in Statecraft *(1995).*

Editors' introduction: After earlier stops in Italy and Israel, in France Secretary of State Rice confronted both a government and a citizenry generally hostile to the United States' military initiatives in Iraq and to Secretary of Defense Donald H. Rumsfeld's depiction of an "old and new Europe." Speaking at the prestigious Institute for Political Studies in Paris, where dissension was high, Secretary Rice advised that "I am here . . . so that we can talk about how America and Europe can use the power of our partnership to advance our ideals worldwide." She concluded, "Our transatlantic partnership" is "strongest when we put our values to work for those whose aspirations of freedom and prosperity have yet to be met."

Condoleezza Rice's speech: Thank you very, very much. Thank you for those warm and welcoming words. And let me also thank the people of France for being such perfect hosts. I've just arrived. I wish I could stay longer. But it's such a wonderful city; it's wonderful to be here. I look forward to my discussions here with President Chirac, with Foreign Minister Barnier, and with others. And—as a pianist—tomorrow I look forward to visiting one of your fine music schools.

It is a real special pleasure for me to be here at Sciences Po. For more than 130 years, this fine institution has trained thinkers and leaders. As a political scientist myself, I appreciate very much the important work that you do.

Delivered on February 8, 2005, at Paris, France.

The history of the United States and that of France are intertwined. Our history is a history of shared values, of shared sacrifice, and of shared successes. So, too, will be our shared future.

I remember well my first visit to Paris—here—my visit to Paris here in 1989, when I had the honor of accompanying President George Herbert Walker Bush to the bicentennial celebration of the French Revolution and the Declaration of the Rights of Man. Americans celebrated our own bicentennial in that same year, the 200th anniversary of our nation's Constitution and our Bill of Rights.

Those shared celebrations were more than mere coincidence. The founders of both the French and American republics were inspired by the very same values, and by each other. They shared the universal values of freedom and democracy and human dignity that have inspired men and women across the globe for centuries.

Standing up for liberty is as old as our country. It was our very first Secretary of State, Thomas Jefferson, who said, "The God who gave us life, gave us liberty at the same time." Now the American founders realized that they, like all human beings, are flawed creatures, and that any government established by man would be imperfect. Even the great authors of our liberty sometimes fell short of liberty's promise—even Jefferson, himself, a slave owner.

So we are fortunate that our founders established a democratic system of, by, and for the people that contained within it a way for citizens—especially for impatient patriots—to correct even its most serious flaws. Human imperfections do not discredit democratic ideals; they make them more precious, and they make impatient patriots of our own time work harder to achieve them.

Men and women, both great and humble, have shown us the power of human agency in this work. In my own experience, a black woman named Rosa Parks was just tired one day of being told to sit in the back of a bus, so she refused to move. And she touched off a revolution of freedom across the American South.

In Poland, Lech Walesa had had enough of the lies and the exploitation, so he climbed a wall and he joined a strike for his rights; and Poland was transformed.

In Afghanistan just a few months ago, men and women, once oppressed by the Taliban, walked miles, forded streams, and stood hours in the snow just to cast a ballot for their first vote as a free people.

And just a few days ago in Iraq, millions of Iraqi men and women defied the terrorist threats and delivered a clarion call for freedom. Individual Iraqis risked their lives. One policeman threw his body on a suicide bomber to preserve the right of his fellow citizens to vote. They cast their free votes, and they began their nation's new history.

These examples demonstrate a basic truth—the truth that human dignity is embodied in the free choice of individuals.

We witnessed the power of that truth in that remarkable year of 1989 when the Berlin Wall was brought down by ordinary men and women in East Germany. Yet, that day of freedom in November 1989 could never have happened without the full support of the free nations of the West.

Time and again in our shared history, Americans and Europeans have enjoyed our greatest successes, for ourselves and for others, when we refused to accept an unacceptable status quo—but instead, put our values to work in the service of freedom.

And we have achieved much together. Today, a democratic Germany is unified within NATO, and tyranny no longer stalks the heart of Europe. NATO and the European Union have since welcomed Europe's newest democracies into our ranks; and we have used our growing strength for peace. And just a decade ago, Southeastern Europe was aflame. Today, we are working toward lasting reconciliation in the Balkans, and to fully integrate the Balkans into the European mainstream.

These achievements have only been possible because America and Europe have stood firm in the belief that the fundamental character of regimes cannot be separated from their external behavior. Borders between countries cannot be peaceful if tyrants destroy the peace of their societies from within. States where corruption, and chaos and cruelty reign invariably pose threats to their neighbors, threats to their regions, and potential threats to the entire international community.

Our work together has only begun. In our time we have an historic opportunity to shape a global balance of power that favors freedom—and that will therefore deepen and extend the peace. And I use the word "power" broadly, because even more important than military and indeed economic power is the power of ideas, the power of compassion, and the power of hope.

I am here in Europe so that we can talk about how America and Europe can use the power of our partnership to advance our ideals worldwide. President Bush will continue our conversation when he arrives in Europe on February 21st. He is determined to strengthen transatlantic ties. As the President said in his recent Inaugural Address: "All that we seek to achieve in the world requires that America and Europe remain close partners."

I believe that our greatest achievements are yet to come. The challenges of a post–September 11 world are no less daunting than those challenges that we faced and that our forebears faced in the Cold War. The same bold vision, moral courage, and determined leadership will be required if we are again to prevail over repression and intimidation and intolerance.

Our charge is clear: We on the right side of freedom's divide have an obligation to help those unlucky enough to have been born on the wrong side of that divide.

This obligation requires us to adapt to new circumstances—and we are doing that. NATO has enlarged not only its membership, but its vision. The Organization for Security and Cooperation in Europe now operates not only on a continent whole, free, and at peace, but beyond Europe, as well. The agenda of U.S.–EU cooperation is wider than ever, and still growing, along with the European Union itself.

We agree on the interwoven threats we face today: Terrorism, and proliferation of weapons of mass destruction, and regional conflicts, and failed states and organized crime.

We have not always seen eye to eye, however, on how to address these threats. We have had our disagreements. But it is time to turn away from the disagreements of the past. It is time to open a new chapter in our relationship, and a new chapter in our alliance.

America stands ready to work with Europe on our common agenda—and Europe must stand ready to work with America. After all, history will surely judge us not by our old disagreements, but by our new achievements.

America stands ready to work with Europe on our common agenda—and Europe must stand ready to work with America.

The key to our future success lies in getting beyond a partner based on common threats, and building an even stronger partnership based on common opportunities, even those beyond the transatlantic community.

We can be confident of our success in this because the fair wind of freedom is at our back. Freedom is spreading: From the villages of Afghanistan to the squares in Ukraine, from the streets in the Palestinian territories to the streets of Georgia, to the polling stations of Iraq.

Freedom defines our opportunity and our challenge. It is a challenge that we are determined to meet.

First, we are joining together to encourage political pluralism, economic openness, and the growth of civil society through the broader Middle East initiative.

The flagship of that initiative is the Forum for the Future—a partnership of progress between the democratic world and nearly two-dozen nations, extending from Morocco to Pakistan. The Forum's mission is to support and accelerate political, economic, and educational reform. Its first meeting in Rabat last December was a great success.

Beyond this bold initiative for reform, in which America and European efforts are fused, we also work in parallel. The European Union has a decade-long experience with advancing modernization through the Barcelona Process.

Individual EU member-states have also been working for years to nurture the attitudes and institutions of liberal democracy in the Arab and Muslim worlds.

And it is not just our governments that are promoting freedom. American- and European-based non-governmental organizations devote huge efforts to the reform process.

Our people exemplify the values of free society as they work in their private capacities. Our societies, not just our governments, are advancing women's rights and minority rights.

Our societies, not just our governments, are making space for free media, for independent judiciaries, for the right of labor to organize. The full vitality of our free societies is infusing the process of reform, and that is a reason for optimism.

Just as our own democratic paths have not always been smooth, we realize that democratic reform in the Middle East will be difficult and uneven. Different societies will advance in their own way. Freedom, by its very nature, must be homegrown. It must be chosen. It cannot be given; and it certainly cannot be imposed. That is why, as the President has said, the spread of freedom is the work of generations. But spreading freedom in the Arab and Muslim worlds is also urgent work that cannot be deferred.

Second, we must build on recent successes by stabilizing and advancing democratic progress in Afghanistan and in Iraq. Last October, the people of Afghanistan voted to set their country on a democratic course. And just nine days ago, the people of Iraq voted not just for a government, but for a democratic future.

All of us were impressed by the high voter turnout in Iraq. Each ink-stained finger belonged to a man or a woman who defied suicide bombers, mortar attacks, and threats of beheading, to exercise a basic right as a citizen.

There comes a time in the life of every nation where its people refuse to accept a status quo that demeans their basic humanity. There comes a time when people take control of their own lives. For the Iraqi people, that time has come.

There is much more to do to create a democratic and unified Iraq; and the Iraqis themselves must lead the way. But we in the transatlantic partnership must rise to the challenge that the Iraqi people have set for us.

They have shown extraordinary bravery and determination. We must show them solidarity and generosity in equal measure.

We must support them as they form their political institutions. We must help them with economic reconstruction and development. And we must stay by their side to provide security until Iraqis themselves can take full ownership of that job.

Third, we are working to achieve new successes, particularly in the Arab-Israeli diplomacy. America and Europe both support a two-state solution: An independent and democratic Palestinian state living side by side in peace with the Jewish State of Israel.

And we all support the process of reform in the Palestinian Authority, because democratic reform will enlarge the basis for a genuine peace. That is why we were supportive of the Palestinian people in their historic election on January 9.

And Europe and America support the Israeli Government's determination to withdraw from Gaza and parts of the West Bank. We both see that withdrawal as an opportunity to move ahead—first to the roadmap, and ultimately, to our own—to our clear destination: a genuine and real peace.

We are acting to transform opportunity into achievement. I have just come from meetings with Prime Minister Sharon and President Abbas. I was impressed with the fact that they said the same thing: This is a time of opportunity and we must not lose it. I urged them to build on this momentum, to seize this chance. And today's meeting of the Palestinian and Egyptian Presidents, the Israeli Prime Minister, and Jordan's King was clearly an important step forward.

The United States and the parties have no illusions about the difficulties ahead. There are deep divisions to overcome. I emphasized to both sides the need to end terrorism; the need to build new and democratic Palestinian economic, political, and security institutions; the need for Israel to meet its own obligations and make the difficult choices before it; and, the need for all of us—in America, in Europe, in the region—to make clear to Iran and Syria that they must stop supporting the terrorists who would seek to destroy the peace that we seek.

Success is not assured, but America is resolute. This is the best chance for peace that we are likely to see for some years to come; and we are acting to help Israelis and Palestinians seize this chance. President Bush is committed. I am personally committed. We must all be committed to seizing this chance.

Next month in London, Prime Minister Tony Blair will convene an important conference to help the Palestinian people advance democratic reform and build their institutions. All of us support that effort.

And we will continue to share burdens that will one day soon, we hope, enable us to share in the blessings of peace between Israelis and Palestinians, between Israelis and all their Arab neighbors.

A G8-Arab League meeting will also convene in Cairo next month. This meeting has the potential to broaden the base of support for Middle East peace and democracy. The Tunis Declaration of this past May's Arab Summit declared the "firm resolve" of the Arab states to "keep pace with the accelerated world changes through the consolidation of democratic practice, the broadening of participation in political life and public life, and the reinforcement of all components of civil society."

If that resolve forms the basis of Arab participation in this meeting, only good can come from it.

Our efforts in Lebanon also show that the transatlantic partnership means what it says in supporting freedom. The United States and France, together, sponsored UN Security Council Resolution 1559. We have done this to accelerate international efforts to restore full sovereignty to the Lebanese people, and to make possible the complete return of what was once vibrant political life in that country.

The next step in that process should be the fourth free democratic election in the region—fair and competitive parliamentary elections this spring, without foreign interference.

In Lebanon and in the Palestinian territories, in Afghanistan and in Iraq, and throughout all of the broader Middle East and North Africa, the nature of the political conversation is changing. Ordinary citizens are expressing thoughts and acting together in ways that they have not done before. These citizens want a future of tolerance, opportunity, and peace—not of repression.

Wise leaders are opening their arms to embrace reform. And we must stand with them and their societies as they search for a democratic future.

Human freedom will march ahead, and we must help smooth its way.

Reformers and peacemakers will prevail in the Middle East for the same reason the West won the Cold War: Because liberty is ultimately stronger than repression and freedom is stronger than tyranny.

Today's radical Islamists are swimming against the tide of the human spirit. They grab the headlines with their ruthless brutality, and they can be brutal. But they are dwelling on the outer fringes of a great world religion; and they are radicals of a special sort. They are in revolt against the future. The face of terrorism in Iraq, Abu Musab al-Zarqawi, called democracy "an evil principle." To our enemies, *Liberté, Égalité,* and *Fraternité* are also evil principles. They want to dominate others, not to liberate them. They demand conformity, not equality. They still regard difference as a license to kill.

But they are wrong. Human freedom will march ahead, and we must help smooth its way. We can do that by helping societies to find their own way to fulfill the promise of freedom.

We can help aspiring societies to reduce poverty and grow economically through sound development strategies and free trade. We must be aggressive and compassionate in fighting the HIV/AIDS pandemic and other infectious diseases that tear families apart, destroy individuals, and make development of whole continents impossible.

Ultimately, we must learn how to put developing states on the path to self-sustained growth and stability. After all, it is one thing to fix a sanitation plant or to repair a schoolhouse; it is another to establish the essential components of a decent society: A free press, an independent judiciary, a sound financial system, political parties, and genuine representative government.

Development, transparency, and democracy reinforce each other. That is why the spread of freedom under the rule of law is our best hope for progress. Freedom unlocks the creativity and drive that produces genuine wealth. Freedom is the key to incorruptible institutions. Freedom is the key to responsive governments.

Ladies and Gentlemen, this is a time of unprecedented opportunity for the transatlantic Alliance. If we make the pursuit of global freedom the organizing principle of the 21st century, we will achieve historic global advances for justice and prosperity, for liberty, and for peace. But a global agenda requires a global partnership. So let us multiply our common effort.

That is why the United States, above all, welcomes the growing unity of Europe. America has everything to gain from having a stronger Europe as a partner in building a safer and better world. So let each of us bring to the table our ideas and our experience and our resources; and let us discuss and decide, together, how best to employ them for democratic change.

We know we have to deal with the world as it is. But, we do not have to accept the world as it is. Imagine where we would be today if the brave founders of French liberty or of American liberty had simply been content with the world as it was.

They knew that history does not just happen; it is made. History is made by men and women of conviction, of commitment, and of courage, who will not let their dreams be denied.

Our transatlantic partnership will not just endure in this struggle; it will flourish because our ties are unbreakable. We care deeply about one another. We respect each other. We are strong, but we are strongest when we put our values to work for those whose aspirations of freedom and prosperity have yet to be met.

Great opportunities await us. Let us seize them, now, together, for freedom's sake.

Thank you for your attention.

(Applause.)

CSIS Conference on Transatlantic Efforts for Peace and Security on the Occasion of Norway's Centennial Anniversary

Richard G. Lugar

U.S. senator (R), Indiana, 1976– ; born Indianapolis, IN, April 4, 1932; graduated first in his class at Shortridge High School, Indianapolis; B.A. in economics, Denison University, Granville, OH, 1954; M.A. and Rhodes Scholar in politics, philosophy, and economics, Pembroke College at Oxford University, 1956; lieutenant, junior grade, U.S. Navy, 1957–60; vice president, Thomas L. Green and Company, Inc., 1960–67; Indianapolis School Board, 1964–67; mayor of Indianapolis, 1968–75; lecturer, Indiana Central University, 1976; professor, University of Indianapolis, 1976; assistant Republican whip, U.S. Senate, 1977–96; candidate for Republican presidential nominee, 1996; chair, Foreign Relations Committee, U.S. Senate; member and former chair, Agriculture, Nutrition, and Forestry Committee; manages family's 604-acre Marion County corn, soybean, and tree farm; awards: Guardian of Small Business; Spirit of Enterprise; Watchdog of the Treasury; and Outstanding Legislator by the American Political Science Association; 38 honorary doctorate degrees.

Editors' introduction: In the fall of 2002, while the U.S. Congress was authorizing President George W. Bush to use military force "to enforce the United Nations Security Council Resolutions" relating to Iraq, within U.N. Security Council debates, France and Germany were expressing their vehement opposition to military initiatives. With the fighting in Iraq continuing, Senator Lugar addressed delegates to a conference sponsored by the Center for Secure Information Systems (CSIS). Although concerned that "rhetoric emanating from both sides of the Atlantic has not helped the relationship" among members of the Transatlantic Alliance, Senator Lugar was "confident that the United States and Europe will work through these challenges." In recognizing the 100 years since the union between Norway and Sweden was dissolved peacefully, the Senator reminded the audience "of how important the Transatlantic Alliance is to our future."

Richard G. Lugar's speech: It is a pleasure to participate in this conference marking the centennial of Norway's founding and the beginning of the close Norwegian-American alliance. I thank CSIS and my good friends John Hamre and Ambassador Knut Vollebaek for this invitation to speak. Dr. Hamre and Ambassador Vollebaek

---

Delivered on March 4, 2005, at the Carnegie Endowment for International Peace, Washington, D.C.

have given generous support to the Senate Foreign Relations Committee and to myself during my chairmanship, and I am grateful for their wise counsel.

It is an especial honor to be with King Harald and Queen Sonja. Their visit to our country has been eagerly anticipated, especially by the many Americans of Norwegian descent who fondly embrace the homeland of their ancestors. We admire the graciousness and leadership of the royal couple. Our warmest wishes are with them and the Norwegian people as they celebrate Norway's centennial.

I also would like to acknowledge the outstanding work of Foreign Minister Petersen. I have had the pleasure to get to know him through several mutual endeavors during the last two years. I appreciate his strong advocacy on behalf of the Transatlantic Alliance and the energy and thoughtfulness that he has applied to leading Norway's ambitious foreign policy agenda.

At the heart of that agenda has been Norway's unwavering commitment to international service. Norway has been a model of global citizenship and peace-making. It has dedicated resources to achieving peace and development that are far beyond its relative size and population. It consistently ranks among the top nations in the percentage of GDP that it dedicates to foreign economic assistance. It is a generous contributor to international peacekeeping missions, and it has sponsored numerous peace negotiations, including those involving Israel and the Palestinians and the warring factions in Sri Lanka.

In Europe, Norway has been a leader in the vital effort to control weapons of mass destruction. Close to its borders it has devoted funds to dismantling deteriorating Russian submarines and to improving the safety of spent nuclear fuel. Norway initiated the important Arctic Military Environmental Cooperation Program, or AMEC, in which the United States, Russia, and Norway seek to address environmental problems associated with the decommissioning of Russia's nuclear submarine fleet. It is also taking the lead in removing and replacing Russia's vulnerable strontium-powered lighthouses in the Barents Sea region. These lighthouses contain radioactive material that could be used to construct dirty bombs. Far from its borders, Norway has contributed resources to the critical work of destroying Russia's massive stockpiles of chemical weapons at Shchuchye, Russia. Norway was the first non-member of the G-8 to join the Global Partnership Against the Spread of Weapons of Mass Destruction—also known as the "10 Plus 10 over 10 initiative."

This short list only scratches the surface of Norway's activism. As we contemplate the future of the Transatlantic Alliance, it is useful to observe how Norway has maintained its strong commitment to the Alliance, while still asserting itself on independent projects and goals around the world.

During the last three years, the alliance between Europe and the United States has experienced severe strains that have caused many commentators to question whether it can survive and, if it does survive, whether it will remain relevant. These are fair questions, but we should resist the impulse to believe that our current differences have no precedent. We should recall, for example, the consuming public debate that occurred in Europe and the United States during the early 1980s over the deployment of intermediate nuclear forces in Europe. The NATO allies had made the collective decision to deploy these weapons in response to the Soviet deployment of SS-20 intermediate missiles aimed at targets throughout Western Europe. But this decision produced conflict in the U.S.–European relationship. Anti-nuclear demonstrations occurred frequently across Europe. On one day in 1983, protests in Europe collectively drew more than two million people. Throughout this difficult period, there was much debate about whether the Transatlantic Alliance would be damaged. But the Western allies maintained their cohesion, and, ultimately, the collapse of the Soviet Union ended the Cold War.

The roles played by Europe and the United States in the world have led to different priorities on some important issues.

The lesson in this historic reflection is not that our alliance will automatically bounce back after periodic internal conflicts. Rather, the lesson is that maintaining an alliance is hard work. No matter how close allies become, centrifugal forces generated by basic differences in the size, location, wealth, histories, and political systems of nations tend to pull alliances apart. Alliances work over long periods of time only when alliance leaders and citizens continually reinvigorate the union and its purposes.

Unfortunately, rhetoric emanating from both sides of the Atlantic has not helped the relationship during the last several years. Some politicians and members of the media in Europe and the United States have promoted caricatures and oversimplifications that appeal to the resentments and prejudices of their electorates. But we must be honest with ourselves that our differences are not merely the result of unfortunate rhetoric. The roles played by Europe and the United States in the world have led to different priorities on some important issues. The alliance will be healthier if we recognize these differences and honestly debate them.

During the last two years, the war in Iraq has been the focal point of these differences. In the United States, the debate that preceded the Iraq war in early 2003 centered on the question of whether the United States should make concessions to world opinion or pursue its perceived national security interests unencumbered by the constraints of the international community. But this was a false choice.

National security decision-making can rarely be separated from the constraints of the international community, because American resources and influence are finite.

Meanwhile, European governments have been slow to acknowledge that notwithstanding anti-American public opinion in Europe, their nations have the same interest as the United States in ensuring that Iraq becomes a stable democratic country that can be a catalyst for positive change in the Middle East.

I am confident that the United States and Europe will work through these challenges. The recent visits to Europe by Secretary of State Rice and President Bush underscored the enduring mutual interests of the alliance and the common bonds of history, culture, and devotion to democratic freedom. We should never forget that the Transatlantic Alliance was founded to defend freedom. At its most fundamental level, the advancement of freedom still should be the core mission of the alliance.

Last November, President Bush asked me to lead the delegation of American observers to the Ukrainian elections. I was inspired by the courage of so many Ukrainians who demonstrated their passion for free expression and democracy. As corrupt authorities tried to disrupt the election and intimidate citizens, brave people pushed back by keeping the election on track and preventing chaos.

On the way home, I stopped in Germany, where I met with Chancellor Gerhard Schroeder. He asked for my opinion on how the Transatlantic Alliance could be reinvigorated. I told him that the answer could be found in Ukraine, Georgia, and other nations that were struggling to establish democracy. The people of Ukraine and Georgia have responded heroically to the hope and justice embodied in fair elections, a free press, free market economics, religious tolerance, and civil liberties. They also want to join a Europe that is whole and free.

Nascent democracies will succeed more readily if they have help from the West. More precisely, they need coordinated help from the West. They need a unified Transatlantic Alliance that can provide a grassroots support system for democracy. Such a system depends on the resources and expertise that can be provided by the entire alliance. In addition, people who are embracing freedom with the hope of gaining the security and economic benefits that come with membership in the democratic club want to see that club unified and strong. The encouragement and inspiration that we can provide is much greater when we demonstrate that the alliance can overcome its internal problems.

Alliance members must understand that the creation and nurturing of new democracies is not a charitable cause. The security of our alliance depends as much on their success as they depend on us. Ultimately, without the advancement of democracy in Eastern Europe, the Caucuses, Russia, Central Asia, the Middle East, and beyond, we will have a very difficult time winning the war against terrorism, maintaining economic stability, ensuring adequate energy supplies, and protecting the global environment. We must expand the community of nations that will be dedicated to global action on these fronts. This means expanding democracy, which empowers people, restrains would-be dictators, and opens nations to cooperation on a range of urgent problems.

The most important of these problems, in my view, is the proliferation of weapons of mass destruction. Along with democracy building, the Transatlantic Alliance must be devoted to the painstaking work of controlling these weapons. Even if we succeed spectacularly at building democracy around the world, bringing stability to failed states, and spreading economic opportunity broadly, we will not be secure from the actions of small, disaffected groups that acquire weapons of mass destruction. Everything is at risk if we fail in this one area.

In the first half of the 20th century, the goal of most disarmament efforts was to prevent war between nations by balancing armaments so that aggressors did not have an advantage. During the Cold War, in the era of Mutual Assured Destruction, arms control often had more narrow purposes. We hoped to limit the costs of the arms race, reduce the prospects of a successful nuclear first strike by either side, and implement confidence-building measures to prevent an accidental holocaust. Ironically, we think of the 1970s and 1980s as the "golden era of arms control" because of the dramatic summitry of the period and the complex arms control agreements struck by the alliances led by the United States and the Soviet Union. But if we are to survive and prosper, we must make our present time the real "golden age of arms control." Twenty years from now, we must be able to look back and marvel at all that we accomplished.

The proliferation of weapons of mass destruction is not just a security problem. It is the economic dilemma and the moral challenge of the current age. On September 11, 2001, the world witnessed the destructive potential of international terrorism. But the September 11 attacks do not come close to approximating the destruction that would be unleashed by a nuclear weapon. Weapons of mass destruction have made it possible for a small nation, or even a sub-national group, to kill as many innocent people in a day as national armies killed in months of fighting during World War II. Beyond the horrific loss of life, proposals to advance the standard of living throughout the world would be undercut by the uncertainty and fear that would follow a catastrophic terrorist attack.

The bottom line is this: for the foreseeable future, the nations of the Transatlantic Alliance will face an existential threat from the intersection of terrorism and weapons of mass destruction. The minimum standard for victory is the prevention of any of the individual terrorists or terrorist cells from obtaining weapons or materials of mass destruction. This is a far more exacting arms control goal than existed during the 1970s and 1980s, when a successful agreement might allow for thousands of new nuclear weapons.

I believe that we can develop the international practices and norms that can almost guarantee that terrorists will not have access to nuclear weapons. In doing so, we can transform our world into a place that is more secure and more connected than it has ever been.

As part of the global war against terrorism, the United States and its allies must establish a worldwide system of accountability for nuclear, biological, and chemical weapons. In such a system, every nation that has weapons and materials of mass destruction must account for what it has, safely secure what it has, and demonstrate that no other nation or cell will be allowed access. If a nation lacks the means to do this, the international community must provide financial and technical assistance.

In 1991, I joined with former Senator Sam Nunn to establish the Nunn-Lugar Cooperative Threat Reduction program. This initiative brought Americans and Russians together to ensure the safety and destruction of the huge stockpile of weapons and materials of mass destruction left over from the former Soviet Union. The program has demonstrated over the last 13 years that extraordinary international relationships are possible to improve controls over weapons of mass destruction.

Working in concert, the United States and Russia have destroyed 6,564 nuclear warheads and dismantled hundreds of bombers, missiles, and submarines of the former Soviet Union that were built to deliver them. The Nunn-Lugar program is employing in peaceful pursuits tens of thousands of Russian weapons scientists who are no longer tempted to sell their knowledge. The program also has made progress toward protecting nuclear material, biological weapons laboratories, and chemical weapons stockpiles. Nunn-Lugar facilitated the removal of all nuclear weapons from Ukraine, Belarus, and Kazakhstan. After the fall of the Soviet Union, these three nations emerged as the third, fourth, and eighth largest nuclear powers in the world. Today, all three are nuclear weapons–free as a result of cooperative efforts under the Nunn-Lugar program.

Beyond statistics, the program has served as a bridge of communication and cooperation between the United States and Russia, even when other aspects of the relationship were in decline. It has improved military-to-military contacts and established greater transparency in areas that used to be the object of intense secrecy and suspicion.

In this context, the decision in 2002 by the G-8 nations to devote $20 billion to securing weapons of mass destruction in the former Soviet Union over 10 years was an incredibly important development. The participation of the G-8 and other allied nations, including Norway, greatly improves the diplomatic strength that can be brought to bear on safeguarding weapons of mass destruction. We welcome not only the commitment of funds, but also the infusion of ideas from allies on how dismantlement efforts can be accelerated.

Now we must not only accelerate weapons dismantlement in Russia, we must replicate our work with Russia in as many countries as possible and build a global coalition to support non-proliferation.

Many questions have been raised about the security of Pakistan's nuclear program. Similar questions may be directed at India's program. North Korea, Iran, Syria, and other nations present unique and difficult proliferation challenges. We cannot afford to be defeatist. Using the Cooperative Threat Reduction model, we should attempt to forge relationships to control weapons of mass destruction in previously reticent or hostile nations.

In addition, we should take opportunities to erect an international system to secure vulnerable stockpiles of conventional weapons. In the Senate, I have introduced legislation modeled on the original Nunn-Lugar Act that targets conventional weapons, including tactical missiles and man portable air defense systems, or MANPADS. Reports suggest that Al Qaeda has attempted to acquire these kinds of weapons. In addition, unsecured conventional weapons stockpiles are a major obstacle to peace and economic development in regions suffering from instability.

My bill declares it to be the policy of the United States to seek out surplus and unguarded stocks of conventional armaments for elimination. It authorizes the Department of State to carry out a global effort to destroy such weapons and to cooperate with allies and international organizations when possible.

Last August, I visited Albania, Ukraine, and Georgia. Each of these countries has large stockpiles of MANPADS and tactical missiles, and each has requested U.S. assistance to destroy them. On August 27, 2004, I stood in a remote Albanian military storage facility as the base commander unloaded a fully functioning MANPAD from its crate and readied it for use. Fortunately, the 79 MANPADS that I saw that day were destroyed on September 2, but there are many more like them throughout the world.

I believe that the Transatlantic Alliance has a window of opportunity to address proliferation threats around the world. We must make the safe storage, accountability, and destruction of nuclear, biological, chemical, and even conventional weapons a fundamental objective of our alliance.

In 2005, in addition to Norway's centennial, we celebrate the 60th anniversary of the end of World War II and we contemplate the 60th anniversary of the bombing of Hiroshima and Nagasaki. These events should remind us of how important the Transatlantic Alliance is to our future. The Allied victory in World War II, for which so many Americans and Norwegians suffered, could not have been achieved without the sacrifice of people from dozens of allied nations. Hiroshima and Nagasaki should remind us that we must have a similar alliance commitment to preventing the next use of nuclear weapons. I am optimistic about what we can achieve together. I am especially heartened, as I am today, whenever I encounter the unfailing dedication and spirit of Norwegian friends.

Radio Address to the Nation

George W. Bush

President of the United States, 2001– ; born New Haven, CT, July 6, 1946, and raised in Midland and Houston, TX; attended Phillips Academy, Andover, MA; B.A., Yale University; M.B.A., Harvard Business School, 1975; F-102 pilot, Texas Air National Guard, 1968–73; oil and gas business, Midland, TX, 1975–86; senior adviser in father's presidential campaign, 1987–88; one of the partners who purchased the Texas Rangers baseball franchise, 1989, and managing general partner of the team, 1989–94; governor of Texas, 1995–2000.

Editors' introduction: On July 7, 2005, terrorists killed at least 52 persons and wounded more than 700 riding on London's subway and bus systems. The attacks reminded Americans and individuals worldwide of the assaults on the United States that killed thousands on September 11, 2001. In his weekly radio speech to the nation, just days after the London bombings, President George W. Bush assured that, "We in America know the sense of loss that our British friends feel at this moment." The president concluded that, "The nation that survived the Nazi Blitz will not be intimidated by terrorists."

George W. Bush's speech: Good morning. Thursday morning, terrorists struck at the heart of one of the world's great cities in a series of bombings that hit London's subway and bus system as thousands of commuters headed to work. We in America know the sense of loss that our British friends feel at this moment. We extend our sympathies to those who suffered terrible injuries, and we pray for the families mourning the loss of loved ones. In this dark hour, the people of Great Britain can know that the American people stand with them.

These barbaric attacks occurred as world leaders gathered in Scotland for the G8 summit. While terrorists were killing innocent men and women in London, leaders at the G8 were discussing how free nations can combat poverty and HIV/AIDS, create a cleaner environment, and improve the lives of people everywhere. The contrast could not be more vivid between the intentions and the hearts of those who care deeply about human rights and human liberty, and the evil intentions and acts of those who rejoice in the death and suffering of the innocent.

We experienced this evil in our own country on a clear September morning in 2001. Since that day, terrorists have continued to kill and maim—in Bali, and Casablanca, Riyadh, Jakarta, Istanbul,

---

Delivered on July 9, 2005.

Madrid, Baghdad, London, and elsewhere. The terrorists believe that free societies are essentially corrupt and decadent. They believe that with a few hard blows, and the televised repetition of horrific images of violence, they can force us to retreat. They are mistaken.

On the day of the London attacks, every world leader at the G8 summit stood with Prime Minister Blair as he said: "Our determination to defend our values and our way of life is greater than their determination to cause death and destruction to innocent people." The free world is united in its resolve: We will never yield to terrorists and murderers. In the face of such adversaries, there is only one course of action: We will continue to take the fight to the enemy, and we will fight until the enemy is defeated.

We are now waging a global war on terror—from the mountains of Afghanistan to the border regions of Pakistan, to the Horn of Africa, to the islands of the Philippines, to the plains of Iraq. We will stay on the offense, fighting the terrorists abroad so we do not have to face them at home. We will continue to deny the terrorists safe haven and the support of rogue states. And at the same time,

---

The free world is united in its resolve: We will never yield to terrorists and murderers.

---

we will spread the universal values of hope and freedom that will overwhelm their ideology of tyranny and hate. The free world did not seek this conflict, yet we will win it.

Here at home, federal, state, and local officials are doing everything possible to protect us from another terrorist attack in America. While we have no specific credible information suggesting an imminent attack in the United States, in light of the bombings in London, we have raised the threat level from elevated to high for our passenger rail, subway, and bus systems. I urge all Americans to remain alert, and to report any suspicious activity to your local authorities.

This week, there is great suffering in the city of London. Yet the British people are resilient, and they have faced brutal enemies before. The nation that survived the Nazi Blitz will not be intimidated by terrorists. And just as America and Great Britain stood together to defeat the murderous ideologies of the 20th century, we again stand together to defeat the hateful ideologies of the 21st century.

The terrorists cannot shake our will. America and its allies will act decisively, because we know that the future of civilization is at stake in this struggle, and we know that the cause of freedom will prevail.

May God bless the people of Great Britain, and may He continue to bless America.

Thank you for listening.

Cumulative Speaker Index: 2000–2005

A cumulative speaker index to the volumes of *Representative American Speeches* for the years 1937–1938 through 1959–1960 appears in the 1959–1960 volume; for the years 1960–1961 through 1969–1970, see the 1969–1970 volume; for the years 1970–1971 through 1979–1980, see the 1979–1980 volume; for the years 1980–1981 through 1989–1990, see the 1989–1990 volume; and for the years 1990–1991 through 1999–2000, see the 1999–2000 volume.

Index